— Kimberley A. Doucette —

GOLDEN CAGES

ILLUSION OF FREEDOM

— Kimberley A. Doucette —

GOLDEN CAGES

ILLUSION OF FREEDOM

To the memory of my nephew
Benjamin (Ben) Lucas Robert Doucette 1999–2020.
Your spirit and presence within me give me comfort and peace.

To my teacher and friend, Noel Milliea.
Your generous and compassionate heart gave me strength to carry on.
Thank you for being my Francis in my Ryan moments.

Chapter One

Honour

THE BLACK OF the night broke and the sun popped up above the horizon. The sun bloomed on the skyline, casting out a rosy glow, like golden petals that had just fallen from a flower and had been placed onto a richly blue-painted canvas. The clouds moved in shoals, like a channel of water that was moving across the stratosphere. Strokes of orange-pink, magenta, amber, and silver twisted and rolled in synch like swimmers performing for the crowd. They displayed both chaos and order.

The days were beginning to feel warmer, like a fire that was just ignited and was radiating off its heat. Unusual spring-like conditions made winter taper out all over Europe. The daily temperatures were rising fast, and yet it was only the end of January.

The sun slanted through the blinds and kissed Ryan's face. He stirred and woke up slowly. The radio blared at its usual time. He had his daily morning routine of coffee, two eggs, and toast. He ran past his wife like he was on fire, jumped in the car, and drove off. Nothing extra-special was seemingly happening that day. Abrupt, focused, and intense was his usual manner.

While listening to sports on the radio, he drove onward; traffic annoyed him as he weaved dangerously in and out of ignorant and impatient lines of vehicles. There were a lot of mornings where he misspent his energy yelling at other drivers for their faults, even though he was manoeuvring his vehicle the very same way. The world was one big race where nobody ever seemed to get ahead.

The clock turned to 4:00 p.m., and he drove back home through the same rude and aggressive lines of traffic. Life was normal: chaotic, listless, routine, and unchanging. His wife called and asked him to stop at the store to grab some milk. He didn't know it yet, but when he'd meet up with Andrew unexpectedly at the grocery store parking lot, life would shift gears and blow an energetic gasket. He'd have no choice but to slow down his acceleration from that point on. The world as he knew it would soon come to a sudden halt and things would never be the same. The next year of his life would be an unforgettable roller-coaster ride.

***

RYAN GRABBED HIS childhood best friend's hand and shook it fiercely. "Hey, Andy! I've been meaning to contact you for quite some time now. I was telling someone about you just the other day and about all your achievements."

"Hey, Rye," Andrew responded with enthusiasm. "I'm happy to bump into you, man! Things have really picked up in my life, that's for sure, and in more ways than you know. I've thought of you every day for the past month. As crazy as it sounds, you've been in my dreams. I was thinking of you just today and believe it or not, I was actually going to go home and call you tonight. Wild or what?"

"Yeah, that's cool. What was the dream about?"

Since childhood, Andrew and Ryan had kept their nicknames for one another, although they always used full names for other friends. They were neighbours growing up and both of their parents would laugh at how they could swear that they were sometimes more like brothers than friends. Yet somehow in their adult years they grew increasingly apart in distance, only seeing one another every few years. Each time they did meet up, it was as though no time had passed and it was as if they'd just be continuing this on-going conversation that never really ended. No distance or time seemed to sever their connection.

"Amongst other important dreams, I dreamt that I sent you to my counsellor."

Ryan laughed, "Yeah? You think I need a shrink, do you? That's intense!"

Andrew smirked and nodded his head. "Yes, I do, actually."

Ryan threw him a grimacing look.

"Seriously, though," Andrew spouted off. "Long story short, I've been working with this Native guy from Canada, and it's been amazing. He's a different type of counsellor. His methods are kind of hard to explain. Let's just say that he's definitely not the shrink type. I think you'd like him. He brought me to a point now that I can see things from a different perspective. He showed me places within my mind that I never even knew existed. I followed his lead and he helped me get lost.

"As I mentioned, it's bringing me back to you, Rye. I keep thinking of you, and somehow, I know you're meant to go see him also. I have a feeling that this guy has a role to play with getting you and me better focused. He'll bring us to a level where we can do something important together, something purposeful. I just don't know what that looks like yet, though I trust it's out there."

This was sounding a bit unconventional, even for Andy. He wasn't the type to ever mess around, so it had to be legit. Ryan felt a pull of excitement without knowing why. Why would they need focus and for what? Life was already good. Wasn't it? "How did you meet him?" Ryan asked.

"Well, it was something like us talking right now. I had a friend who went and he told me all about it. I saw the changes he was going through, the gusto, the passion, and I wanted some of that in my life. I ended up going too, and uh, what can I say—I'm really glad that I did. You might think that I sound crazy right now. I probably would have dismissed this if I hadn't experienced it for myself. It's not exactly something you can explain in words. I just have this knowing that we were meant to reconnect on a deeper level at this very moment and have this talk. One day we'll sit together and talk about that reason on a much bigger scale."

As random and alien as all of this appeared to be to Ryan, there was something hauntingly familiar in this conversation. It always felt that way when he was with Andrew, though he would never admit it. It was as if some of what they were talking about was something he knew would happen even before it occurred. Flashes of images, feelings, thoughts, and even colours were swirling in Ryan's mind as Andrew kept talking about how his life had improved. It was as if Ryan had dreamt of this event before.

Andrew discussed his new love for life, his work, and his mental clarity. All at once, Ryan felt a twirl of emotional shift happen within his core. He could now swear an oath in front of a courtroom that he had indeed had this conversation before. It made him feel uncomfortable. Later he would find out that the name of this phenomenon was called "déjà vu," and that it was a sign of being on the right track. Confidence was something he lacked. He was never one to talk a lot unless he'd had a few drinks beforehand, even with Andrew, with whom he felt the safest of anyone. He remained speechless, took a breath to relax, and took in the rest of what his friend had to share.

Andrew went on about getting out of the head and living from the heart. This sort of talk sounded almost like a foreign language to Ryan. He had no clue whatsoever as to what he would help his buddy with later on. Still, something pulled on his heartstrings, urging him on to find that enthusiasm within himself. He wanted some of that gusto and passion, too...maybe later.

"Thanks, Andy. I can't say that I'm really interested in this right now, but I will keep it in mind." Ryan sounded a bit like someone shrugging off a door-to-door vacuum salesman.

Andrew smiled oddly, "You will be." Andrew passed him one of Francis's business cards. "Oh, and by the way," Andrew asked, "did you see that sunrise this morning? An amazing one, eh?"

"No," Ryan admitted, "I never noticed a thing." He shook his head laughing. "Have you gone off your rocker?"

"Nope!" Andrew flashed a sudden naughty look, knowing that it would stir up curiosity in his friend later on.

***

RYAN FELT TINGLES through his whole body the entire ride home. It felt like ants were walking on his flesh. He brushed them away wildly. His skin was nearly raw from rubbing his arms.

That night while the kids and his wife were sound asleep, Ryan himself couldn't even catch a wink. The fear processing part of his brain wouldn't shut off and was on overdrive. Speculative questions with open-ended thoughts started formulating in his head. "What would it be like if I went for this counselling? How would my life change for the better? How much better would or could life get than this?" Ryan rehearsed mentally and emotionally. He kept seeing himself meeting up with Andrew again someday, also a changed man and feeling just as happy as him. It was as if he were already embracing a future event that was happening right then and there.

Over a period of hours, his emotions took a violent turn. A light switch had been turned off and suddenly what started out as insight and excitement turned into an unilluminated gloom. Ryan caught himself embracing his deepest and darkest fears. Thoughts rolled around tumultuously, like continuous storm clouds hovering and stuck between two mountain ranges, fighting their way through and breaking free into the vast stratosphere. It was almost daylight when he finally fell asleep.

Upon waking, Ryan felt as though he was hung over. Some strange depression overtook him. It made him feel alone, lethargic, and draggy. "How is it possible that someone could change your life for you? Life doesn't work that way. Andrew has seriously lost it. Nobody could change me. I have no reason to change. I'm happy just the way I am. I don't need any stupid counselling."

Nothing smelled or felt right on his palate when he ate. The bitterness of his own reality had an overpowering taste.

Whenever any possible or sudden changes came into his awareness, Ryan's body often suffered with headaches or nausea. Depression usually followed, and this was no exception. His mother was the same. He had gone for help before and the doctor said, "It's hereditary, and these pills will simply contribute to a more normal state of mind. This medication is effective for fear, anger, overthinking, anxiety, or addictive craving; in fact, it can be tried for any emotional disorder." Though he got the prescription filled, Ryan chose to suffer through his anxiety phases, allowing them to pass without medicating. Toughing it out was his way, no matter what he was going through. He only wished that he had a way to stop himself from feeling, in general. He knew from experience that no one had a magic remedy to make things better. "What if this Francis guy tries to push another prescription on me?"

RYAN VIEWED HIS future emotionally as though he were looking through and comparing it to different camera lenses of the past. The more he tried to un-memorize the bygone days, the more the past haunted him. Unresolved issues, such as what might have been and what never came to pass, were chasing him down. He turned to look at them, but none of them had a face.

It wasn't until the beginning of April that he decided that he had had enough and that he either had to fix his situation or get out of it. Ryan was calmer now and wanted to call that counsellor. He had misplaced the card that Andrew had handed him with the contact information on it. A part of him awakened on that fateful evening, and he tried to force that part back to sleep, but he just couldn't. A major part of him felt heavy and exhausted. It wasn't possible to carry the struggle of wanting to push everyone away any longer. Everything within his marriage was failing, his emotional state had plummeted, his mom was feeling left out, and he needed help.

WHEN ANDREW PICKED up the phone, he seemed to know exactly what Ryan was going through.

"I got a feeling that I need to tell you that awareness starts to change you, Rye. Don't be discouraged if your old self puts up a fight. It's not easy to dismantle the old you. After some work—and it'll be work!—you'll find that the memory of the old self ends up being like another lifetime. The ego will try to stop you before you even begin to process anything logically. Eventually you'll be able to look back at life without an emotional charge. I think they call it wisdom." Andrew chuckled.

"How do I prepare, Andy?"

"Keep your mind focused on what you want, and get clear on what that is. Francis will set you straight pretty fast if that focus is off, trust me on that one. My advice to you is to be very clear about why you're there from the moment you walk in his office door or you'll be sorry in a hurry. I would give you more information, but in my experience it's better to leave you with that and send you in to see him as is. No matter what happens, trust the process and don't give up. At first, you'll feel at odds with being there, but over time and after a few visits, you'll thank me. Trust me this once, please.

"We can talk after you see him. I'll be waiting with my ears opened wide. I can't wait to see where life will take you from here. You may have to take time to let it all sink in, and I trust that eventually it will. I just hope the ego doesn't hold you hostage for too long, man. If you need my help, let me know. Don't hold it all in like I did and hang onto suffering longer than you need to. I'll always be there for you, with anything that you need. Remember that." Andrew left it at that and gave Ryan the contact information.

Ryan stood stunned and confused for a while before going back to work. *What the hell am I about to get myself into?*

Holding onto the number for another three tedious weeks, Ryan finally called to make an appointment with, in his words, "this mysterious enigma of a counsellor dude called Francis."

The first counselling session happened differently than what he had expected. It was a complete disaster, really. He was mortified after it finally ended, upset with himself for making the biggest mistake of his life. He went in very sure of why he was there and left feeling that his words had been torn and barbarously mutilated. It proved to be yet another day that would change his life and his attitude toward it forever; he just wasn't aware of that yet and wouldn't be for a while to come.

***

RYAN LOOKED AT his calendar to make sure he had the right date, "Yes, okay, it's April 24th." He entered the office promptly at 3:00 p.m. by the door labelled "Francis S. MacDonald."

"You aren't how I expected you to look. Francis MacDonald? That sounds Scottish, not Aboriginal."

"What did you expect?" Francis asked

"I don't know. I figured you'd look a bit more, umm?"

Francis looked at his client with a levelling glare, as if to be scanning him from head to toe and reading him psychologically.

Ryan squirmed uncomfortably in his chair, like a kid called to the principal's office at primary school for having gotten caught for smoking in the bathroom.

"Were you expecting me to look more like a savage?"

"Well, I wouldn't say a *savage*... that's a bit extreme...but at least with a feather on your head." Ryan thought he was being funny, but failed quickly.

"Does the business jacket and jeans combo bother you?"

"No, it's just distracting, I guess."

"What are you wearing?" Francis pointed out Ryan's outfit.

"I'm wearing jeans and a shirt. Umm, I'm sorry, it was stupid of me. I mean it's the 21st century. I don't know what I was thinking. Maybe I'm nervous. I admit, though, I was hoping to see you more natural or maybe I'm looking for the word "traditional"? It's probably because of movies and television shows I've watched."

"So, you came to see what I would be wearing based on television shows?"

"No, no, I didn't mean it that way."

Francis decided to give him another chance. "Then why did you come?"

"I heard good things about you. It's not like me to just blurt things out. I'm usually the listener, not the talker. I feel quite embarrassed now. Honestly, I just shocked myself."

"Okay, no offence taken." Francis continued to gaze solidly into Ryan's eyes.

"I guess I just thought you would be different."

"What we think and what we know are two different things. One is based on experience, the other on either imagination or past programs. Now you know based on experiencing it for yourself. Don't you?"

"Yes, I do."

"So again, why did you come?"

What could Ryan say? He felt scolded and his ego was a bit wounded. He was feeling frustrated and his patience was being stretched like a rubber band about to snap. It was apparent that he needed to stay calm and take back control of this conversation. He tried but instead ended up blurting out something he would regret even worse. "I came to uh, to get help for my wife."

"I see. Your wife can't talk?"

"No, she can, I just need to know how to help her. So, I came for her. Oh, this is just not going how I expected it to. I can't seem to find the right words today."

"Expectations are a killer, aren't they?"

The room went silent and Ryan suddenly heard the clock ticking noisily above his head.

Francis allowed it to tick for a time before finally speaking. "So, you came to honour her?"

"Honour her?"

"You came to honour your wife by coming to fix yourself."

"No, no!" Ryan thought he'd better explain things better. "I came so I can help her fix herself and help her eliminate some problems in her life that have affected our marriage and how I feel about her. I have no idea what you mean by 'honour.'"

"I see that, yes. So, you are not her problem?"

"What? Her problem? No, no, I'm not the problem. She has a problem. Sorry I got you confused here."

"Hm? Yes, I think she might have a big problem."

"Yes, that's what I meant. Problems with her, I mean herself, her family, problems with life. She's just not happy. Her family is always trying to control her. We live with my family, thank God. The hard part is that she doesn't see how good we have it. It's like she struggles no matter where she is. So, yeah! Problems."

Silence once again entered the room. The clock was beginning to sound like an electric hammer driving nails up against Ryan's head. He explained himself further so that Francis would see how normal he was. The conversation had just started on the wrong foot and he was determined to fix it. He restarted as though nothing had happened. "My mom is helping with everything. We live downstairs and my parents are upstairs. My mom comes and does everything for us; it's great."

"Everything, eh? So, why is this great?"

"Yes, everything. I mean, she cooks, cleans, and cares for our kids. We don't even have to do laundry. It's perfect, really. My parents love our kids. We have freedom for other stuff. We get to vacation every year with them and they take care of us and the kids. It's Heaven, really."

"I see."

Ryan remembered what Andrew had told him about staying focused on why he was there. He decided to give Francis more details so that he could know how to help Clara. He was feeling a bit more in control now. "My wife's family always gets in the way. They want us to live near them or to visit more. It's so far away, though, at least an hour's drive. I mean they could just come to us. It would make more sense because I don't want to leave my parents alone, as they need my help now. To be honest, I'm happy that her family doesn't come over very often, as it just makes things easier, and we are happier without the intrusion."

"Your parents need you? Or you need them? I'm confused, here." Francis crossed his arms and leaned backwards slightly in his chair.

"Yes, they need me. They did so much for me in life. I want to give back to them now. My mom would be lost without me for sure. We are her whole life."

"Why would your wife's parents not coming over make you happy? What's the problem with them being there?"

"Well, her mom thinks she owns the place when they do come. She wants things done her way, and wants to take care of us. She expects to be the one cooking, and then my mom gets upset because she feels like she is being shoved aside. It's not right and not fair at all to my mother to be put in that position. Mom's upset for days afterwards, and it's just not right."

"And what does the lady of the house do when her mother comes?"

"You mean my mom? I just told you about her, she gets upset. It starts off okay and she's happy at first. Then something always happens that hurts her feelings. She becomes distant and stays upstairs. She stays quiet, but she mumbles to herself, and paces like an animal in a cage. So, needless to say, I'm always happy to see my mother-in-law go."

Francis pulled his arms in tighter and leaned forward slightly, now resting his elbows on his legs. "Oh, I meant the lady of your home, the part you live in. That is your wife, isn't it? Or do you all sleep together in one bedroom?"

"No...oh my God. That's funny! Sorry, I should've explained myself better. My parents live upstairs. I think I told you that it's two apartments. It's like two separate houses in one."

"So, like I asked, the lady of the house, being your wife, the one who lives in your part of the house, what does she do when her parents come?"

"I don't know...she acts funny. I used to argue, but there's no use. Her mother always wins. My wife says her mom is so good, so nice and has done so much for her that she could never say no to her. She actually wants her to feel comfortable in the house when she visits. She would never dare complain about her, I think. I don't get it. I wish her mom would..."

Francis cut in. "She says these things about her family, or you say them about her family?"

Ryan realized that Francis must be viewing him as some kind of liar.

Francis continued to ask questions in order to better get to know his client. "And, how does she react when your mother is there?"

"My wife seems vacant and upset. She leaves the house more lately. I guess she's just busy with other things. My mother helps her so much and gives her total freedom, so she's able to go and do what she wants. In my opinion she should be happy about that and grateful, but sometimes she isn't. She complains that my mom is there too much, and that she's smothering her into submission. I mean sometimes it's a bit much, I admit, but I appreciate my mom because it really allows my wife freedom, like I mentioned."

"Freedom?" Francis placed his thumb under his chin and then his pointing finger over his mouth. He looked at Ryan inquisitively while rubbing his lips left to right.

"Yeah, she's free to go and be happy because my mom does everything for her. I think she should love her for that."

"Before she embarked on this, uh, *Freedom*, how did she react toward your mother?"

Ryan continued to explain things in more detail to be helpful. "Well, that's part of her other problem that I sort of mentioned. She told my mom that she was controlling and this really upset the whole apple crate. She sees me as spoiled. It got ridiculous at one point. She even went so low as to get upset several times because of the laundry detergent and softener my mom uses...something to do with the chemicals, maybe. My mom also uses mothballs and other things to make sure our stuff stays nice. My wife doesn't like them and complains. I don't see the big deal. My mom does a better job than her anyway. It was a terrible ordeal for a month with mom crying non-stop until I stepped in and made things better. Now she does stuff for us again, but my wife just stopped talking and now spends more time outside the house. She won't drink with me anymore, either, and she refuses to go places unless I drag her out. She even pulled away from our best friends."

"Aren't mothballs proven to be poisonous?"

"What? No! I grew up with them. It hasn't affected me any."

"Are you sure about that?" Francis paused a moment. "Mothballs have been banned in some countries because of studies that have shown that they may be harmful."

"I had no idea."

"Now you do have an idea. So, did you honour her request to get rid of the mothballs?"

"There you go with that 'honour' word again. I don't know, I think my mom still uses them. Anyway, I'm a bit confused, here. I came to talk about real problems, not about mothballs or about my mom's traditions. No one has died from mothballs!"

"Again, studies have shown that they may have caused complications that lead to deaths. Obviously, your wife's research must have proven itself to you. You must have asked her why she didn't approve of them, right?"

The clock ticked even harder now. Ryan wasn't about to admit that he hadn't ever asked her why. He just wanted peace in the house and for his mother to be respected.

Francis decided to set Ryan up to focus better. "Tell me more about the relationship with your wife in the beginning."

"It used to be good. Things changed after we had our second baby. She doesn't want me to touch her anymore."

"And how are you handling this?"

"I don't know. I'm okay. I'm the same."

"Same as what?"

"The same as before," Ryan couldn't hide the frustration now building in his voice.

"And who were you before?"

"The same person that I am now...I don't know!"

A long, intense pause filled the room. Ryan continued on reluctantly, "I loved my wife when we met. We were out a lot with friends, always having fun. Now she doesn't want to be out with any of those friends, like I mentioned. I just want peace again and for things to go back to normal. She judged my friend's wife, Gloria, for not being nice. She claimed she wasn't her friend or something strange. She doesn't want to be around Gloria anymore. I don't know what happened. Gloria is so nice and so beautiful."

"Beautiful?" Francis was now raising his eyebrows and leaned forward again to observe his client more closely. He had just hit the nail on the head. Ryan could pretend all he wanted but the guilt was becoming obvious. The signs were all there.

"Yeah. She always looks perfect. Always smiling and always has perfect hair, clothes, makeup. You know, beautiful. My wife is probably jealous of her."

"I see. Yes, that tells me a lot."

Another awkward silence entered the space.

"And, your wife?"

"What about her? Yeah, back to her. So anyway, she has many problems and I don't know how to help her."

"Do you see your wife as beautiful?"

"Well, yeah, she is beautiful, of course. She just..." Ryan paused a moment to clear his throat. "She isn't happy."

"We know your *friend's* wife's name, and that is glorious." Francis said it sarcastically while gesturing quotation marks in the air with his fingers to make a point. "I think that maybe we forgot to honour your wife at the beginning by presenting her name?"

Ryan froze in fear.

Waiting a moment to see first if Ryan would say his wife's name, Francis continued. "Do you tell her she's beautiful?"

"Who, Gloria?" Ryan's voice was heated. His hands were getting sweaty and clammy.

Frances chuckled to himself. He couldn't hold back. This conversation was getting just as tedious to him as it was to Ryan. What should have been a simple conversation was turning into major triggers for his client. This was obviously going to be another wild horse to break in. Francis could tell from the get-go that Ryan was hiding the truth even from himself. He had seen this attitude time and time again and knew exactly what direction to go in order to hurry up this process. He'd lead him down a bumpy road that would help them get down to the bottom of the real core issues that caused Ryan to act the way that he did toward his wife. A woman as patient as she would have to be to put up with the likes of him was surely worth the effort.

Ryan was clearly confused and felt foolish. The look on his face showed that he had no idea where this was going.

Francis used that confusion to his advantage. He knew that this guy needed to step out of his comfort zone as quickly as possible or he was going to end up like a hamster spinning on the same wheel and getting nowhere. To get him there faster, he knew he had to squeeze him a little more. "How often do you tell her she's beautiful?"

"Wait a minute. Who are we talking about, here?"

Francis's voice remained smooth, calm, but commanding. "Your wife, the one you dedicated your life to, the one you live with. I'm not talking about Gloria and not about your mother; I'm referring to your wife! Do you tell her she's beautiful?"

"Well, yes, of course I do." Ryan was beginning to feel like he was on trial and ready to plead the fifth amendment, guaranteeing his right to silence. He looked around as if to be seeking out where his lawyer was hiding. He needed help fast before he blurted out any incriminating information. His face was now as red as a tomato.

Francis used a commanding tone. "When? And how often?"

"Probably when we go somewhere special. Where are we going with this?" The room was uncomfortably still. Ryan fidgeted around and scratched his skin, like a druggie fresh off crack. He sat up and composed himself in the chair before continuing on. "Maybe a couple times a month. Like normal, I guess. But probably if she wasn't complaining so much, I'd tell her more often. No matter if I do compliment her or not, she acts up." He mockingly gestured quotations in the air to mimic Francis's earlier actions. He was surprised himself by his actions. He was usually such a well-mannered guy, but there was just something about this counsellor that seemed to bring out the worst in him. "It's almost like she's upset when I tell her or she just doesn't believe me. I end up feeling like an asshole for trying."

"Maybe it's because you don't know her name. What do you call her? Hey you? Or hey, wife?"

Ryan laughed nervously. "Sorry, yeah, her name is umm, umm," he stammered. Thrown off, his mind went blank for a brief moment. "Umm, Clara." He paused to catch his breath. His chest was tightening up from being so nervous. It was heaving up and down. "Seriously, though, when I do compliment her, she asks me what I want from her. So, I tell her what I want and what I like to see, for example, what Gloria wears or how she does her hair. I like it and I want her to do that but she refuses to. I mean she asked me to tell her what I wanted from her, right? So, her refusing to change anything makes me tired of trying. No matter what I say or do for her, nothing seems to help."

"So, Clara isn't beautiful, then?"

"Of course, she is, I just told you that! She could just be better, is all." Ryan murmured something inaudibly under his breath.

"What you're saying is that the other woman is the example that you want her to follow?"

"Yes, basically. If you put it that way."

Francis resolved to press forward. "Why?"

"Because the other woman is always beautiful, and so therefore she's happy. If she could be like that it would make me happier. Okay? Anyway, what does this have to do with my friend's wife? Can you help me or not?"

"With what? To help you fix Clara's hair? Or to help her know what to wear? I'm not a stylist, sorry."

"No, no, I mean can you do something? Can you help me so that she has no problems anymore?"

"Yes. I think something will happen. I can help you if you want help. Do you want help?"

"Oh, great! And yes, I do want help. What now? What's our first step?"

"I want you to bring me two rocks."

Ryan paused to check if he heard him right and then laughed loudly. "Two rocks?"

Francis looked at Ryan matter-of-factly. "Yes, two rocks."

"For what reason?" Ryan cocked his head sideways like a curious dog.

"For meaning and purpose."

"Okay...seriously, two rocks?" Ryan blustered forward from the chair and stood straight up, now throwing both hands into the air like a child about to have a tantrum.

"Yes."

"That's ridiculous!" Ryan plunked back down in his chair shaking his head no.

"Is it?"

"Where would I find them?"

"What? Rocks? Wherever you look for them. Somewhere outside I presume."

"What does this have to do with helping me help my wife?"

"Your beautiful wife Clara, you mean? Do you wish for my help?"

"Yes, I do. I already said that I did."

"Are you sure?" Francis relaxed into an intense stare.

This was obviously some stupid trick but Ryan had never backed down from a challenge, ever, and this wasn't going to be his first. "Yes!"

Francis confronted his client with a fierce look. "Are you willing to do the work that I'll be asking you to do?"

"Yes. Obviously. I'm here, am I not?" Ryan wasn't about to let anyone get the best of him. He sat forward glaring back at him, and nodded his head as if he were playing centre in basketball and letting the referee know it was okay to throw the game ball up in the air.

"So, I'll see you again next Monday, then, same time, with two rocks."

Ryan suddenly lost his enthusiasm. He couldn't hide his insecurity any longer. "Okay, but I'm not sure if I understand. This isn't why I came. A rock or two has nothing to do with my marriage."

"It was an honour, brother. See you in one week."

"I'm not your brother!" Ryan collected himself and softened his voice. "What kind of rocks am I looking for, exactly? I mean, how will I know if I have the correct rocks?"

"You'll know."

"I thought this was supposed to be an hour session? We only spent a short time, here. Maybe half an hour? What about the rest of the hour?"

"The trees and birds will be there to witness the rest of the hour while you find those two rocks. They're wise, those rock people. You should listen to them closely when they speak."

"Who is wise? What are you talking about? Who will speak to me?"

"The rock people…"

Francis looked at Ryan as if he should know what he was talking about.

Ryan was still lost. "Rock people?"

Francis crossed one arm over his chest and grabbed his client's hand and hugged him with a crossed heart and walked out of the room with no excuses and no explanation.

Left feeling royally confused, Ryan had no idea what to do next. Was this some kind of joke? Should he let himself out of the building? He took a minute to breathe, and bent over to brace himself on the chair in front of him. He cackled out loud like a clever jackal about to collaborate with an evil sorcerer. He took a moment to look around the room. Where was Andrew? Shouldn't he be coming through a door to reveal the candid camera that he had secretly placed in the room somewhere?

Was it possible, Ryan thought, *that Andrew knew about his cheating on Clara? Had Francis somehow reprimanded him and put him in his place? Was Clara setting this whole thing up through Andrew?* Ryan shook his head and walked to the car, feeling a bit dizzy. His attention was diverted to the fast-approaching headache rolling in like a storm cloud. Francis's words rang through Ryan's mind over and over as he drove home. "Yes, something will happen…" Something had just happened for sure. Ryan had just made the biggest mistake of his life.

RYAN STRUGGLED, REASONING out how Francis could have twisted his words that way. "Generally, I have nothing to say about the world around me. I stay low in the workplace putting in my days and going home to exercise and then relaxing afterwards. On my time off, I play sports and hang out with friends. Between that, Clara, and the kids, there isn't much more I need in my life. Maybe I really don't need these sessions. Perhaps I went so that I could see that everything is perfect as is."

If only he could get Clara to change, things would be different, easier, and he wouldn't have to cheat. Like he told Francis, she wasn't who she was at the beginning of their relationship. The attraction to her wasn't the same anymore. Nothing he did to change that feeling worked and no convincing himself brought back that desirability. "What about Mom, though. If I don't try and fix this, it will break her heart." Something had to give.

"This guy came so highly recommended by Andrew," Ryan explained to Clara. "You really should go see him. I met him the other day and I think that he'd be a really good counsellor for you."

Clara had no interest and refused the offer flat out. She was tired of Ryan trying to change her and she avoided the conversation by busying herself for the rest of the week. Ryan almost decided not to go back. But the embarrassment of being considered weak in Andy's eyes cut too deep.

Chapter Two

Shiny Rock. Dull Rock

I T WAS SUNDAY afternoon, and Ryan had one day left to get the two rocks. The week seemed too short, and he still had no idea why he would be asked to do something so trivial. Clara and the kids were busy doing their own things, so it seemed as though it was now or never. Packing a lunch, he threw it in his backpack along with some water and headed to his old childhood hangout.

Old memories of rough splashing, joyous summer afternoons, and jumping into the small pool of water came to mind. He and Andrew had spent hours of fun there throwing the slimy mud bottom at one another and then burning off the leeches that had decided to use them as hosts for nutrients. It used to seem harmless back then, but now the thought of bloodsuckers on his legs gave him body shivers from head to toe.

Tall trees and low shrubs were spidering out over what was once an opening in the trail. Long ferns that were once fiddleheads in the early spring swayed back and forth in the warm wind. A frog hopped noisily into the pond, making Ryan realize he was there already. The water moved silently, forming small undercurrent swirls that eventually lingered off somewhere, showing up in random areas here and there.

Ryan found the remnants of an old rope that they used to swing from. It was now frayed and tattered after so many years of exposure to the elements. Time was a foggy haze that lay over his connection with things from the past. Those old days seemed like another life-time now. The space around the area began to lighten up with the cheerful chirps of birds all around. He got suddenly annoyed with the loud disruption.

The light slanted through the trees, pulling his attention suddenly downwards to what looked like a moss-covered floor with lichen-covered slabs of rock sticking out of it here and there. They looked similar to rolling hills Ryan had seen while on long drives in the country. A small lizard scurried as he walked closer to view this incredible green blanket that time had laid over top of the earth. It was quite magical, actually, as though he had walked into another world, a kind of fairyland, not that he would ever admit it. He had never realized before how the trees grew in patches or in circular formations around the pond.

Ryan spent a few minutes sitting there searching for flat stones to try and skip on top of the water. He used to be a champion at it, and seemed to have lost his touch somewhat as an adult. He quickly got frustrated after a few tries and chucked a random rock into the water instead. He whipped another stone, which plopped into the liquid, now causing a slight reaction in the water. The ripple pulled him in toward it, like he was being sucked into a kind of vortex. It was as if he had a moment where he was seeing things in dream form. Colours were slightly faded and he went into a kind of trance while he sat there.

Things got weird. So much so that it took the breath right out of him. It was as if tiny waves were travelling outwards in a circular formation, reaching out into some kind of force field. He could tell that things could move and exist but go nowhere and yet everywhere all at once. He had to shake his head so things would look less foggy. Was he losing it?

Ryan looked off to the woods. It seemed he could suddenly zoom right in and hear certain sounds, like dogs barking, birds chirping, and then an emptiness such as nobody's ever heard. Then something different came, a warmth like an overwhelming feeling or a whisper. Not by his ear but something deep inside. He couldn't exactly make anything of it but he could feel it. It was like being in a movie watching everything in slow motion.

Ryan hadn't let his mind wander like that in ages. It scared him when he went off in that way. These types of things used to happen to him a lot but he found ways to avoid feeling so much. It was one of the reasons why the doctor prescribed him pills that time. A shiver suddenly went up his spine toward where the skull connects, creating a muscle spasm. He shook his head to loosen his neck muscles and threw another rock into the pond, hoping to shift back to reality.

Maybe the kids should know about this place. Clara likes these kinds of settings. I could bring them here sometime. Maria forbade him years ago from coming here after she found out about the leeches in the water. Most of his childhood outings were kept secret so as not to upset her. Ryan heard his mother's voice in his head, "Proper leisure pools are cleaner, safer, and save time."

Nature outings that were off the beaten track weren't exactly encouraged. He eventually caved and became a man of the concrete jungle, vacationing at hotels, enjoying an easier life and making fewer waves with his mother. Clara wasn't ever impressed by it, though. "I can't stand the places that are more about flash than substance," she'd say. "Leaving the city for resorts isn't a real vacation." *Whatever that meant.*

The birds chirped loudly suddenly. Ryan realized that he hadn't listened to the birds in quite some time. Had car sounds become more normal to him? A strange comfort that soothed and conditioned him to accept the real world? Whatever the case, he was eager to get out of the woods and more than willing to go back to it.

Ryan threw more stones into the pond. He wished now that he had shut his mouth about Gloria. *What was I thinking?* he murmured to himself. *Maybe I was a bit shut off emotionally and tuned Clara out intentionally, and the kids, too. I don't know! I'm not sure of anything anymore.* He whipped another rock into the water.

In that office, something sinister had happened. He'd had no control over himself or his words. Maybe Francis would see him in a different light this time around. Ryan shook his head. He hadn't come here for this. He just needed to get those stupid rocks and get the heck out of there. He tried to stand up but felt gravity holding him in place, forcing him to sit for a while.

"Place of innocence. Place of innocence." Who was saying that? It was as if Ryan heard a loudspeaker from above. He looked all around, expecting to see someone else there; but there was no one.

Ryan picked up a rock again to busy himself. He decided that he would teach the rock-skipping skill to his kids someday. *Maybe if they did things that I liked, then I would spend more time with them.* He wasn't even sure anymore if he knew what he liked. The things that he used to do upset his mom, so to keep her happy and live peacefully, he jumped into work and exercise because she approved of and encouraged those things.

Was he keeping busy at work to avoid his life? Out of frustration, he threw the rock into the woods. He was losing his grip and was unable to stay focused for one solid moment.

A LARGE CLOUD ROLLED in unexpectedly and shaded the entire area. The beautiful bright blue of the afternoon faded into darker tones and then into ugly, deep greys as if an angry night sky were already inching in. Ryan felt a chill from the sweat that had formed on his back while walking and his skin was cooling off rapidly. He got an overwhelming feeling that someone was watching him, and he stood up abruptly to look around. Again, there was no one. His heart was now beating fast. Thunder rumbled overhead. His mind sobered, as if to be coming back from the haziness of a long-forgotten memory. *Two rocks, for God's sake. That's all I have to do and then get the hell out of here. Think, Ryan, think!*

Francis wouldn't let him off easily if he came unprepared this time. How that guy knew things, he wasn't sure. That man had peered into Ryan's soul the way that a cat would look intensely at a mouse before pouncing on it. It left Ryan feeling vulnerable and alert all at once. He wouldn't be caught off guard a second time. He was too embarrassed to call Andrew to look for the cheat-sheet of "How to handle the Francis Class 101." "Okay," he sighed aloud, "there are rocks everywhere. How to choose two that would have meaning to Francis? That is the real question. I can do this."

Ryan waited and stared at the ground for a while. Nothing popped out at him, at first. Then he saw several different stones that interested him. One was shaped like a mountain range. One looked a lot like an umbrella, and another strangely like a Halloween cat with its back hunched up. He was surprised that so many stones could be exposed in one small area like the pond. One looked similar to a shoe, and beside it, another like a boot. He recalled that someone had lost a shoe somewhere along the trail and he almost tripped over it on the way in. Maybe he was getting some sort of sign? Not that he believed in signs.

The thunder rolled overhead and spoke authoritatively the way that natural forces occasionally do. Thundershowers were forecasted to hit, but not this early. He had better get out of there.

Within thirty seconds, big droplets of rain started coming down hard over Ryan's head. So hard, in fact, that he had no choice but to grab his belongings and go. He wasn't going to leave empty-handed, though. Lightning lit up the now blackened sky, striking downward with huge bolts that left flashes lingering in the air. It was as if time had stopped and a cloudburst had fallen on top of him. He struggled to grab two random stones and headed out of the woods. The strikes seemed to have arms reaching outwards, much like tree branches. He realized that it wasn't just an ordinary thunderstorm. High winds nearly knocked him over. Multiple strokes of light hit down all around him in a series of spurts, as if aiming straight for him.

At this point, Ryan was absolutely terrified and truly concerned for his life. When he felt and heard the thunder this time, it clapped so loudly and so close to his head that he thought for certain that this was the end. Frozen in fear, his legs almost gave out. *What the hell? Did I just...* He was distracted by the warm liquid running down his leg and into his socks. This wasn't the experience he was expecting when he set out on this innocent little journey. He then ran as fast as he could to get back to his house.

Trees violently slapped and whipped Ryan's face as he got closer and closer to the end of the wooded area. One last large clap of thunder rolled overhead that made his knees shake and buckle.

Overlooking a tree root that was sticking out of the ground, he snapped down hard on his shoulder on one of the roots and cracked his head on a rock. The lights stopped flashing and the roaring thunder lingered for a bit but eventually faded out.

***

RYAN LAY UNCONSCIOUS for nearly an hour before he came to. Meanwhile, he had a vision of walking toward a beautiful sunset over a river. It was as if he was a part of it, *one* with it. He melded in with his surroundings. He took time to feel the serenity of the moment, to admire and take in all the beauty that engulfed him. It was just something that happened every single day, yet he never took the time to notice it before. A voice came again and told him that he would now begin taking in more. He'd soon be noticing more things about the world and about himself.

It was true. After that event, he started seeing everything differently. He'd continue to get flare-ups of imagination...flashes of things...seeing things as plain as day, and then suddenly they would be gone. He saw a woman's face, for example, and then moments later that woman was near him offering help.

Ryan snapped to when he suddenly heard the sounds of someone walking their dog on the nearby roadway. He coughed from the humidity that hung in the air. It was so thick you could almost see it sparkling in the dim sunlight. He called out for help with a weak and raspy voice. "Help! Somebody? Help me, please."

"Are you okay? Can I help you?" A gentle, slender, blonde lady stood over Ryan looking very concerned.

Ryan could barely hold his eyes open. Blood had trickled down his face, and he looked a mess.

"I'm Hannah and I can help. Do you need an ambulance?"

Ryan shook his head no and sat up quickly in response, now leaning to one side. "I got caught in the storm and fell trying to get out of the woods. I hit my head and am just a little dizzy. I could use some help getting up, is all."

Hannah ordered him to stay put and called her husband, Ricky, who arrived shortly after with his Ford pickup truck. Ryan reluctantly accepted their help and grabbed the two rocks that were now next to where he was sitting. He shoved them in his pants pocket.

Arriving home, Ryan offered to pay them for their troubles, but they refused and said that it was the right thing to do. He waved them goodbye, thanked them for their kindness, and was just relieved that no one was home. He had time to compose himself and wash the blood off his head and face before the family came back from shopping. He took out the rocks, set them on the table, threw his wet, stinking clothes in the washing machine and jumped into the shower. He decided he'd keep the whole rotten experience to himself.

***

RYAN STAYED AWAY from the family and kept to himself that evening, like so many evenings before. He remembered asking Francis how he would know what two rocks to pick and the answer was only that he would know. He looked down at the stones, now in his hand. One was shiny and one was dull. They were different from the ones he had seen at the pond and different again from what he would have chosen. One had contents of pyrite and the other was a plain old sand rock, which he knew from the few lessons he had in school on the subject of geology. Why it would stick out in his mind was beyond him.

He tried to go to sleep but he lay in bed wide awake, shivering into the night. He tossed and turned, trying to tune out old echoes of the past. One memory was of his grandfather yelling. It scared Ryan to see such violent expression toward his father. "I pissed myself that time, too! Mom re-dressed me and made me swear secrecy not to upset the men." He had totally forgotten about that.

An unexpected tear flowed down Ryan's face as he thought about the eerie repetition of having to hide his shame again today. He was pretty sure Hannah and her husband could smell it off of him today. He wanted to sit in the back of the truck but they insisted that he stay in the cab with them. He laid awake most of the night feeling insecure and weak. His head throbbed into the wee hours of the morning.

THE NEXT DAY, Ryan headed out to go to the scheduled session with Francis. He checked his calendar and the time to be sure he had everything correct.

After his shocking experience in the woods, he was afraid of what would happen next. He looked a bit like a sulking dog licking its wounds in the corner. He didn't have the energy to hold the façade that he assumed the first day. Francis was waiting for him at his desk with a much softer expression on his face than the first time they met. Ryan adjusted and held himself as steady as he could, hoping that Francis wouldn't notice his injury. The bruise from the fall was hidden by his brown wispy hair. His head was still pounding, and his shoulder drooped a bit, as it was still tender; it took everything he could muster to try and keep himself aligned in a proper, composed stance.

Francis looked him up and down, and offered him a chair. Ryan sat down slowly and carefully.

"How is your head, brother?"

Ryan snapped to attention. "My head? How do you know about my head?"

Francis looked at him strangely. "A lot of thinking this week?"

"Oh, ah, yeah! I thought a lot, yes."

"How is your beautiful wife?"

"She is well. Thank you. I mean, Clara is well."

"Good to hear it. No better feeling than honouring the woman of the house, eh?"

Ryan paused a moment. "Yeah, uh!"

"And the two rocks?"

"Yes, I have them." Ryan was trying to be as clear and concise as possible without sounding too overly robotic. He wasn't going to get caught in another trap.

"Interesting experience this week, eh?"

"To say the least, yes. I'm not exactly sure what happened this week but umm..." Ryan looked at Francis, surprised, wondering where his words were coming from. In fact, he hadn't planned on saying anything at all.

"Looks like you found the perfect rocks, brother."

Ryan looked down. He hadn't realized that he had the rocks already in his hands. He must have grabbed them automatically from his pocket and didn't notice it. "How do you know they're the perfect ones?"

"Because something happened."

"Yeah, about that. Umm, a lot happened while I was getting them." Why couldn't he just stay quiet? *Damn*, Ryan thought to himself.

"Good. Now, see these pots over here? Come to the sink and help me." Francis pointed toward the soil and a scoop, and told him to put some dirt in the two pots that he had provided for him.

"What's this for?"

"For planting."

"I know, but why?"

Francis ignored the question. "Now take these seeds and put some in each pot."

"What do these seeds grow into?"

"Plants," Francis answered honestly, though it sounded sarcastic to Ryan. "Later I'll ask you to put the rocks in the two different pots so you'll know which one is which. For now, you can think about it."

"What is this exercise for?"

Francis continued on as if Ryan hadn't spoken. "Water one each day and leave out the other one. Do not water the second pot."

"Which one do I water?"

"The one that needs to be nurtured."

Ryan felt like he was a four-year-old again. He was uncomfortable not knowing the exact details of what was happening or why. "Wait a minute, this makes no sense. Obviously, one will grow and the other won't."

"Yes, like everything in our lives, what grows depends on what we feed it."

"What do I do with the one that isn't watered?"

"Take it home too and put your attention only on the one you are watering. Bring them both back once the one you watered germinates and grows into something."

"We are not ending our session here, are we?"

"Do you want to?"

"No." Ryan stood with one hand on his hip as if standing his ground. He waited for Francis to speak first.

"Then go sit down."

Ryan's fake charade was suddenly squashed. He decided to try and check his attitude a bit. He could see that Francis wasn't so snarly when he took a calmer approach. "Something happened yesterday that I want to talk about. A lot of things happened, really." Ryan rolled his eyes at himself. Again, why couldn't he just shut his mouth?

It was too late; now Francis was curious. "Memories?"

"Yes, for one." Ryan wondered how the heck Francis knew things. Was this guy psychic or something? He decided not to ask and kept talking. "But more than that. I mean, did you see that lightning and hear that thunder yesterday? I got caught in it. In fact, it scared me so bad that I fell and I got knocked out cold."

"I did see it. Did they speak to you?"

"Did who speak to me?"

"The rock people."

Ryan expected to get a better reaction than that. "I just told you I got knocked out. Were you listening to me?"

"Yes."

"Okay. Well, if you call me hitting my head on one of those rocks speaking to me, then yeah, they spoke."

"It sometimes takes a good hit to get our attention."

"Yeah, okay! I never heard of anything called rock people before, so I'm not sure what you mean." Ryan thought for a moment. "Umm, actually, I heard a voice that said, 'Place of Innocence.' I heard it outside my head. Where that would come from is beyond me." Ryan felt heat in his face from the embarrassment of just having admitted that out loud to someone. He kept the rest to himself.

Francis continued forward, unruffled by what he just heard. It was as if he was expecting Ryan to say all that. "The important part is where it brought you."

"Then I had that storm situation happen and it brought me back to a rather uncomfortable memory."

"Yes, you were brought back to the place of innocence."

"Yes, back to my childhood, which I hadn't thought of much. Well, those times not ever, actually. I haven't thought of my grand-father on my dad's side for many years. He was a difficult man. He lived with us. My grandmother died when I was a baby." There was something about Francis that pulled words out of him. It was getting rather annoying.

Francis got Ryan focused again. "Like your parents now live with you, your grandparents lived with them, eh?"

"Yes."

"How do your kids react to your parents being there?"

"My dad stays quiet. He's good to them when he does talk. My kids are okay with him. He was different when I was young. Nothing like his father, but he had some anger bouts, too, I guess. My kids don't see any of that, though. My mom is more active in their lives; she runs the show, as we determined the last time I was here."

"Now your mother covers both your father's tracks and yours, eh?"

Ryan snapped forward a bit and grabbed his shoulder. He had forgotten how painful it was to move too quickly. "What does that mean?" he asked while rubbing his arm.

"Your anger—she hides it for you. She's doing a good job, I see. And she tries to cover Clara's pain that's caused from your anger and by her control over Clara."

"Oh, wow! Where are you getting that from?"

"It's obvious."

"Obvious?"

"Don't you think it's time you dealt with all that anger?"

"I wouldn't exactly call myself angry." Ryan folded his arms like a kid refusing to play a game that he was losing.

"What was the storm about then?"

"A weather system," Ryan confirmed. "A freak storm. I mean a storm that was forecasted, but not scheduled to be that bad." He unfolded his arms again and wiggled in his chair uncomfortably.

"Sometimes that's how anger comes. It rolled right in, eh? Our emotions affect the world around us, including the weather...just so you know."

"The storm came from my emotions? Yeah, right!"

"It seems you have a gift of transferring some of that energy up into the weather system. So, yup!"

Ryan rolled his eyes and scrunched up his face to show his denial. "I don't know about that. Like I said, it was just a freak storm that came suddenly. There was absolutely no sign of clouds when I walked to the pond, and where I got the rocks. I wasn't there very long. All of a sudden, I was over my head in danger and the next thing I knew, well you know..."

Francis spoke calmly. "Nature sometimes helps us release when we can't let it out through emotions. Call it Earth Repair."

"That's a strange thought. If that was the case, I don't even know what I had to release. It wasn't my anger that I remembered, afterwards, it was my grandfather's. I don't even remember ever getting angry in my childhood, maybe a bit in my adulthood, but I wouldn't exactly call it a problem."

"Yours came out in different ways, brother. Your anger comes from women, not men."

"I'm not angry at women." Ryan looked shocked. It was as if someone pushed him. He tilted back slightly in the chair.

"But you are struggling over women's issues right now, brother, aren't you?"

Ryan decided Francis had won that battle and didn't bother fighting him on that subject. "Yeah, about the women thing, umm?"

"You made some mistakes?"

"To say the least, yes."

"And so now what do you want to do about that?"

"I would like to repair it or at least see if it's worth salvaging."

"Are you ready to do the work? Or let me guess, do you want to blame that part on Clara also?"

"I think I would like to keep her out of it for now. Thanks." Ryan felt shameful suddenly.

"Your call, brother."

"I'm scared to ask about how I'm angry at women, but something tells me that I had better ask here rather than allow nature to teach me this week."

"Your mom."

"My mom? Maybe I *shouldn't* have asked. What do you mean?"

"You have a lot of respect for her. You cover for her a lot, I can see."

Ryan pounced, suddenly feeling protective of his mother. "It's the right thing to respect her and care for her!"

"No, I mean you cover her back, like she covers yours. Your words just now are a good example of that. Imagine if her anger was ever unleashed. That would be a big storm, eh?"

"My mom is never angry, though. She is the nicest person in the world. She's always smiling and dresses beautifully. She does everything perfectly right, if you know what I mean. She gets upset sometimes but not angry."

Francis shook his head and smiled. "Pepsi or Coke pours out real nice into the glass, doesn't it? But if you shake up the can or bottle beforehand, what happens?"

"It fizzes up." Ryan looked at his counsellor with squinted eyes. Where was Francis going with this?

"Yup. And if your mom was ever shaken up like the can of Coke? As I mentioned, that would be a great big storm."

"I get your point, but she would never really fizz up because she doesn't really show it when she is upset."

"Again, another example of you two covering up for one another."

Ryan never thought about things like that before. This guy was certainly unique. Andrew did warn him. He paused for a while staring intensely at Francis with his eyebrows squeezed together till it caused a crease, like the fold on a lizard's elbow. He looked around the room to see if this guy had any credentials. He remembered Andrew talking about the ego stopping him. He decided to continue despite his misgivings.

"So, you are saying that my mom keeps things from getting shaken up to not let things get stirred up?"

"I'm saying that sweet things like Coke fizz if you shake them."

Ryan busted out laughing. "Where is this going?" He murmured a few choice words under his breath. "Mom is an angel, even if she is sweeping things under a rug a bit."

"A bit?"

"Yeah, a bit! It still doesn't excuse Clara getting so upset with her. It's not right!"

"I would be upset too, if someone was controlling me all the time."

"Wait a minute, cool it down here a bit!" Ryan couldn't hold back his reactions anymore. "Control? Dare I ask? Where are you getting all of this from? I told you, she only wants to help us, so we'll have a good life; that isn't control. She's like an angel."

"You told me everything I needed to know in our last session about your life with Clara. I know a controller when I see one. You can't fool me, brother."

"I'm confused. So, Clara is the controller?"

Francis gave out a bellowing laugh. "Are we in the same conversation? Your *mom* is the number one controller. You're the result of that control. You are controller number two, aiding and abetting your mom, who is teaching your kids to become the next phase of controllers."

"That was a joke, right?"

"Want to continue the session?"

"Yes."

"Remember, you are now becoming the second controller in the house."

"Can you walk me through that part so I can understand?" Ryan was curious how this would all play out. "Because I completely disagree with you. I'm never around enough to control anyone and my mom is anything but a controller."

"Where is Clara in your life? Where is she in your household? Who runs the kitchen of her life? How should Clara dress again? Like Gloria? How should Clara wear her hair today?"

Ryan stopped him there. "Okay, okay, I get the point. But I don't stop her from doing what she wants. Clara does everything on her own. She chooses the kids' activities; she chooses for herself. She has an easy life. She should be more grateful and respectful and not so mean about my mom. That's my whole point."

"Single moms have a lot of responsibilities, yes."

"Single moms? What are you saying?"

"I'm saying that Clara is a single mom living in your mother's house. There's no man of the house from what I can see. Am I wrong?"

"What are you talking about? There's my dad and I!"

"And the kids? Are you an example to any boys in the family?"

"Well, our five-year-old boy is pretty strong-willed. He seems to be our little man. He gets what he wants when he wants."

"Yes, he's being shown early how to control and disrespect women."

"Okay, I'm really confused here. Controlling and disrespecting women? That's over the top now. You're really starting to piss me off!"

"Good! And yes, he is being groomed to disrespect women just like you do."

"Come on! That was unprovoked and uncalled for and you know it!"

"So, I must be wrong then. You never did anything to disrespect the women in your life?"

Ryan felt a panic coming on. "I need a break. I think I need a drink of that Coke or Pepsi you talked about. Got a vending machine?"

"I keep lots of Coca-Cola in that fridge just over there. Please go and help yourself."

Ryan opened up a can and took a long drink. He needed a moment to focus and regain a bit of composure. His heart calmed down after a drawn-out breath. He counted to ten in his head before he spoke again. "So, what's Clara in all of this?"

"She is the woman losing patience with you while you figure all this out."

"I can see this will take a while by the looks of it."

"One storm at a time, brother."

"Why do you keep calling me brother?"

"Because every man is my brother from another mother."

"What?" Ryan decided to just move forward and let that comment rest. "What exactly do I need to work toward as an end result here?"

"A happy wife."

Ryan laughed out loud. He was beginning to relax and understand Francis's style a bit. He was obviously the hard-ass cop type. Ryan saw this kind of character in the movies but figured it was just an American crime film thing. There was just no good-cop coming in for relief, is all. "Okay, funny guy, I mean what is the end lesson? Because I can see here that you're trying to take me down a road that I never asked to go on."

"I asked you if you were willing to do the work, did I not?"

"You did. So, what exactly is the end result that you are leading me toward so I can get this over with?"

"Freedom."

"What kind of freedom? I told you my mom is there through thick and thin, and I have all kinds of freedom in my life because of it."

"Freedom from your mom and dad's programs and the tools needed to clear and then choose your own patterns. Not to mention a restarting of your relationship with Clara, without those programs and without your mother ruling the roost. A happy wife is a happy life, brother."

"I don't get this whole thing about freedom or programs. I can see how people affect one another but I don't have programs. My life is great. Clara is the problem that I just need to have cleared up."

"Are you sure about that?"

"Yes. I can see clearly what's going on in my own life and I think I'm the one that's okay."

"Okay, boss!"

"Don't call me boss!"

"Okay, brother."

Ryan couldn't help but laugh. This guy was relentless.

"We'll see if you are okay or not. Just so you know, the toughest fall the hardest."

Ryan scoffed. "Huh! Just so you know, I don't expect to fall or to fail."

"In time you'll see it for yourself. Denial is a big step to get past. The more open-minded you become, the deeper you'll go and the faster you'll move forward. Move quickly and soon you won't know yourself. In a good way, of course."

"Believe me, I want to get through all of this as fast as possible."

"Are you sure about that?"

"Yes, I am."

"Okay—I'll put in the request to go even faster, then. Just so you know: it may be a bumpy ride. Get your seatbelt on."

"Okay, whatever. I just don't see that I have that much that needs to be changed, if I'm honest."

"If you want to move through it quickly, then you better start having different questions or a different focus to work on. Not to mention the fact that the more you fight it, the bumpier the road gets."

Ryan decided to go along with Francis's game; obviously he was having fun toying with him. "Okay, how do I begin a new relationship with Clara, then? How is that for a focus?"

"Good—and you do that by healing you."

"Healing *me*? You jumped from honour, to anger, to mom being a controller, to me controlling, and then me teaching my boy to disrespect women. Now I need to heal myself? You've got to be kidding me! This is getting more confusing by the minute."

Francis smiled playfully. "Now you see how much work you need to do. You have to heal the control, the anger, and clear the patterns. Yep, that's a lot of programs to deal with. So yes, time to heal yourself."

Ryan threw his arms up in the air. His shoulder hurt terribly and a burst of anger flooded through his veins, leading him to slam his fist on his knees like a madman. Grabbing his shoulder to try and stop the pain, he searched for the door and felt that he was trapped like an animal in a cage. He looked up at Francis with rage and frustration. Suddenly, the anger disappeared and all that was left was this feeling of being completely alone and lost. A huge tear rolled down his face and dropped at his feet.

Francis allowed some time for Ryan to collect himself again before he spoke. "Another Cola, brother?"

Ryan had a frog in his throat and could barely speak. "Yes, please."

"It has been a while since you allowed yourself to feel that emotional pain, hasn't it? As men, we are sometimes expected to hold all of that in. I'm happy for you to finally feel all that frustration. It's a good sign. You finally got to let it out without someone covering it up for you or babying you through it. You were probably taught that men would be angry if you got upset, weren't you? You aren't used to feeling so much, are you?"

Ryan felt the throbbing again as he shook his head no. "I don't think it's a good sign at all. Not for me it isn't."

"You've been expected to be a good boy your whole life and to submit to the household program and to hide anything that would bring shame to the family. Anything out of that pattern couldn't fit into that box.

"Clara is made up of a different program and so maybe this is why she doesn't fit into your household. You're doing real good, brother...amazing, really. I haven't broken a horse in so easily in quite a while."

"You mean you wanted me to be angry? That is just mean!" It took everything in Ryan not to throw a punch.

"I wanted the real you to have a safe place to begin finding your freedom, brother. Real freedom. You can't do that by holding things in as tightly as you've been for so many years."

"But I feel terrible. My shoulder is killing me today, and I haven't even told you the extent of my experience at the pond. I mean, it's all very embarrassing."

"You don't have to tell me. There are some things we are meant to be able to keep to ourselves unless we want to speak it. That is freedom from having to do something. The freedom you'll have some day is called 'freedom to,' meaning freedom to do what you choose. When you have freedom to do what you want based on expectations of others, that isn't a freedom, brother.

"Your mom set you up really nice, it's true. She gave you everything to comfort you into a life that would keep you close by her side and wouldn't stir things up too much. She also ensured that you would always need her. She did not offer you the freedom needed to allow you to see what life would be like with other viewpoints, other experiences, and other patterns...a life that you could choose for yourself."

"I don't know what to do now. Remembering the past wasn't fun. Experiencing what I did in the thunderstorm sort of conjured up stuff that isn't comfortable and now I have to deal with current stuff. And sitting here with you is no fun, either. It's the worst part of it all, actually!"

Francis chuckled. "Good for you, brother, for feeling comfortable to speak that way about me."

"What?"

"That is real freedom. Healing isn't always comfortable. I read somewhere that if we had a good day every day, it would be a great set of days. It would be a good life. We wouldn't learn a lot, though. Today and the thunderstorm day are also great days. Great days to learn and grow, that's what makes the difference. Sometimes people live in what I would call a controlled atmosphere. Those are good lives also, but they are often lives lived inside a box. I'm here to get you out of that box. If I make you uncomfortable, then I take that as a compliment. It means you are learning something."

"You want me uncomfortable? That is crazy to me. And I'm learning nothing here because your words don't make any sense to me."

Francis continued. "When we live in a box and never get outside of it, then we also don't learn how to deal with anything outside of what we consider to be our normal. We become closed-minded, and that doesn't leave much room for acceptance of anything or anyone new in our life. We start to expect things. For the most part, everything we do expect will and does happen. This is kind of like living while asleep opposed to living awakened. The problem with that is when something or someone new is introduced into our life, we are often unaccepting. To accept that new thing or person means that we have to change. To change means that we have to live outside that box. We feel unsafe, unsure, and scared, and sometimes even angry toward our new environment or new people entering our life. The black sheep comes into the crowd and everything goes awry, doesn't it?"

Ryan's mind was everywhere at once. He thought about his own life and how maybe it was kind of true that he was living in a controlled atmosphere or controlled setting. Francis waited for Ryan to speak. "I had no desire to have an outburst like that, but you just pissed me off, Francis! I see now that you were goading me to try and get me to react. I may not like your methods, but I guess you're trying to help in a roundabout way, and I'm sorry for my explosion. It was uncalled for."

"Again, you're doing real good, brother. I'm proud of you for speaking up like that. You're in a safe place here to do that. And remember, you asked for this to go fast. I'm just honouring your request."

Ryan was relieved to know now that Francis wasn't as hard as he let on he would be at the beginning. "I can't believe I'm saying this, but thank you for understanding and not getting upset also. So, what's next? Are we going to talk about Clara? To be honest, I'm not up for that right now. I'm feeling really tired and drained, I didn't get much sleep last night and this session has given me a lot to mull over. Could we end this conversation with something easier for me to handle?"

"Okay. The first thing I want you to do is to take another look at these pots of plants that you put together today. Put one rock in each planted pot so you know which one is which. Choose which one you'll water."

"Well, that's an easy one. The pot with the shiny one. Wait! Maybe the other one. I get a sense that this is some kind of test or trick or something. Yeah okay, I choose the sand rock one."

"Okay, I see."

"If I chose wrong, then tell me." Ryan waited to see if Francis would give him the right answer. He didn't. "I'll take the shiny one then. No, no, no! Okay, going back to my first thoughts. No, umm, wait—which one was I thinking first? I'll take the plant with the dull one." Without knowing for sure why, Ryan grabbed the pot with the sandstone rock as his official choice, hoping to please Francis.

"Okay, the sandstone one it is. Take them both with you, and only water that one, never the other one. Our sessions are done or on pause until you get some growth in your plant. Just come in when you're ready to see me next. No need for an appointment."

"What if you're busy at that time? How long will it take to grow? Why don't we book right now, just in case?" Ryan wasn't exactly sure why he was suddenly begging to come back.

Francis smiled. His plan had succeeded. He knew by pushing a guy like Ryan, it would challenge him enough to come back. He had no intention of tricking him; he genuinely saw good in Ryan, that was all. Now how to help him draw that part of himself out was clear. He had a hunch that Andrew would help him adjust before the next session, also. "Just come. Like I said, that particular session you won't have to book. I'll be here."

"How do you know? What if you're not here? Or with another client? How will I know what time or what day to come? Usually, I book things ahead of time so I know what to expect. I'm a schedule guy. How will I know when to come?"

"You will just know. Let go of control and let's see what happens. I have a feeling it'll work out beautifully in more ways than one."

Ryan took a deep breath. The unknown was scary for him and he was realizing for the first time that he liked the controlled atmosphere after all. Francis crossed one arm over his chest and grabbed Ryan's hand with the other. He hugged him with a crossed heart, making sure not to hurt his shoulder. He walked out of the room like in their first session, saying nothing, making no excuses, and disappearing mysteriously.

A strange feeling came over Ryan as he downed the last swig from the Coke can. He sat listening to the last of the bubbles as they fizzled out. His ears rang with the silence in the room and from the headache that still lingered. So many thoughts rolled around in his mind. Were the pots about Clara and Gloria? Was Francis playing some kind of mind game? Were they about Clara and his mom? Was he really a controller? Was he really angry? Again, tears welled up in his eyes and he took a deep breath to push them back inside before walking out the door. He wanted to get out before any other feelings washed over him. He had had enough.

Chapter Three

Moving Forward

RYAN LEFT THE pot with the shiny stone out on the back doorstep where it wouldn't get wet. He entered the house quietly and put the other pot on the windowsill where the sun came in for a good part of the day. He'd be sure to only water one of them.

A few minutes later, trying to make sense of everything that had been happening in the sessions, he decided to call Andrew. "Hey, Andy, wow, you really sent me to a drill sergeant, huh?"

"Don't give up, please, Rye—trust me, you won't regret it in the end, like I told you before. You'll get used to him pulling out weeds. Do you see now why I couldn't really explain anything in the beginning?"

"I would say that if you had explained it to me, I wouldn't have made an appointment. That's for certain," Ryan chuckled.

Andrew knew his friend needed consoling. "Look, I know you're feeling frustrated and vulnerable right now. It's not something that I'd ever experienced before, either. This guy seemed like he was from a different universe. Francis seemed cruel at first, but after a while I realized he was just talking without any filters; he called it as he saw it. He spoke with authenticity. In the places of my life where I felt emptiness, he was speaking with wholeness. No one I knew ever approached me that way before. I took offence to his honesty, and I saw a pure act of love as competition. I felt like there was a war up against me. Later, he helped me tame that part of myself that was trying to stop me from moving forward. The part of me that I didn't realize was sabotaging my own happiness. I know now that part of me is called the ego. He'll get into all that with you."

"Tell me what to expect. I do much better if I have the curriculum laid out for me."

Andrew sighed and took a moment to think. "Expectation is a killer. When we set ourselves up for what we want to hear, we also set ourselves up for disappointment. I tried playing that game at first. I learned that what we want isn't always what we need."

"But that's exactly it. I went for a reason and he hasn't even started helping me with *that!*"

Andrew laughed. "I know. I know, the reason is for you to help Clara. I don't even have to ask. If I know Francis like I do, he made one thing clear. We can only help ourselves."

"Well, he didn't put it into those words exactly, but yeah, okay, I guess he did enforce the fact that *I* might be her problem." Ryan laughed realizing how silly that sounded.

"Okay, so now that's important," Andrew explained. "Clara has her own stuff to deal with and once you dissect your own inner world, what you'll find is that her issues start to be dealt with automatically. Especially if you have anything to do with being her problem."

"Do you mean if I go and do this counselling, Clara will change?" Ryan liked the sound of that.

"Yes, she'll have reason to change because she'll feel safer because she won't be the only one working on herself. Do you know what I mean?"

Ryan murmured in agreement. "I kind of get what you're saying, but I still feel like I'm wasting my time there. I still didn't get what I came for."

Andrew stopped him there. "You'll know what I mean later on. For now, remember, I went there for my own reasons and he saw right through them. You need to understand that he sees underneath our programs and belief systems. He sees our potential, too. Instead of taking years to sort through the layers of programs to get to the bottom of it, he goes right to the root system and hauls out the weed causing the problem."

"You wouldn't have time for a beer, would you? I would love to talk more." Ryan needed a personal connection in order to understand further.

"I don't drink alcohol anymore, Rye, but I'll meet you tomorrow and pay for your lunch down at Sam's Diner if you're available. What time would be good for you?"

Ryan shook his head in disbelief. Andrew never ceased to surprise him. He used to drink like a fish.

***

"ARE WE GETTING old?" Ryan laughed.

"You are," Andrew laughed back. "I love the home cooking here, and that we aren't a number to the waitresses. They know our names here."

Ryan couldn't argue. Sam's *was* nice. He was surprised that this place had lasted. Nothing had changed. The steel stools still lined up with the counter overlooking the waitresses, who were busying themselves. The booth tables lined up as they always had. The same ladies who worked here when he was a kid were still serving.

"So, I have a few more questions for you about this Francis guy. It's funny, you know: Yesterday you described it as him pulling out weeds. That was a good one because he has me gardening and picking rocks, for God's sake. I think you sent me to the local greenhouse expert, not a counsellor."

Andrew laughed and then called the waitress over for some green tea for himself and allowed her to ask Ryan what he was drinking. Ryan decided nervously to take the same. He felt uncomfortable with Andy's choice, yet didn't want to be the one sticking out like a sore thumb.

"Okay, same for me—tea it is," he laughed nervously.

A new lady came to take their order for lunch. Andrew rebounded back into the conversation as soon as she left. "Francis is a gifted one. He'll help you put it all together at some point."

"To be honest, I find that he's too pushy!"

"Francis is like the sunrise, something you can rely on to be there when you need it after a dark night. Something you can't appreciate unless you take time out in your day to really look around and pay attention."

Ryan laughed and shook his head again. "Andy, I don't know about you, man. You've changed."

Andrew thanked him for the compliment and carried on with the conversation. "How have you been doing with emotions?"

"Well!" Ryan sighed, "It's been rough."

Andrew explained that when he began his own self-journey, the shift of awareness caused him to be more empathetic to the world around him. "I had to separate myself from people for a while to figure out what was mine and what wasn't. I was feeling things out of this world. I had to learn not to share too much of my energy with the people around me. It's also when I put down the bottle."

"So, what's the point of no alcohol? Wouldn't getting drunk help?" Ryan was getting more and more curious.

"After I started my journey and the road got narrow, I wanted to *feel* even more."

"That makes absolutely no sense. Sorry, man...I mean one day you feel 'off' so you cut out normal things? For what? To feel worse? Alcohol was invented to cheer people up and to help us *not* feel." Ryan's voice was slightly defensive. "Are you trying to push some kind of cult onto me?"

Andrew smirked. "Yes, the spaceship leaves tomorrow. Have your bags packed."

Ryan laughed but he felt anger rolling forward inside him like a fast train. He wasn't even sure why he was so upset. Maybe even offended.

Andrew kept moving forward, asking more from Ryan. "What kind of emotions were hitting you, Rye? You may as well spit it out if you want my help. Be clear with me, otherwise you're just wasting time, here."

Ryan respected the fact that Andrew was being straight up and so he decided to tell him the truth. "Well, I may as well be honest and tell you. I got nothing to lose. Clara and I haven't been as intimate as we used to be. I guess it stopped after I had a thing with Gloria."

Andrew nodded, folded his arms, and leaned forward so they could speak lower while the waitresses were around them. "Yup, I saw that coming. Go on."

"Tom and Gloria were always around us. We did everything together. Our kids are the same age, and so we ended up in the same vacation areas, even. My parents took our kids while we left on vacation evenings. Maybe at some point Gloria and I would sit alone as Tom and Clara would grab the drinks. At the pool they'd swim, or one would swim and the other would head to the hotel room for something. It seemed more and more that Gloria and I had small moments alone. It seemed to be normal at first. Maybe it got too normal.

"One comfort led to another, and one night when Clara got tired and headed to bed early, and Tom got called to the hospital for an emergency, Gloria and I found ourselves alone. An opportunity presented itself. I can't say I'm proud of it or that I got that much satisfaction out of it, to be honest. At first, we kind of brushed it off like it never happened and for months we all still hung out. Months turned into a couple of years, and opportunities sprung up here and there.

"Things got tricky. I put a stop to it when I realized Gloria started seeing it as more than just a thing and got emotional and stupid about it. She started contacting me unexpectedly. I told her it was just a physical act and to let it go. She finally got the point and backed off just recently. It wasn't worth losing my friendship with Tom.

"Clara had no clue, but she got increasingly colder with me. Over time, she stopped wanting to hang out with Tom and Gloria anymore. I still meet with them. Clara does come when I force her out, but she has some kind of attitude now and it drives me insane. I mean I love how Gloria looks and I admitted that to Clara so maybe she felt jealous of that. For sure I know she never caught on to the sex thing and probably never will."

Andrew listened intensely and only adding, "Clara's body knew what her mind didn't, brother."

Ryan sat silent for a moment, thinking about what Andrew had just spit out, not to mention the fact that he called him "brother" like Francis did. That was just weird. Had he just confessed all of that out loud to Andrew? Clara's body knew what her mind didn't? What did that mean?

Andrew remained still and silent. He didn't judge nor support Ryan. He just sat there like a witness, taking it all in.

"It was an honour hearing your story, Rye. I believe you're onto something. The answers are all there."

Puzzled, Ryan looked at Andrew. "Answers? I asked no questions."

Andrew smiled compassionately and explained that he would be thinking of Ryan and his family and sending good thoughts their way. "I'm looking forward to hearing about the next part of the journey. May your road narrow quickly."

Andrew seemed to know a lot more than he was saying, and Ryan was starting to get uncomfortable with that. He felt stupid suddenly for speaking as much as he had.

Andrew felt Ryan's apprehension and decided to say a bit more. "Can you promise me something?" Ryan nodded his head in agreement. "Go back to Francis. Put your guard down. Think of it like, the more you stay open, the faster you get through this thing so Clara can choose to change for herself. Can you do that?"

Ryan sat there in silence for a moment. He took a long, drawn-out breath. "Okay. But I don't exactly know how to do that."

"You go in with no expectations, no attachment to the outcome, and you let him lead more. Let your mouth open up and just speak without a filter."

Ryan just nodded again in agreement with pursed lips and squished eyebrows.

"Can I ask you something before we leave?" Andrew asked.

"Yes," Ryan agreed hesitantly, knowing almost immediately that he should have said no.

"I'm really not teasing you here, but did he make you cry yet?"

Ryan stood up slightly and waved for the bill.

"No, really—I'm not trying to make fun of you; I went through it, too. Did he break you?"

Ryan smiled shyly and nodded yes.

"Good!" Andrew was delighted. "This means that the next session will go a lot easier."

***

IT HAD BEEN eight weeks since Ryan had last seen Francis. In the meantime, he could see that the plant had grown. He had been busy, yet uninvolved. Even sports seemed to get set aside as he dealt with things. Deep down he knew he was making excuses for not going back to Francis. He hadn't wanted to look too closely at the situation, denying any wrongdoing on his part, feeling sorry for himself for being stuck trying to please the two main women in his life.

After a few more pep talks with Andrew, Ryan was beginning to let go of his hesitations and to feel more courageous or enthusiastic about helping himself. They met up to talk each week, going over some of the concepts that Francis had brought up in the first two sessions. Today had been one of those days. They had a long breakfast at the diner. Ryan asked every question he could, to try and know what to expect from the sessions.

"It doesn't work that way, Ryan. There is no one set agenda when it comes to Francis. It happens as it goes. He doesn't plan when or how he'll say stuff. He bases it on your questions and your energy."

"My energy? I have been a nervous wreck, so I hope he doesn't base it on that. How long is it going to take for me to feel like I'm getting results? I don't want to go in and feel like an idiot again."

Andrew knew he was being prodded for reassurance so he was honest. "There was no real set time for anything in Francis's world. It was around the third or fourth session that I had a major turnaround. I have a feeling this meeting tomorrow is going to be one of those turnaround moments for you, too. I would go back if I were you. I'm telling you, something is going to shift"

"What do you think my shift is going to be?"

"Ryan, if I'm honest with you, I get the sense that Clara's going to be your turnaround."

"What do you mean by that?"

"Okay, we both know you cheated on her, but if we put that aside, I think you love her a lot deeper than you know. You were not yet put in a position of losing her. I think you would have crumbled in a snap and grovelled at her feet for her forgiveness if she had found you out."

"I wouldn't exactly crumble, but I admit, yeah, disappointing her would suck, but grovel? Come on!" Ryan laughed at the thought.

"I know you better and for a lot longer than anyone else involved in this situation, Ryan. You were one of the most sensitive and sensible kids I knew growing up. That's why I stuck with you. Okay, you were a competitor but never ever a cheater. If anyone played against the rules, you were the first one to take it up with them. The person you hated the most was a liar and a cheat. So yeah! Once you tap back into the real you again, you'll be grovelling. Enjoy your session tomorrow. You'll be happy you went back, trust me."

RYAN CAME HOME from seeing Andrew with a lot on his mind. He just wanted some peace and quiet. Clara and the kids were in the backyard filling up a new pool that she was setting up as a surprise. He felt a bit upset with her about not talking to him before making the purchase.

"What is this?"

Clara smiled and asked him to go grab the lunch she had made. There were sandwiches waiting on the table.

"Mom will have lunch for us in an hour. This is crazy and I'm not hungry. I just ate. I had a late breakfast with Andy."

Clara smiled and explained, "She'll have to be okay with me making food for my own family, today of all days."

Ryan brought the sandwiches out grudgingly, soon forgetting his anger as the kids crawled all over him. They laughed and giggled with excitement, hoping he would throw them in the pool. "It's freezing cold! Wait until tomorrow," Ryan grumbled.

Clara smiled and shook her head no. Later she and the kids got their bathing suits on and she threw Ryan's swimming trunks at him. They stayed in the pool for only a short while, but their smiles told him to keep his mouth shut. It was nice to see Clara beaming for a change.

RYAN'S MOM WAS quite upset that evening.

"Mom, cool down!"

"Who does she think she is?" Maria was infuriated. "Nobody told me anything. We could've been invited downstairs. I would've brought the food down. She acts like she owns the place. And you! You ate what? Sandwiches? That isn't even real food. She doesn't know what she's doing. She's never cooked in her life. No wonder she only made sandwiches."

Ryan felt a twinge of exhaustion. He was surprised to see his mom acting like this. "Mom, don't you think you are being a little unfair? Like I said, I'm sorry. I'll deal with her. Now calm yourself and don't get so upset."

Maria put her hands out in front of her as if to say stop and looked out into the distance. "I just want to have peace in my house, Ryan."

"I'm sorry, Mom." Feeling helpless, he turned and went back downstairs.

Confused about the whole situation, Ryan wasn't sure what to say. Today had been the first time in a long while that he had seen Clara so happy. She had a new shine in her eyes that he wasn't quite able to place. He wanted to consider the teachings he had gotten about letting her run her own household and he hadn't wanted to take that away from her. Yet it hurt him to see his mother hurt, too. Maybe they needed a bit of a break from the regular routine?

"Mom, tomorrow we won't be coming up here for supper. I just want to let you know out of respect. I just need a little peace for myself, too, so I'm ordering out. This way no one cooks for a day. You can come down if you want to, but me and my family are eating downstairs tomorrow. It's just one day, so don't worry. I love you, Mom, and I appreciate everything you do for us."

Maria turned away to wipe off the table and shifted sideways to speak to Ryan. "You guys enjoy, I'll be fine. We still have some leftovers from today since no one came to eat here. We'll use those up. Have fun, dear."

Ryan was relieved that his mother was so understanding. He felt bad for putting her in such an awkward position. Maybe Francis was wrong about his mom—she was uncomplicated and understanding after all. He was clearly causing unneeded trouble.

When Ryan came down, he saw that Clara had fallen asleep while sitting on the couch. She still had a glow about her even in her slumber.

The five-year-old was still bouncing around like a monkey. Where did all of this energy come from?

The nine-year-old smiled and said, "Thank you for making Mommy happy today, Daddy. She just needed to play, and the water wasn't too cold for her. Now let her sleep and help me put little Ryan to bed."

Ryan got shivers down his arms and legs as Angela guided her brother into the bathroom to brush his teeth. He caught on for the first time that Angela's name sounded a lot like angel. Did both kids age and he missed it? Maybe he hadn't been around as much as he should have been. He was often there in the body, just not always available on a conscious level. Tonight, there in the moment, it felt good.

"Doesn't Mommy look beautiful today!" little Ryan blurted out while pulling up the covers on his miniature car bed.

"Umm," is all Ryan could muster up to say back. In all honesty, he had no idea what Clara was wearing.

Angela tucked little Ryan in and kissed him on the forehead. "Yes, Honey, she is beautiful as always. Now sleep well and we'll see you in the morning. Now how does that rhyme go?"

Little Ryan blurted it out before he had a chance to say anything. "Good night, sleep tight, don't let the bedbugs bite..."

Ryan was astonished that little Ryan was able to talk so well. He followed Angela into her room and helped her up the steps to her bunk bed. She asked him to pass her the book she had been reading. "Unicorns, huh?"

"Yes," Angela said, "unicorns, Daddy. They help a poor innocent girl. Her daddy died and so her and her mommy lived all alone. The little girl finds a unicorn in the forest and has a secret relationship with her. Her mommy stopped believing in unicorns a long time ago. It's a bit sad. The girl won't give up on her mommy. Do you believe in unicorns, Daddy?"

Ryan jerked back and let out an unexpected whimper and answered back with a shaky voice, "I don't know. I mean, I *want* to believe, Honey. I want to." Not even sure why he said that, he started to tuck her in nervously.

Angela pushed his hands away and pulled the blankets up by herself. "Don't worry, Daddy. Like the unicorn told the girl for her mommy, I'll believe *for* you. Now you go get some sleep. Tomorrow is a new day and you'll need your rest."

Ryan shut out the main light and went out to the living room. He turned the television off and sat for a long time staring at Clara in silence. Her hair was lighter, almost blonde, and cut differently. Her dress was lovely, and simple. He hadn't taken the time out to really notice her lately. She was looking really good.

"Why was she so happy today? And why was she so dressed up?" A twinge of jealousy shot through him. Was she involved with another man? Deciding not to wallow too long in his perplexity, he took a blanket out from the chest and laid Clara down, reclining her into a more comfortable position on the sofa. Sound asleep, she squirmed and snuggled into the blanket as he shut the lamp off next to her head.

Now heading to the shower, Ryan couldn't pinpoint what he was feeling. For the past weeks he had taken in everything that he had learned with Francis through Andy's coaching, but it hadn't quite jelled together yet. He was questioning everything in his life, including his fatherhood.

A fit of anger hit him like a shot. Earlier his dad had just sat there as his mom scolded him about Clara's making sandwiches. *Why didn't Dad say anything? Was Mom in the right? Should Clara really need to ask to make food for the kids and me? Maybe Francis was right. Mom does wear the pants. Is there a man of the house? Have I been wrong this whole time? Do I need to make a few changes?*

This mind yo-yo-ing between thoughts was enough. It was time to get some needed sleep. Hopefully his counsellor would be there. Francis did say to just show up. Ryan would take his chances. Something would happen.

By the time Ryan was up and ready the next morning, Clara and the kids were already out for the day. He decided to leave a note for Clara, to say that he had told his mom that they wouldn't be having supper upstairs that evening and that he would be getting takeout for them to eat at their place tonight.

WAS IT REALLY almost July already? The pot of plants had grown into a type of flower that he was unfamiliar with. Maybe Francis would know what sort they were.

Chapter Four

THE TWO WOLVES

"HEY, HEY, SOMETHING told me to come into the office today! Good timing." Francis was a bit extra-vivacious today.

"Yeah, you told me to pick a day and just come in. I was going to call in to see if you were here but decided to take my chances."

"Yes, I was off on vacation for over a week and just got back yesterday, so it's good timing. I see you brought your plants. Marigolds! Wow, nice choice."

"You gave me the seeds, so why are you so surprised?"

"I had no idea what they were," Francis admitted. "They were just seeds that I had lying around. I see you left the other pot unwatered. Why?"

"Umm, because you told me to!" Ryan threw his arms up in the air in disbelief. Was Francis senile or something? Was it the right choice to come back to see him? He took a deep breath and decided to put his judgments aside. There was no going back on his promise to Andy.

"Ah, yes, and you listened. Great! Now put them both right over here."

Ryan placed the two pots on the countertop.

"So, where do we begin today, Ryan?"

Ryan found it odd that he was asking him where to begin. "I don't know what to say. I think I have stuff to share, and yet nothing really happened. I can thank Andy really for helping me make some small steps forward. You could say he got me past a few hiccups."

"Yeah? Well, the smallest steps are sometimes the most important ones."

Maybe he did have something to ask about after all. "I had the roughest dream last night and I'm freaked out about it. Maybe we can start there?"

"Okay, tell me about your dream."

"I was on a beach with Clara. It was magical, warm, and like the perfect day. It was as if I had everything I had ever wanted. Then the mood changed from relaxing to suddenly being intense. Clara spoke up loudly and asked if I trusted her. I told her I did, and then she yelled, 'Then run!' She grabbed my hand and ran into a building, demanding that we not take the elevator. We climbed the stairs and got to the top floor, which seemed to take forever. When we got there, we looked over and watched people being engulfed and swallowed up by the water. They were all being washed away in a massive tsunami, like the real ones you see that have been caught on camera. It came in a series of waves for a period of about half an hour, or so it seemed.

"I can see why they call it a 'wave train' because no single wave could make an impact like that. It felt so real, as though I was actually there. We were the only survivors except for one old man who stood there across from us. We were all knee-deep in water. Waves reached the top of our building. The structure itself was still standing strong. The water had rolled in and was now receding.

"The man looked at me hauntingly yet said nothing, as if I should know what he was thinking. The look on his face was so intense. Clara just stood in awe. She glanced at me a few times but mostly stood looking over the side. She never seemed to notice the old man. I woke up sweating."

"Wow, what a great dream! There's a lot in there."

"I would say a lot of water." Ryan could feel less stress today and he was happy to be leading instead of Francis. He felt more in control this way.

"You had a lot to wash away," Francis explained.

"A lot of what?"

"Well, water is a symbol of emotion."

Ryan decided to create a rapid reroute in the conversation. "That old man was creepy!"

"A wisdom keeper, eh?"

"He was wise because he saw the water coming and went to the top of the building?"

"He was wise because he could watch the memories without the emotional charge. He witnessed them for you."

"I don't know what you mean by that. It wasn't a memory. It was an event happening in real time, but it was in dream form."

"The water in the dream was a representation of what was built up inside you. The higher the water, the deeper the memories affecting you in this reality or real time. The parts of your physical life finally washed over you."

"Okay, I guess. So why would Clara say, 'Do you trust me'?"

"She was the one that was awakened and sensed the danger ahead."

"Obviously." Ryan rolled his eyes. "Thank God for that, but how did she know to run up there?"

"Everyone is at different levels. She had obviously been up there before and was down on your level for your sake. Pretty patient woman, if you ask me."

"Why wasn't I leading her? It was my dream."

"Because you were learning to follow her instinct. It's a sign of what's to come."

Ryan cocked his head back a moment. He stopped a few seconds to reflect. "Before I went to sleep, stuff happened that could be connected, I guess. A sort of fight happened between my mom and me about Clara's making a meal for me and the kids. The kids afterwards acted so adult-like, it floored me. Like *they* were the ones leading *me*. It was as though my daughter was the parent, not me."

"Yes, they say that the teacher will appear when the student is ready."

The words caused Ryan's eyes to flutter for an instant. He shook his head back and forth involuntarily before speaking. "I started seeing Clara differently."

"It took a whole eight weeks to get there, eh?" Francis refocused and directed Ryan to review his homework assignment. "So, let's look at those marigolds, shall we?"

"I was right, then? The pots were about Clara and my mom?"

"One pot was Clara, for sure."

"And the other pot?"

"Other women."

"Every other woman? Or a particular woman?"

"Any woman you put before Clara."

"So why not water that other pot?" Ryan couldn't help but ask questions. "The seeds sat dormant and that makes no sense. Why couldn't I have watered both and taken care of both?"

"You could have."

"But why didn't I?"

"Because Clara was the one who needed you. The other marigolds are someone else's responsibility to squirt moisture into. Don't you think?"

Ryan's face twisted with disgust. "Oh...you got me there!" He laughed and covered his mouth feeling ashamed, exposed and shocked all at once. "Francis, you turn words around like a Rubik's Cube expert."

"Thank you, and to solve that cube, we first need to figure out the format, don't we? The easiest method is to divide it into layers. The trickiest part is going to be for you not to mess up the pieces already in place."

"I never did get all sides of that cube mastered."

"Something tells me you are about to mess up one of those sides now with your next question."

"I need to know more about these pots. This wasn't about my mom at all, was it? You did know about Gloria!"

"No, but now I do. Who does this 'glorious' Gloria belong to, anyway?" Francis threw more quotation marks back up into the air.

"That would be my friend Tom, as I mentioned before."

"Your friend? Well, now you know who that other pot belongs to."

"Oh! Umm, yeah! I hear you."

FRANCIS DECIDED IT would be a good time to redirect his client. "Did you see that poster on the wall?"

"The one over there? Oh, yeah, that must be new."

"New to the room, yes. It's a teaching that has been around for a long time, though. Give it a read."

Ryan took a few minutes out to read the poster.

The Story of the Two Wolves: A Native American Parable

An old Cherokee is teaching his grandson about life. "A fight is going on inside me," he said to the boy. "It is a terrible fight and it is between two wolves. One is evil—he is anger, envy, sorrow, regret, greed, arrogance, self-pity, guilt, resentment, inferiority, lies, false pride, superiority, and ego."

He continued, "The other is good—he is joy, peace, love, hope, serenity, humility, kindness, benevolence, empathy, generosity, truth, compassion, and faith. The same fight is going on inside you—and inside every other person, too."

The grandson thought about it for a minute and then asked the grandfather, "Which wolf will win?"

The old Cherokee simply replied, "The one you feed."

"Wow, that is simple but powerful. I never saw that story before."

"Does it explain a few things?"

"Yes, it does." Ryan felt that this was perhaps that "aha moment" that Andrew told him would happen in the third or fourth session.

"And so, which wolf have you been feeding?"

"I was feeding a bit of both, I admit."

"So now when it comes to Clara you know what to do."

"Yes, I think I do, thanks. Can I ask now about the rocks?"

"Do you have to ask?"

"I think I got the answer already."

"Yes, I think you did, Ryan."

"The shiny one was Gloria."

"In that case maybe you didn't totally get the point. The shiny one was your ego drawing you to what separated you from your own spirit. Clara stopped being shiny when you stopped taking care of her, brother."

"You can say that again."

"Clara stopped being shiny when you stopped taking care of her, brother."

"Okay funny guy. I didn't mean to actually say it again."

Francis spoke firmly, "Say no more than what you mean then, brother."

Ryan locked his lips tight and nodded his head rapidly to show that he clearly understood. He wanted to avoid Francis's serious tone. "Tell me then, why did I get myself into the Gloria situation in the first place? You can't say it's because I was a controller?" Ryan regretted his words the moment they came out of his mouth.

"I can."

"How?"

"You have control over the two wolves, don't you?"

"Yes. I mean I do have a choice." There was no avoiding that one.

"Yes, and that choice controls the outcome, right?"

"Are you going to tell me next that I have to tell Clara what happened between me and Gloria?"

"No."

"Good. But wouldn't it be the right thing to tell her?" Ryan paused and squinted, surprised by his own sudden moral switch over.

"Do you want to tell her?"

"No, I don't. I mean not now, anyway. I think I have something I need to do first."

"The right thing to do would be to give Clara back her shine that you snatched from her and gave instead to Gloria. Then you'll know how to proceed from there."

"And how would I do that?"

"By letting Clara be the one to lead you."

"Is this where my mother comes in?"

"You already have that answer."

"Okay, I get that part, but I want to go back to the idea of my being a controller. How is my mom not the controller?"

"She is. We went over that already." Francis looked at him sternly as if to warn him not to backtrack too far.

"Okay, yeah, but yesterday I came to the realization that she was acting less like a controller and more like a victim. I feel bad saying that."

"Your mother *is* a controller and a victim, too."

"How can she be both at the same time?"

"How can you live two lives and have two women? It just happens. Victimhood is a wolf we choose to feed or not to feed, just like control. They often go hand in hand."

"Okay, I get that, I guess."

"Does your mom have a good golf swing?"

"What? I don't understand. Why do you ask? My mom doesn't golf. Should I take her golfing?"

Francis chuckled at the fact that Ryan still didn't catch on to his diversions. "I read somewhere that people who practise suffering and victimhood are neurologically doing the same thing as someone who is practising their golf swing every day. They get better and better at it. Breaking the habit of victimhood is as hard as breaking a drug habit. Once you have mastered being a victim, it's a skill for life and isn't easily forgotten."

"Oh, great! But I don't want to force my mom to change...or to change myself, for that matter."

Francis smiled gently. "You can't do things the same way over and over and expect different results, brother. That is insanity, as Einstein taught us. Besides, you have to figure out your own choices and allow your mom to choose hers. We need to allow others their own process.

"I have to warn you, though, now that you're becoming more aware of your own choices, your mom will begin swinging you like a golf club to retrain you back into submission. As you become more aware, you'll enjoy the game less and less. Getting past that and not getting stuck in the middle of her victimhood traps can bring you more enjoyment in the end. However, it's going to be like that Rubik's Cube you mentioned earlier, except the colours will keep changing on you. You'll have to pay close attention to the original cube if you want to master this one."

Ryan looked concerned. "I see that maybe it's not going to work out in the way that I had expected, and I feel torn. I still don't want to hurt anyone."

"Trying to please everyone will just make things harder for everyone involved, and in the end, you'll be the one in trouble. Controllers often get away with not taking their own responsibility. You take your own responsibility and let your mom take hers."

"What would my future look like, though, with an upset mother?"

"It would be a new future with new emotional experiences and an upset mother," Francis explained.

"But that isn't the future I want."

"There are three futures you can choose from."

"I have three futures?"

"Everyone has three futures."

"We do? What are they?"

"The first one is, if nothing changes, then nothing will change."

Ryan never heard anything like this in his life. It was interesting, however. "Okay. And the second one?"

"The second future consists of change. If something changes then something will change, along with it. I suggest the second future over the first."

"So, I can change things for my mom?"

"Worry about yourself and forget about your mom for now. When you change something in your own life, something will change for you. Her future is hers to choose, remember?"

"Okay, and the third future?"

"Well, you screw up."

"Oh, great, and what then? It just ends there?" Ryan felt utter disgust.

"No. You choose to feed another future. Another wolf."

"Wait a minute. What are we talking about here? Do you mean we have a third wolf like we have three futures?"

"Yes."

"Is there more to this? Are we talking a grey wolf?"

"A grey wolf, eh? I like that." Francis could see that Ryan was ready to hear more. "Okay, so imagine, this grey wolf then is an individual who has been in the world and has had some experience. Screwing up has taught him to be stronger and hopefully wiser. He was born as a white wolf, innocent to the world, and has become blackened by experience, which causes him to become grey now.

"After screwing up, we feed the grey wolf the positive traits. Innocence is once again possible, just on a different level now. He knows better because of experience. He melds innocence with experience. He is the white wolf again, but now with the knowledge of the grey wolf. We are less likely to make the same mistake twice if it hurt enough the first time around, right?"

Ryan nodded. It was obvious that people learn from their experiences, but, he wondered, how could you combine innocence with experience?

Francis could see the wheels turning in Ryan's mind. He decided to push a bit further. "We can also start feeding the positive aspects again to the white wolf yet act as the grey wolf from experience. Do you follow me?"

"Yes, but what if you wasted the first three futures?"

Francis scoffed. "You're still stuck there?"

Ryan couldn't stop there. All pistons were firing at once. "It's like a genie in the bottle and you wasted the wishes, isn't it? It messes up everything. I don't understand how we are allowed another choice? It doesn't seem fair."

"We're always allowed three new futures at every turn in our lives. Even when life is good, we can choose to go for something that is bad for us or we can choose what is good."

"An example would be good right about now."

"Well, what future did you create when you cheated on Clara?"

"Well, I would say the third one. I screwed up."

"Yes, you did. You fed the black wolf and as a result, that's the wolf that got stronger."

"I think that I would like to change that to the second future now. If something changes, then something changes. Which means I would need to feed that white wolf again."

"This is quite the jump from eight weeks ago, don't you think?"

"Yeah, I guess. I just want to make things right, even if I don't know yet what that is. Maybe it's because of Andy—he reminded me that I would have taken up arms against a cheater before."

"Great, so you screwed up and now you want to make a change, so that something can change. How does that future change, then?"

"If something changes? I don't know." Ryan was scared to get the wrong answer. "I just know that after reading that story today, I want to turn away from the black wolf altogether. I think I want to become the white wolf totally, but I know now from what you are saying, that I can't do that. My best bet is to accept the grey wolf and work on feeding the white wolf again."

Francis was happy to see this shift and wanted to draw him in deeper. "Exactly. The white wolf, once having experienced life, never becomes innocent again. However, he does gain a higher awareness in its place. That's the merging of the two wolves. William Blake would call that a higher innocence."

"Do I really have to deal with that black wolf at all? Is that even wise?"

"What you do with him is up to you, brother. Would you rather that Clara and the kids deal with him for you? If you don't deal with this in some way, that black wolf gets transferred onto your children and your children's children. If you can't face the black wolf, then you can't give your kids proper teachings for their future. Use the experiences you got from the black wolf and turn it into higher awareness.

"Imagine your boy having a dad who faces himself and gives his son teachings of how to respect women and how to respect himself? A dad that admits he merged the innocent wolf with the experienced wolf and is now the great grey wolf working on himself. Stories help kids learn before they're offered a chance to mess up their own futures."

"You have a point there."

"Merge the two wolves together. Live like no black wolf could ever take you over again."

"How do I do that?"

"There are always going to be black wolves in every future that would love to take you over, brother. Just stay aware of the teachings that the first black wolf gave to you. The master, the teacher is your black wolf. It knows the darkness within you more than anyone. Make friends with the dark parts of yourself and you'll know how to avoid the black wolves of the future."

"To be honest," Ryan admitted, "when I think back now, I feel like an asshole. I knew better than to cheat." Ryan sat for another moment. Francis allowed him his own space without consoling or guiding him. Ryan couldn't help but think of the repercussions of his mistake and how lucky he was that it wasn't out in the open. "How did you become so wise, Francis?"

"I stopped being an asshole."

Ryan laughed out loud. "What? You were an asshole?" He couldn't believe it.

"The bigger the ego, the bigger the mission."

"So, you learned to feed the right wolf once you realized your wrongdoings? You have me curious, now. Are you a grey wolf still?"

"I'm now a white wolf."

"How do you know?"

"I forgave myself."

"How did you do that?"

"I lived in a way that I knew I could trust myself, and because of that, the black wolf can't get me."

Francis seemed so smooth and solid. No one could have guessed that he once had past issues. "Wow, that's big. So, you changed your life after that?"

"Yes, in more ways than one."

"Then you were able to help other people?"

"Yes. Experience and healing ourselves helps us see for others."

Ryan was even more curious now. "How did you heal?"

"I found an ex-asshole like me and I asked him for help."

"And so, the cycle continues, huh?"

Ryan laughed again. Curiosity had the best of him now.

"What did this ex-asshole teach you?" Ryan asked.

"He, like many elders before him, follows the seven sacred teachings that serve the white wolf. These include Love, Respect, Courage, Honesty, Wisdom, Humility, and Truth."

"Those are nice. Why don't you look typical native?"

"Why don't you just get to the point?" Francis looked a bit like a wolf for a moment, warning Ryan to back off.

"I'm just curious, is all."

"I'm not sure what 'typical aboriginal' is supposed to look like these days, but in my case, my ancestors conceived off reserve, so to speak. I guess that you'd call it a mixed bag."

"Okay... So, how did you heal?"

"I learned first that I had been living alone and separate like all white men do. I became aware of myself and others by changing my thoughts and actions, inspired by those teachings."

"All of this after you met the ex-asshole, huh?"

"You're a quick learner, I see."

"What do you think was your biggest teaching? I mean what did you learn on a personal level? What did you have the hardest time learning?"

"I see you are using your gift of control to drive the subject away from yourself again, brother. Is this session about me or about you?"

"Sorry."

"I had a hard struggle learning about control, if you really want to know," Francis confessed without shame.

"Really...what about it?"

"I had to learn that we should only control ourselves and no other and to let no one control us. I learned to respect others for their choices and not take them on as my own."

"I don't know if I'll ever get this whole concept of control. You got me messed up over that."

Francis continued. "I learned that if we choose for ourselves each day and respect others by asking them what their choices are, then we have it beat. Each day is different, so we should never assume anything. We should take each day as if it were a new beginning. Also, we should ask before taking anything out of someone's hands and only give advice when it's asked of us.

"These are the beautiful lessons I learned from the black wolf. If I hadn't experienced the negatives in my life, then I wouldn't have come to appreciate the positive aspects of the world I live in now. Without night, we wouldn't see the value in day, right?"

"Right. It brings me back to what happened this weekend. I can see now how I tried to take Clara's choice away from her. I took the buying of a pool for the kids from her. Then my mom tried to take her choice of making sandwiches away. I can now see that it was her way of celebrating with the kids about the pool. My mom and I took that away from her and made the situation about us. So, we became victims when Clara was just being herself. Or at least she was trying to be herself. And then we accused her of being the controller."

"Now we're getting somewhere, brother."

Ryan suddenly looked like something bit him. He jumped up and looked all around him as if searching for the culprit. "Oh, my good God! I just realized something even bigger. Francis, I got to go!"

"Why? What did you forget?"

"Yesterday was Clara's and my tenth anniversary. Damn! Both my mom and I forgot."

"You *are* an asshole!"

"Yes, I am! Now I know why Clara was all dressed up and why she had actually bought the pool. It was a gift for me and I complained instantly about it, and Mom made such a big deal about Clara making sandwiches. I wasn't paying any attention to the date whatsoever. That isn't like me. Can we make an appointment for next week at this time?"

Francis looked at his calendar. "We can." He helped Ryan gather his things so he could get out the door.

"Are there any stores open for a gift this time of night?"

"I believe they're all closed."

"What the hell am I going to give Clara to make up for this one?"

"There is a nice pot of marigolds with a rock sitting inside it right here." Francis offered him his silliest grin.

Ryan laughed. As foolish as it sounded, he grabbed both pots and ran out of the door.

Francis ran out to the car while Ryan shuffled around trying to put his seat belt on. "Wait, wait, Ryan! I just came back from vacation, as you know. I picked up an extra gift while there. I just wasn't sure who it was for. I see now it's for Clara. Give it to her from you and don't mention it came from me."

Ryan squinted at him and gave an impish smirk. "Are you actually helping me conjure up a lie here, Francis?"

"There are some things that are okay to keep to ourselves when they're for the highest good of everyone involved, brother. You just need to know to never take advantage of that knowledge. It's a duty as men to honour our women, and I'm asking that you allow me to honour Clara with a gift from you. This is one of those moments where a woman would rather be remembered than forgotten, don't you think?"

"Good point, and yes, I agree. Wow, thank you! What is it?"

"Open it up and you'll see. Tell her this, 'It came from the deepest waters of my soul.' Remember those words."

Ryan opened the small jewellery box and saw a beautiful pendant in the shape of a dragonfly and made from coral and mother-of-pearl. It was connected to a sterling silver chain. He murmured the words to himself so not to forget. "It came from the deepest waters of my soul."

"Dragonfly means 'wisdom,' by the way."

Ryan read the inscription on the back out loud. "Wow, it says, 'The Wisdom Keeper.' Connected perhaps to the old man in my dream?"

"Yes. I recognize him now."

"You do? Maybe he was some creepy angel helping me out and came to save my ass! Clara had an early morning, and I haven't seen her yet today. She fell asleep last night before we got to say anything about the anniversary. I did leave a note to say that I would pick up supper tonight."

"That note might have saved the day—however, you're still an asshole! Now go! Get out of here and feed the right wolf this time."

Ryan drove off with relief in his heart and a permanent smile on his face. He had the takeout food to go and pick up, and some grovelling to do. Andrew was right after all, the thought of upsetting or losing Clara was unbearable and shook him to the core. "Damn, he won that one!"

Chapter Five

Dragonfly Wisdom

RYAN ASKED THE kids to go upstairs to his parents' place. He had a surprise for Mommy and needed a few minutes alone with her. Angela winked and shuffled over to the wildflowers near the house, then ran with her brother up the stairs to bring the oddly ordered floral arrangement to Grandma.

Ryan was nervous but knew that if there was ever an important milestone in his life, this was it. There was an urge within him to make things right. He pulled the small box out of his shorts pocket and handed it over to Clara and offered an awkward smirk. "I meant to give you this yesterday, but you fell asleep." Lying to her seemed opposite of what he understood as honour but he agreed it was best she didn't know he forgot her on such an important day.

"You did remember!" Clara shone as bright as a sunbeam that had just peaked through the clouds. "It's beautiful! Thank you. Where on earth did you find this?" She grabbed the necklace and put it on immediately, running to the mirror to check herself out.

"Umm, it came from the deepest waters of my soul?" Ryan was hoping he had the right words and that it hadn't come out too much like a question. He was beginning to trust Francis's intuition over his own, not that he ever saw himself as intuitive.

Clara turned back to Ryan as though the house was on fire. "What did you just say?"

"The deepest waters of my soul?" Ryan explained or repeated... he wasn't sure how she had perceived it.

"I can't even believe what I just heard you say." Clara almost squealed. "I had a strange dream last night about this actual necklace. You and I were on a beach and suddenly you asked me if I trusted you." Her whole demeanour changed and she became suddenly very intense and serious. "We ran into some building to avoid a major catastrophic tsunami. We made it to the top just in time before everyone else was swept away. I was so upset in the dream. I just hung over the side of the building, wet to my knees. The water had splashed up to where we were standing, though the building wasn't being destroyed or washed away, or anything.

"I turned back to you so sad, especially after seeing all those people die. You were just staring at me as if you were a wise old man. You knew something that I wasn't aware of. Like some big secret that I wasn't in on."

Ryan gulped and thought to himself, *Yeah, I'm aware of the fact that I just lied about the necklace, not to mention the Gloria thing.* His throat suddenly felt tight.

Clara continued telling him about her dream. "You had this exact necklace in your hand. Your arm was extended out as if to be giving me the necklace. You told me that everything from now on would be all right. You told me not to ask questions, just to trust. That bad things sometimes happen for a reason. I asked you where you got that necklace from and you spoke the exact same words that you used just now."

The couple repeated the words together, almost simultaneously, "It came from the deepest waters of my soul."

Was Ryan that old man in his own dream? Or was it someone else? Maybe Francis? One thing was clear, he had to make one of the most grown-up decisions of his life. Make a move, or lose it all. Those dreams and the dragonfly necklace were telling him something. Should he tell Clara the truth?

Clara stood staring again into the mirror marvelling over her gift and thinking to herself, *I can't believe he said those exact words just now from my dream. It's some sort of sign. Should I try and work on this marriage? Or am I being told it's done? He does seem to be changing.*

Ryan stood back and watched her face glowing, as she beamed another brilliant smile. She wasn't doing a thing for a moment and yet it was as if she poised herself in such a way to be holding the universe together. He tried to think back to one gift that especially pleased her like this one did. She had never fussed over anything before except her engagement ring.

A sharp pain pierced Ryan's heart. He thought to himself, "I may very well lose out if I don't swallow my pride. Why did I stop seeing her beauty? Is this because of her or me? I used to adore her. When did I switch from that faithful guy in love, to suddenly thinking that she was just pretty ordinary? They say beauty is in the eye of the beholder, but what made my perspective change that much?"

Ryan suddenly phased out like he did at the pond. Time seemed to stop and everything went completely quiet in his mind. He let go and just observed, while entering a space of neither here nor there. Things suddenly became crystal clear, as if the universe had finally offered to sporadically unravel the mysteries of life and answer all his questions. A download beamed down, and like a broadcast from heaven, the truth was revealed. Some random voice spoke to him that didn't sound either male or female. "Beauty is a vast, unmerited, and prejudiced gift given at random by some unseen force, foolishly, unjustly, and then judged recklessly by beholders such as yourself." In no uncertain terms, the universe had just slapped him across the face.

No one would believe it unless they saw it themselves, but Ryan was suddenly transformed in that moment. He took another breath, and in that very instant, he became a new man.

It was like some miraculous natural process was happening, of disconnecting from the old parts of the self, like a snake shedding its skin or a tree shedding its leaves. As much as he fought the process, he couldn't stop the progress of seasonal changes that were occurring in his life. He was coming out of the long, dark winter of the soul and was now entering the springtime of his life. The seeds he would choose to plant at this very moment in time were vital to what type of growth was to come.

Ryan knew then and there, that there was a major probability that by admitting his faults Clara would leave him. Did she deserve better? Maybe so. Perhaps he needed to allow her the opportunity to make her own choice in the matter. Hearing all that talk lately about honouring women was foreign to him, and yet today, as he stood there, now focusing on her and seeing her shining so brightly over a simple necklace, he was humbled. The time to tell her was now.

Words rolled and swirled around in his mind. Now standing up, Ryan grabbed Clara's hand, and blurted out long overdue words. "I'm sorry, Clara, for not being awake, and for stumbling through our lives thinking that was how life was meant to be. I realize now that I... we...were only existing. I'm sorry for being selfish and inattentive. I'm sorry for not being the husband and life partner that you needed me to be. I'm sorry for not being as present as I should have been in our children's lives. I've made so many mistakes, big ones. God! I can't even tell you. I want to..."

"Shh!" Clara stopped Ryan from speaking any further. He had never spoken so much to her at once. It was almost overwhelming. "I made some mistakes too, Ryan."

"You did?" Ryan staggered.

"I did."

Ryan peered deeply into Clara's eyes allowing the heartfelt words to pour out of him. "You can ask me what you need to. I don't care about the past, but honestly I'm scared that if I tell you, I'll lose you."

"Shh!" She shushed him again to keep him from saying more than he should. She wasn't even sure if she believed anything coming out of his mouth. "I already know, Ryan. A woman just knows. Please, just listen and hear me." Clara took a deep breath. "My mistake was pretending, and not wanting to admit to myself that things weren't right between us. Things haven't been for a very long time. I chose not to say anything to you about it, nor about my other fears and doubts."

Now queasy, Ryan couldn't believe what he was hearing.

Clara continued. "My mistake was not telling you what I needed and wanted from you, from our relationship and for our family. I hated you for it and I know we have a long road ahead of us, good or bad. I can't go on pretending anymore. I can't continue living like this, as though everything is okay when it's obviously not. I want more, Ryan. I need more for myself, and for our kids. Hopefully, we can figure out where we go from here, to grow from this experience, maybe to forgive one another, and to choose a direction that is right for everyone."

A sudden sense of urgency spilt out. That was a lot of words, and Ryan only took half of them in. He needed a diversion and quickly. "I don't want to seem insensitive and cut off our conversation, but I need to get something for you that I left outside. I'll be right back. Will you wait for me?" He didn't wait to see if Clara agreed or not and ran like a bat out of hell, out to the car. He grabbed the two pots of marigolds and hurried back inside again. He tried to catch his breath while explaining, "I planted these seeds and have been watering and growing this pot. I think it's the right time now to give it to you."

Clara listened patiently while Ryan explained further.

"These flowers are called marigolds. Do you know what marigolds represent?"

Clara whipped her head from side to side, clueless as to where her husband was going with this.

Ryan continued to explain. "I looked them up on the Internet on the way home tonight. They symbolize cruelty, grief, and jealousy. They can also mean strong passion, as well as a desire for riches. Somehow, they just turned out to be appropriate without my knowing it. I'm pretty sure I might be the black wolf aspect of this situation and you're the white wolf."

Clara looked at him puzzled, "The *what* wolves?" She shook her head to let him know she wasn't following.

Ryan laughed, "Never mind! I've been the darker aspects of the marigold. I'm cruelty."

Clara sat attentive, trying to piece it all together. She had questions. "Why do these pots have rocks in them? Why is one not growing?"

Ryan thought carefully before he answered. He needed to speak up now, knowing well that this very moment would change everything or nothing. He was aiming for future number two, being that if you change something, then something will change. Bravery was key, and she deserved better than a lying thug, so he had to tell her. Yes, she knew something but he wasn't sure if they were talking about the same thing. She may not know with whom he had cheated. He finally managed to spit out words. "The pot with nothing turned out to only be something shiny, Clara. It nurtured nothing inside of me. It left me, and others, lonely, lost, and empty."

"And what are we to do with this empty pot, Ryan?" Clara's eyes were squinted now with intensity.

"Well, I was thinking I need to bring it there to her, or maybe to him." He paused a moment before continuing. "To, um, Tom."

Clara put her hand up to stop him from speaking any further. To hear Ryan admit her suspicions to be true was too much to bear. Tears flooded down her sweet and now scrunched-up face as she sobbed and whimpered like a dog left out in the cold. She kept her hand up in the air, waving it occasionally as if to be warning him to leave her alone and not touch her. She thought silently for quite some time.

Ryan knew best not to interrupt her while she processed. His whole body shook while shame, anger, and heartbreak landed at his feet. Seeing Clara so sad, knowing that he had hurt her so deeply, and that she deserved so much better was insufferable. The only thing that he knew to do was to be there for her, to sit by her side and be silently supportive, no matter what she decided after their talk. He deserved everything she could possibly hit him with.

Clara finally spoke up. "In some ways I should make you do it, but I think I need to take some of the responsibility for this. I want them both to stay here, Ryan. Both pots of plants."

Ryan stayed quiet. In the back of his mind, he realized the pots were also the two wolves. Clara wanted to merge the two without even knowing what it meant.

"I'm a part of that past now," Clara lamented. "If we're going to make it, I have some things that I need to say and ask of you."

He looked at her surprised. "What? Are you saying what I think you're saying? Are you willing to give us another chance?" He wiped his tears and felt hope as he continued. As much as he once considered the affair with Gloria as just a thing, it was now an albatross around his neck. "Clara, I want to be a better man, a better husband, and a better father. I want us to learn and grow together, to make better choices, and to *live*, not just exist. I want us to be each other's best friend, partners in life and love, to be..."

Clara lifted her hand and stopped Ryan. This was all a bunch of bull to her. Clara wiped her tears, feeling scared, angry and hopeful all at the same time. Wanting to be perfectly clear about her intentions she declared, "Even if we're not going to make it work between us, I still have to say it." She paused a moment. "Don't ever ask me to spend time with them again! Got it?"

Ryan nodded his head yes, immediately knowing she was referring to Tom and Gloria.

Clara's voice suddenly got stronger. "Don't ask that of me. Ever! I don't want you to want to spend time with them, either, but if you choose to, we can't make this work for sure. Neither a marriage nor a friendship could work between us if you go back there! This isn't because I want to control you—this is because I need to be a priority in your life, not just in words, but in actions."

Ryan tried to speak again and was cut off quickly.

"I don't want you to say anything right now, just please listen without interrupting until I'm done." Clara paused a few minutes to think. She gestured with her hand again for Ryan to back off while she composed herself first.

Ryan knew if he didn't give her space, there would be hell to pay. She rarely got upset like this. He had learned in the past that when she blows, she blows. He held back and remained silent.

Clara cleared her throat. She felt as though now was the time to address the elephant in the room. She continued with her part of the conversation. "It isn't just about 'her'—it's about my place in our relationship. It's also about your mother and every other woman who has stood between us all these years. I'm grateful for everything that your parents, mostly your mother, have done for us but I can't be a wife and mother in my own home while living under the same roof as her and put up with all of this nonsense from you."

Clara didn't want to say this next part in anger, so she took a deep breath first. "This isn't just your fault. I chose not to say anything, in order to keep the peace. If you are truly being honest with me and really want things to change between us, and if I could make a wish, it would be..." She took another pause, "...it would be to rebuild our relationship from top to bottom. I would want to start over at zero. I want time to learn to be my true self, and share my life with someone. If that person is you...I mean, I can't say so yet. I need someone to go on dates with, to laugh with and do things together, to connect with nature, and I need my own house, too."

Ryan nodded his head hurriedly to assure her that he was listening, even though he was having a hard time staying present. He knew enough not to put his own issues on her shoulders. She needed to get things out. He hung his head like a scolded puppy and remained quiet.

Clara kept going. "I would want to tell you and show you that I love you and our kids. I would want us to be a real family, though I make no promises. I would need for us to be a priority. I would need for us to make decisions together. I would want us to be each other's best friend, too! I would want us to truly learn to communicate with each other, in good times, and in hard times. I would want us to be free, yet to choose to be together, and to be who we are meant to be. I want a balanced life. I want this with all of my heart, but I can't and won't do it alone and I don't want anything less!" Clara stomped a foot on the floor to show that she was serious. "If we both work on ourselves individually and we both still want the same thing, as we work on our relationship, then we might be able to make it work for ourselves and the kids. And if we can't come to an agreement, then we'll have to come to an understanding, so we can end it properly. I'm well aware that divorce may be the answer."

Feeling hope and remorse all at once, Ryan agreed. *Did she mean it? Could she want to try again? Or was she suggesting that we might have to end it? Should we end it? Would that be the appropriate thing to do after such a betrayal?* Awestruck by this strong woman before his eyes, he made a silent vow to do everything in his power to never let her down, to never let himself down or his family like this again. He decided to hold the intention that it would work out and that this was a beginning and not an ending.

After allowing a time of silence to be sure she was finished speaking, Ryan finally found the appropriate words to say to Clara. "I want to live a life of integrity, to be more mindful and awake like Andy has been teaching me to be. He helped me understand that I want to figure out who I am now and what I want to be. I want to be someone that I can recognize and respect when I look in the mirror. I used to be a stand-up guy and I want to see that again. I know it won't always be easy. I want to thank you for being open to even considering to try and make this work. Friendship, marriage, whatever, just don't give up on me yet, Clara. I won't force it, though I will be solid in whatever version of me that you choose to be with. I feel so honoured and blessed that you still choose to be around me while we sift through all this. I don't deserve you, but I do love you."

Clara was now feeling overwhelmed and exhausted, yet lighter and happier. The emotions shifted within seconds. She brought the pot with no flowers over to the sink to water it. She placed both pots back on the shelf where the first one found its blooms. "I want to be the shiny rock in your life again, Ryan, or at least in my own life. I got that when I saw the dull one in the flowered pot. You saw me as dull. Frankly, I saw myself that way, too. I've felt so alone, and lost, not just with you, but with myself, too. I have shut myself off, not truly living or feeling, just existing. I want to recognize and respect that person I see in the mirror, too. I want to figure out who I am now and who I want to be."

Ryan interrupted her so he wouldn't lose track of his thoughts. "I screwed up and I see that now. I promise you I'll work on myself to try and understand how I ended up becoming that kind of guy. I guess I just needed something in my life where I felt I didn't have responsibility or like I was the one in control or something. I can't explain it.

"Gloria helped me go to a place where I didn't have to feel. Obviously, you cause me to feel, and I can't always handle that. I never set out to hurt you, I swear I didn't. It's just more like I fell into some kind of dark hole without even being aware of it. I got swallowed up inside there. Now I need to find my way out." Ryan felt love and gratitude as he opened his arms and gestured for her to come to him for a hug.

A bit pressured, Clara drew toward him tentatively. He held her tight for the first time in a very long time. As much as it hurt her, his words rang true. She could see partly why he did what he did. She still blamed it on herself, and her inability to be a better woman for him. If only she was good enough or looked better externally, maybe he wouldn't have strayed.

WITHOUT WARNING, ANGELA and little Ryan whipped the door open. Clara jumped back quickly, brushed herself off, and wiped her eyes to hide the waterworks. The kids were carrying an oversized chocolate bar. It was already opened and partially devoured.

Ryan questioned them. "Let me guess, Granma and Grandpa sent that one down knowing that we haven't had supper yet?"

Little Ryan gave him a thumbs up as he forced a large piece of chocolate inside his mouth.

"Come here you little squirrel," Ryan said, now picking him up and swinging him around almost robotically and out of nervousness. He didn't know what else to do. He knew enough to take the pressure off of Clara and to try and help eliminate a bit of the awkwardness they felt. Finally, he remembered the food. "I got us some takeout tonight—if that's okay with everyone?"

Clara tried her best to act like everything was normal for the sake of the kids. She couldn't even think about eating yet. She wanted to avoid sounding bitter even though she was and couldn't hide it. "I thought your mom would be making supper as usual."

"I guess you didn't find my note, then," Ryan explained. "I let Mom know we had our own thing today and I can see now we need to do our own thing more often. What do you think about that?" he asked, hoping to neutralize things.

Clara was about to say something smart and decided to fake a smile instead. Her thoughts strayed. She started thinking that her dream of not asking too many questions was helpful. She decided to follow that advice, but was glad to have still said enough in order to not explode. On one hand, she wanted to hit him, or yell at him. On the other hand, it was a relief, in a strange sense, to know that her suspicions were correct. She was unsure of what tomorrow would bring, but she felt more hopeful than she had in a long while.

Ryan interrupted her trance, "I loved the pool, by the way. Thank you, everyone, for surprising me yesterday," he chirped with a fake delight, even though he hated those types of pools. "I was in a kind of shock, I think. I got to give Mommy her surprise today. What do you think, guys?"

"Wow, Mommy!" Angela declared, all the while feeling suspicious of the lie she detected. She was no fool. He wasn't this chipper yesterday. She kept up the front for her mother's sake. "Just like in my book about the unicorn. The girl in the book keeps seeing a dragonfly."

"Oh, wow, that's nice, Angie." Clara was surprised that her daughter was this intelligent. She was coming around and feeling calmer and more able to be in the conversation. "I wonder if the dragonfly has any meaning?"

"Yes, it does," Angela volunteered while looking back skeptically at her father. "The unicorn said that the dragonfly teaches us about wisdom. That people get old and they forget about the things they used to believe in, like unicorns. With age, the dragonfly becomes more colourful and beautiful. When people grow old, their colour is called wisdom. Sometimes they have to make some mistakes in order to gain it, though."

Both Ryan and Clara looked at one another and could barely hold back their awkward laughter. This was the icebreaker they needed to shift the mood. Ryan was obviously caught on a hook. If Clara hadn't twigged to the fact that he forgot their anniversary, Angela certainly had.

Little Ryan jumped into the conversation also, telling them about his recent dragonfly find. "It was green, and I saw through its wings. It was all shiny."

"Yes," Angela reported, "that's called 'iridescence' when you can see through it; or you can call it 'transparency,' if you like." She whipped around, shooting another dirty look at her father, like a dart thrown toward the bull's eye. She was a good shot.

Ryan looked at Clara with wide, surprised eyes and chuckled, "Transparency, huh? Another brilliant one who can spot a truth from a lie. Help! I see that I'm surrounded. How old is she, exactly? I thought we had a nine-year-old girl. I had no idea that we were raising a university student already!"

Angela bleated, while waving her father away like an annoying fly, "Oh, Daddy, don't be so silly! The unicorn says that nature is our teacher. There are many beings out there just waiting to talk to us. They help us know right from wrong. There are some things in nature, Daddy, that are just too beautiful not to notice, don't you think?" She stared at him now with folded arms.

Ryan was distracted internally for a moment, "Beings waiting to talk to us? Rock people?"

He shivered a moment with emotion while reaching out to grab Angela and hug her. He then called little Ryan over to do the same. He sank his head downwards into their backs and suddenly cried outwardly like a baby. They looked at one another, baffled by their father's random behaviour. Ryan was finally able to speak. "See that woman sitting here with us? She's the most beautiful thing *I* ever saw in nature. As I get older, the wiser me sees beauty differently."

Clara felt upset, knowing that what he was saying couldn't have been true, or he wouldn't have gone for Gloria instead.

"I've made some mistakes," Ryan continued, "and I almost got too old to believe, so the unicorn had something right, Angela. Tell her thank you next time you see her. I want to believe in innocence; tell her I'm trying. Tell her I'm sorry for the things that I've done to lose my innocence. And losing the respect of the woman I love. I've got some making up to do for that."

Clara knew his words were really being directed to her and this made her even more upset. She hid her face so it wouldn't show outwardly.

"Why are you crying, Daddy?" asked little Ryan.

Clara thought that she was the one to answer, but suddenly felt emotionally numb and couldn't find words for her son.

Angela looked at her mother to try and figure out what the problem was.

"Mommy is just a little mad at me right now for something I did wrong," Ryan explained instead, while taking his own responsibility.

"You weren't sharing nice?" Little Ryan asked curiously.

"That's right. I wasn't letting mommy have her turn." Ryan's eyes were bloodshot red now.

Angela knew to be consoling. "Don't worry, Daddy, I'll teach you how to be nice."

Ryan watched helplessly as the innocence drained out of Angela's eyes. He felt like a jellyfish stuck on shore being hit by the rays of the hot midday sun.

Angela stood silent and stared sharply at her father. She understood more than her brother did, and from the look on her mother's face, she knew that it was a big problem, not just something about sharing or forgetting an anniversary. "Are you guys going to get a divorce?" she asked.

Clara knew not to let the conversation go any further until they had had more time to talk again in private, but she wanted to be both comforting and honest. "That isn't what we want, honey. Sometimes Mommies and Daddies need help, too. We're going to get that help so that we can figure things out together and for our family. Some things may need to change, but it'll be better for us all." She hugged Angela and gave her a kiss and a reassuring smile. She then diverted the situation by asking Ryan what he had brought for supper.

"Anyone hungry for pizza? Or should I say cold pizza?" Everyone nodded their heads in agreement.

Clara said, "Great! I'll heat it up while you set the table, Ryan. Kids, go wash your hands. We're having supper downstairs tonight!"

Ryan had an epiphany as he chewed into the crust. "I have a special place nearby that I've never shown you guys. I was thinking that we could go there sometime soon. Maybe we will find unicorns there, too," he chuckled. "It's a special place with a pond. We can pack a lunch and have a picnic. It'll be fun! What do you say?"

"Yippee, an adventure! This is gonna be so much fun!" Angela said while squeezing little Ryan's arm excitedly. She only wanted everyone to be happy. She shoved the fear of her parents' potential divorce deep inside. It wasn't something that would resurface again until she was much older, as a trauma to heal.

WHILE GETTING READY for bed, Ryan shared a bit more with Clara. "I know that you've been too patient with me, Clara, and it isn't fair of me to ask any more of you. I know now that it wasn't right or even healthy of me asking you to change yourself. Especially when I was the one living two separate lives, not you. I'm sorry I did that to you, both lying and then shoving it onto you to go for counselling instead of me. I want to find out who I am, and what made me want to do something like that, so I don't ever have to say sorry again. Not to you or to anyone."

Clara took in his words, saying nothing. She was feeling a bit numb.

Ryan was so emotionally tired and raw that he fell asleep in what seemed like an instant.

Clara remained awake, staring at the ceiling. She could barely believe what had conspired in the last few hours of her life. Ryan never ever spoke so clearly or said so much in one conversation. She had said a lot, too. She was so used to pulling words out of him like a dentist pulls out teeth; it was always an ordeal and never worth the effort. Though a bit weary, she liked this new Ryan. They both needed to make big changes, and it would be far from easy.

Would he follow through and keep helping himself? Only time would tell.

Chapter Six

SIGNS AND SYMBOLS

"HAHAHA, LOOK WHAT the cat dragged in."

"Yeah, the lion almost got me. Thanks for saving my ass last week."

"It helped us both, brother. What one can't do for themselves on their own journey, sometimes gets healed in someone else's journey."

Ryan tilted his head wondering what was behind that statement. What was Francis's story anyway? Maybe one day he would poke around for more details. Today he'd stick to his main focus. "I told Clara about Gloria. She's actually a much smarter woman than I gave her credit for. She said she knew and kept it to herself until now."

"Oh yeah? Wow! Sometimes the body knows what the mind doesn't."

"That statement sounds familiar." Ryan paused a moment. "Oh, and also, something freaky happened that I want to talk about."

"Yeah? What happened?"

"Clara sort of had the same dream that I had about the tsunami. Somehow that dragonfly made its way to her dream before it even found me."

"Dreams have a way of bringing things to the light and joining all worlds big and small."

"It's amazing but alarming for me at the same time. The words you told me to use with her, 'the deepest waters of my soul.' Well, she dreamt of them also. Can you explain *that* to me?"

"There is a special window that opens sometimes, and a breeze comes in, whispering messages from a different place than where we are right now."

"Okay, whatever. I'd just like to get my head wrapped around us having the same dream."

"To understand dreams, we first need to know that they're a part of our instincts. As humans we've forgotten this. We often shut off our response to the world, and therefore our instincts. Dreams help us figure out what we haven't taken notice of while we're awake. It's important for us to pay attention to dreams. When we do, we can navigate better in our physical world."

"How did we end up losing our instinct like that?" Ryan asked.

"We embraced our rational side a little too much. Sometimes our mental mind is so clogged up that we don't see what's right in front of us."

Ryan understood the basics but wanted to grasp things on a deeper level. After this week's dramatic experiences with Clara, he was willing to go all in or nothing. "Why wouldn't it all just come while we are awake, though?"

"As we've been learning, brother, our mental mind gets in the way. The subconscious has an opportunity to kidnap us while we're sleeping. Dreams try to knock some sense into us while the mental mind is at bay. It prevents the mind from causing any more problems. Besides, while we sleep, so does the ego."

"Problems like what?"

"You can either have a tsunami in your dreams, or in real life you can get hit with thunderstorms. Which one would you prefer, Ryan?"

Ryan looked at his mentor with wide open eyes. "Oh, my God! I'll take the dreams, thank you!"

"When we sleep, automatically we balance between the mental, physical, emotional, and spiritual selves. We should be doing that on a conscious level when we're awake. When we deny emotions during the day, those emotional things get dealt with in dream form. Dreams or symbols within them can be helpful, and we need to see them as positive signs. Dreams are a way for our spirit to align with our body."

"I still don't understand why Clara and I had the same dream?"

"Your higher self spoke to you and to Clara at the same time. What it had to say wasn't able to come out or get through to you in this reality, so something had to be spoken in the dreamtime state instead."

"My what? Higher self?" These were all new concepts. "Oh, never mind, forget it. I'll ask this, though: how do you fit into that picture buying the dragonfly necklace and knowing the right words to say? I mean you are as creepy as that old guy in my dream."

"Sometimes missed messages get sent out into a kind of cyberspace. Whoever has their spiritual computer open at the time, gets the message. I happened to get your messages for you. I was tapped into my higher self, so I guess I was the one actively online. That or the universe knew you wouldn't even bother to open your inbox. They sent it to me to deliver the message to you."

"So, your computer was open for me?"

"I don't own a computer."

"Okay, funny guy. How could you be open for my stuff to come to you?"

"You came and asked me for help, didn't you?"

"Yes," Ryan confessed.

"Let's say, by agreeing to my help, that you were put under my radar. Unluckily for me, the cyberspace government connected us, and I paid your taxes or arrears for you. Now you owe me one, brother!"

Ryan had to chuckle at how Francis was so quick at coming up with these types of jokes. Somehow it made it easy to understand concepts that otherwise would be hard for him to catch onto. "If I can't always get a message when I'm awake in my physical world, then how can I dream more to get these messages?"

"It's not about dreams or having to dream in order to get the message. It's about being more aligned with yourself while you're awake. Like any kind of muscle, if you work on it, that instinct gets stronger."

"Okay, that makes sense, but if I want to dream more, what muscle do I work on?"

"Your spiritual muscle needs the workout."

"I don't really believe in the spiritual stuff, remember?"

Francis snapped him back to focus. "Do you remember that I mentioned the emotional, physical, spiritual, and mental selves?"

"Yes, I remember."

"You need all four of these to make up a whole person. If you break them into equal parts, then you have four pieces of a pie. It's simple mathematics. Each of those four pieces equals 25 percent each of who you are. To have balance, we need to exercise all four muscles. Otherwise, one section is weak. When one falls, they all fall."

"Okay, I'm following."

"Congratulations, you just graduated Grade 2 and now welcome to Grade 3."

Ryan smiled shyly.

Francis continued with the lesson. "You'd have to keep all the pieces of pie balanced at 25 percent each every day, nothing less and nothing more. Once you do that, you'll be in alignment and less distracted by overindulgence in one area or the other. Too much physical, makes for cramps in the body. Too much mental, you go nuts. Sound familiar?"

"Yes, and too much or too little emotion you can become angry or end up feeling nothing. I learned that one." Ryan cringed, having admitted that.

"You may graduate Grade 3 quicker than I thought! Too much spiritual and you can become a balloon flying too high and you'll soon need to ground yourself. So, don't worry about not believing in God or spirituality. It's about learning to believe in yourself while becoming a spiritually based being."

"Isn't that the same thing?" Ryan asked, rolling his eyes. He continued on without allowing Francis to respond. "So, I have a question. Is it better that I get myself more acquainted with or get to know the part of me that is awake? Is that what this is all about?"

"No, that person will drive you crazy for sure. It's better to forget who you are. That is part of becoming conscious. We learn to unlearn ourselves. Then we get to know ourselves."

"That makes no sense at all. Sorry. I'm supposed to be awake but I'm not? Dream but not dream? Get to know myself but forget who I am? Huh?"

"Follow my lead and I'll help you get lost."

"I heard that one before from Andy; now I know where from."

"The person you knew for thirty-five years turned out to be an asshole. Follow his lead and you'll get your ass kicked over and over again."

Ryan let out a cackling laugh that sounded a bit like a crow cawing. "True enough," he admitted.

Francis spoke in a smooth and steady voice. "Forgetting who you were is about letting go of the belief systems that were shoved onto you by your family, community, and the world around you. Half of you is your parents' beliefs and the rest of you is your community's beliefs. By the time a person becomes aware, how can he or she know themselves? You need to get through that tangled mess to find yourself. So, trust me, forget who you are, and you'll find it easier to tap into that innocence again."

"How can I do that? I mean, let go of these programs and find that innocence?"

"Start watching the program around you, become aware, watch your words, don't judge, yet become aware as to who you speak like and act like. Find out who you are at the core. Who you are at home? Who you are on the job? Who you are when you're alone? Once you can separate all of those parts of yourself, you can begin identifying what parts are useful and what parts of your attitude that just need to go into the trash. You need to be aware to become aware. Got it?"

"Yes."

"Good. Once you become aware, then it's easier to catch the ego when it starts to run the show. It's an autopilot glitch that the Creator hasn't worked out in us yet."

"I think maybe I'm on the recall list." Ryan laughed at himself.

"I think so, too!" Francis didn't even crack a smile, which made Ryan laugh even more.

Francis paused and took a conscious breath before continuing on. "See, the brain begins to change your desires the moment you become aware of old behaviours. You started doing this already. Once you became aware of doing wrong, that's when you began wanting different things. Awareness changes you."

"Andy said that would happen. It makes sense now as to why I have this sudden moral switchover. I convinced myself in the past that what I was doing with Gloria was normal and the right thing to do. Once I saw that as a wrong action I wanted to try again with Clara and redeem myself, but only when I saw it as wrong, not before. It's like I changed overnight."

"Yes, brother, that is exactly it, and the more aware you become the bigger the changes that will occur. Becoming aware of who you are at home, at work, with friends, with your parents, kids, and wife, etcetera, is exactly what I'm referring to. These are all separate parts of you. We'll get deeper into that the further we go. For today, we'll stick to understanding the autopilot. The autopilot has many facets to watch out for, so you don't end up getting something you don't want. Like that kick in the ass that you got this week."

"Yeah, that kick got me right where it hurts. I came to the realization while you spoke, that it's while I'm around my parents that I go into autopilot. I'm robotic around them, in a sense."

"Family members are our blind spots and our best teachers at the same time. They have a beautiful way of pulling us backwards into old programs. I want to dig deeper into the root of the original issues that occurred in you, and to do that we first need to focus on family."

"It's as if I act a certain way when I'm around family," Ryan admitted, "and I don't know for sure, but I think I brought that down into my house with Clara. I shut off as a kid because of stuff that happened with my parents and within their family feuds. It's been easier to live numb and it may be the root cause of my issues. Even with my ability to see all this clearly, I don't know if I'm alert enough to pilot my own plane without crashing. I think I liked autopilot."

"I'm certainly not going to volunteer to be your passenger in that plane anytime soon! Yikes!"

Ryan laughed.

Francis resumed his teachings. "Opening up your ability to feel again and not go crazy will be a challenge. That need to shut down is a program and a belief system that can be changed right now as we speak. Change your belief, change your body's reaction to the emotions of what is happening around you, and then your life changes. Got it?"

"No, I don't understand."

"The key to understanding is seeing that the body and the body's emotions run the show, not necessarily the mind. Otherwise, you have no peace. The world has been filled with people who would love for you to remain sleeping and unaware. One black wolf pulling you toward the dark side is all it takes. Every war has two sides."

"So, Clara and I are two opposing sides, looking for peace. I went on autopilot with my parents, and from there it caused me to go on autopilot with Clara and again with Gloria. I don't want to be like that anymore. God, and I don't want that for my kids. I want them to have respect in their lives no matter what they believe in or what life they choose. I want to help them learn to feed that white wolf."

"You call on God a lot for someone who doesn't believe in Him."

Ryan looked at Francis inquisitively. He thought back to what he had just said, seeing only now that he did use that "God" word a lot.

Francis carried on with the discussion. "Just saying! Saying God without meaning is an example of an autopilot word that you let drive your airplane. We use many of these autopilot words without realizing it. It's up to you to use it or not, just be conscious that each time you say it, God or the Creator, as I call it, hears you and answers you. Start listening and you'll hear what heaven has to say back to you."

Francis kept his focus and resumed. "Let's get back to you not wanting to affect your kids. Luckily, children today came with an upgraded system and they're smarter than us. We affect seven generations after us, and we have a responsibility to ensure they're taken care of and taught how to take care of the seven generations that come after them. If we respect ourselves, we respect them."

Ryan couldn't hold back his bubbling emotions. "Seven generations? Excuse the extreme language, but 'F'..." He decided not to actually swear after that autopilot word lecture. "That would mean that seven generations of stuff that people in my family avoided dealing with got mixed into my life. That really sucks. If sleeping people raised a sleeping society, then their behaviours got passed down to me."

"Yes, maybe, and guess what? You just graduated to Grade 4. Who is talking and where did you put Ryan?"

"I don't know, it's just starting to click together, I guess." Ryan paused a moment before continuing. "For a while I thought you were ranting, but I can see you meant that sleeping people affected others who were once awakened and kind of pressured, lured and even captured them and forced them into a sleeping state."

"You got all that from what I just spoke about, eh?"

"I guess, yeah. It is what you meant?"

"Indirectly, yes."

"Maybe I was making it up in my head as I went along," Ryan laughed. "I'm not sure how I came up with that, if I'm honest, but yeah, that's where my brain landed."

"It's called reading between the lines, or maybe you just put the Lego pieces together. The junior edition!" Francis couldn't hold his face straight any longer.

"Maybe I'm seeing that I captured Clara. She often claimed that she used to be awake and instinctual. Now I know what she meant by that. My life choices, my attitude, and my mother captured Clara in all directions. I can see now that she was put in a cage of sorts."

"You got it! Another Lego piece, maybe. It was a nice-looking cage, with all the bells and whistles, but a trap all the same. A golden cage."

FRANCIS PAUSED FOR a moment, as though he was deciding whether he should continue on or not. He nodded his head as if listening to someone's advice from the sidelines and then gazed into the distance for a while. Once again, he started looking at Ryan and went on. "The lives of your kids were also captured inside one of those golden cages. They see the world from the perspective that they were given. They will stay in those same patterns and same lifestyles if they don't know any better. You want to go in one direction, Clara wants to go in another, and their grandmother wants it her way. To keep the peace, you all follow what your mother wants. At least until now. How can the kids see what true love is if they aren't brought up in it? How can you teach them to respect others if you don't show respect to your wife? How can they learn if your mother doesn't truly show respect to you or your wife?"

"Good point," Ryan intervened.

Francis continued. "In our culture we teach Respect, Honesty, Trust and Love. They're as important to make us whole as the mental, physical, spiritual, and emotional parts are for our balance. Actually, as we share about them, they're often one and the same. We share this as a part of what you would call a medicine wheel. If we don't respect, then we can't be honest. Without honesty, we can't be trusted nor can we trust others and therefore we don't know love in its truest form.

"With the Gloria situation as our example to dissect, you had strayed emotionally from Clara before you chose to cheat. Even though deep down you knew it was wrong, you did it anyway. Sensing this, Clara knew that she couldn't trust you; love was blocked as a result and cannot be present until she's fully respected. If you are lucky enough to have her in the future, that is. With this act you teach the kids at the same time to disrespect her. She becomes everyone's easy target, doesn't she?

"I would bet anything that when your little boy doesn't get his own way, he has tantrums with her and acts up? He is likely as sweet as pie with his grandmother because she gives him what he wants. Chocolate is always the winning example."

"Yes, he does that a lot. He gets into trouble at kindergarten as well. He only acts good for my mom...you're right. Chocolate is indeed the winner. Now I know why. Wow!"

"Like with Clara, it'll begin with healing yourself and becoming a good example for him. He's the environment that's raising him."

"Can we go back a bit? I think I need to digest that part for a while."

"Okay, lead me to where you want to go."

"First I want to ask why you said that in your culture you share. You said that instead of using the word teach. Why is that?"

"Very perceptive, brother. We are all teachers. As we share our experience, it becomes a teaching for others around us."

"So, like everyone is a leader in a sense by what they choose to share?"

"Yes, that's a beautiful way of putting it. Thank you for sharing that observation with me. And also, by sharing our knowledge, it gets transferred down through the next generations, to the new leaders of tomorrow."

"Okay, wow, that's nice. So, secondly, can I ask more about dreams?"

"Yes. Absolutely! Give me an example of what you want to know about."

"I often dream of the same scene all night. Not really remembering anything when I wake up. I just know in the morning that I had a dream that seemed to last forever. I wake up exhausted. Any ideas?"

Francis continued, "Remember I said that we should be aware, and remain on a conscious level when we are awake?

"Yes, I remember."

"The problem is that sometimes we deny emotions during the day. Emotions can be helpful for us to understand our life experiences. Emotions sometimes come in our dreams instead of when we are awake. We need to see these dreams as positive signs." Francis could sense that Ryan needed another approach to fully understand what he was talking about. He knew exactly how to apply it in a simpler form. "Have you ever played Pacman?"

"Pacman? You mean the actual Pacman game?" Ryan was surprised Francis thought of that game. It used to be one of his favourites.

"Yes, the actual game."

"Yes, I used to play that with Andrew a lot when we were kids."

"Remember trying to beat the game and going to bed and dreaming of it?"

"Oh my God, yes, I did do that." Ryan took a mental note of that autopilot word "God" popping back up again.

"It's common, with kids' minds especially, because they're so open to learning and developing. They take in everything around them, and the neurological connections are happening at every turn because they're so vulnerable and susceptible to everything around them. Games are like the real world for them, which is a big reason why we should watch what games kids are playing.

"Anyway, back to dreaming of Pacman. We go to bed and dream all night about the problems we saw during the day within the game. We can virtually problem solve in our sleep. Some dreams we remember and some we don't."

"Really? Wow, cool! I didn't know that."

"Yes, really. Strangely enough, studies have shown that when we go to bed and dream of a game, we can wake up and beat the scores or get through major levels without having practised with our physical body. Only the spiritual body practised while we slept."

"That is really cool."

Francis knew he had warmed Ryan up enough with Pacman to help him now apply it to his original question at the start of the session. "Furthermore, I dreamt of the dragonfly necklace before I bought it. I didn't know who I was buying it for when I purchased it, but just by meeting you, you became a part of my awareness. We were in the same Pacman game, so to speak. Being aware and allowing you to talk in that first session allowed my mind to start processing from a waking state, as though I were in the Pacman dream figuring out what route you needed to take before you knew you needed to take it. Somehow, even though a part of me was unaware, I knew only to purchase the necklace. As a result of listening to that knowing, you won that level of the game."

"Wow, yeah! That is exactly what happened. I most certainly did. This explanation brings it all into perspective, Francis. Thank you."

"You are most welcome."

"How do other symbols fit into dreams? I dream a lot about animals."

"Now we're talking! Animals are one of my favourite subjects. It's my forte, as the French would call it, or my strength. Give me some examples."

"Okay, bears, eagles, dogs, cats, monkeys, foxes..." Ryan blurted them out as if he had a list in front of him already written out and was reading from it.

"Animals have great meaning. A bear could be showing a great healing to come. An eagle helps you to see above your situation. It offers majestic views of your life and gives you a higher perspective or a bird's-eye view on things. Dogs remind us to be loyal to those we love. Cats show us things about our own confidence levels or of those around us. Monkeys adapt to life situations. They may fall, but they brush themselves off and get back up in the tree where they belong. This is a teaching we should all learn from. Fox also teaches us to adapt."

"Oh my God, how do you know all that stuff?"

"It's simple."

Ryan laughed hysterically. "Well, it's not simple for me. Okay, let me think for a moment. Snakes and spiders make their appearance from time to time, also. They scare me."

"Snakes and spiders represent hidden fears or phobias, but these critters can help us bring those fears up into our awareness, so we can overcome them. Fight those fears, master them, and you master yourself. From there we can become greater warriors in life in any area we choose."

"Wow, that's cool."

"There's more."

"Really? Like what?" Ryan couldn't wait.

"Elders say that the snake, with its bite, invited humans to get creative and to invent a powerful anti-venom from the snake's venom. If we take this into past experiences, then what or who bit us in life usually had many wisdoms for us. They were our teachers by hurting us. Good or bad, we can use this knowledge that we obtained to heal ourselves. From there we can share these wisdoms with others based on our own experience. In this way we help others heal also."

"And what about spiders?"

"Spiders are masters of communication. They weave words of wisdom into our body and allow us to feel the words that we'll then use in masterful ways to reach others. For the spider, his home can never be broken because he'll always repair it, even if he must do so by starting again from nothing. Home goes with him. He teaches us to enjoy the short time we have here in this home, the one we call Mother Earth. He also teaches us to do what we can to repair the damage done to the Earth and to build thoughtful communities."

"Does it mean something when you see animals in real life?" Ryan asked. "I saw a frog and a lizard the day I got the two rocks for the pots."

"Yes, in real life they have just as much meaning. Consider this. If we saw life as a dream and dreams as real life, we would easily interpret their meanings, because we would be far enough removed from the circle of emotion to grasp those meanings."

"I love that. And all this talk on animals I have to say is really fascinating to me. I would love to know more," Ryan explained, hoping it would make Francis continue on with the subject.

"I'm glad we figured out one of your interests. Animals are a wonderful way to start finding meaning and purpose in the world around us, as well as from dream form. Just look at their habits, habitats, what they do, or don't do. There's so much we can get just by sitting back and observing them. Take your frog, for example. Any kind of hoppers like frogs, kangaroos, grasshoppers, or rabbits are all signs that things are moving forward. They can only hop forward and never backwards. That's very significant. They tell us unequivocally that we are about to make great leaps forward. They also remind us to keep things on track, because once we do jump forward there's no going back, especially when it comes to making mistakes. The lizard is a sign to pay attention to upcoming dreams, by the way."

"Wow, this is amazing stuff. I could listen all day."

"We have a new step coming—you know that, right?"

"I had a feeling you would say that. Can I have it the easy way this time?"

"You always do."

Ryan put his hands in prayer position as if to be pleading. "No more thunderstorms, right?"

"Sometimes a good bolt is needed in order to wake up, remember?"

"Oh, God, now I'm scared."

"God, eh? Take a couple of weeks to stir things up and shake up that can of cola we talked about."

"I already did stir things up. The last can sprayed out over my whole life and I'm in a sticky situation because of it." Seeing that Francis was serious, Ryan straightened up in his chair to listen. "Okay, what do I do for homework this time?"

"I want you to stay aware for the next period. Be present in everything that you do."

"Okay that sounds easy. What do I become aware of?"

"Pay attention to the programs we've talked about. Watch the world around you. See how you feel now that you have woken up a bit. Remember, you're making progress, but you're not exactly healed yet. Try not to get too cocky, if that's possible. Stand still and watch, viewing your parents' programs and how they affect you. Sit back and watch Clara and the kids. See what kind of world they live in. Also, I want you to look at society's programs; identify them."

"That's all?" This was going to be a cinch, Ryan thought.

"Do you want more?"

"No! I'm all right with that and I can do it."

"Then I want you to report back to me and tell me what you get from it."

Ryan grabbed Francis's hand and crossed his own over his chest and hugged him. Francis jumped up and received the gesture with an eye-to-eye smile. Ryan felt as if strength was being poured into his chest from Francis. He stood tall and took a deep breath then turned and left, saying nothing more.

Chapter Seven

Be Present. Be Aware

CATCHING GLIMPSES OF the programs in his life wasn't quite as easy as Ryan thought it was going to be, especially with his household being under siege. Torn between wanting to make lasting changes in his life and wanting things to stay the same, the unknown was crippling. Now that the cat was out of the bag with Clara, there was no going back.

Clara had supper waiting for him when he arrived home from work one evening. The kids were at a birthday party. Ryan was distraught and didn't speak much during the meal, and was barely able to eat what Clara had made for him. He was obviously having one of his mood swings and it wasn't worth her time or effort to try and probe him. Neither of them had spoken a word for a couple of weeks now. What could be said, anyway? She allowed him his own process, and simply cleaned up the plates, making her way outside to enjoy the beautiful colour display that had overtaken the evening sky.

How was it that Clara was taking the situation so smoothly? Was she just hiding what she really felt? At some point he knew this would all have to come out. Maybe she was waiting to see what Ryan would do. She must be holding onto a lot of anger inside, he figured, and how could she not? These thoughts about him cheating were constantly in the back of his own mind, so they were surely in hers as well. Nothing had been fixed; it was all just set aside for now. This was the arrangement while he worked on himself, yes, but it felt like he was living in a hell in the meantime. The silence was deafening.

Maria, too, had been quiet these past weeks and kept making excuses for not having them over. Ryan felt squished in between two pieces of bread and he was the sandwich about to be eaten. They were all just a bunch of strangers living in one house suddenly. How was Maria going to take the news of him cheating? Should he even tell her? She had been there for him his whole life. He'd be such a disappointment to her if she found out.

His heart ached, feeling that he had suddenly abandoned his mother. It left a gaping hole in his chest. Something had to be done, and Maria would want to know what had brought on these changes. Maybe it was better not to share all of it with her; it was between him and Clara, after all. He wanted to be mindful of what it would do to his wife, to have someone else know about his affair and possibly blame her for it. His mother would criticize her for certain. It was best to stay quiet about it for now.

Mental exhaustion knocked Ryan down for the night. Hours later, he awoke panicked and sweating. "Maybe I really did make a wrong choice in not allowing mom to cook for my family that day. Two weeks is a long grudge to hold. God, what have I done?"

Suddenly, a voice came to Ryan and jolted him as if a fire truck had just rushed through his bedroom. "Enough!" the voice demanded. "Do you not find it strange that you had very little guilt until recently about cheating on your wife and now you are feeling sorry for your mom? Where are your priorities?"

Where on earth did that voice come from? Ryan's heart raced wildly, and he leapt out of the bed as if to be chased by someone's ghost. "What the hell was that?" he whispered with a panicked breath, trying not to wake Clara up. She was now lying still and fast asleep, unaware of anything happening around her. Ryan shook his head. Now feeling as hot as a furnace, he went out into the living room to cool down. He had made a decision that he would ask his mom to cook for them tomorrow and he'd apologize. Feeling satisfied by this, he headed back to bed.

The alarm blared non-stop the next morning and Ryan forced himself to wake up and shut it off. Clara came rushing into the room. "Sorry, I woke up early and wasn't thinking to shut off my alarm."

Ryan rolled over and plopped the pillow over his head, a sign to Clara of one of his stress-induced migraines coming on.

Clara came back a few minutes later, "Here," she said, "this painkiller and also a coffee might help with that. Don't forget to drink lots of water today. It's going to be a hot day. You are probably a bit dehydrated."

Ryan knew he had a challenging task to attend to that day. He called in sick at the office and took the day off to try and figure out how to do damage control and handle the situation.

***

"I'M SURPRISED TO see you home from work, Ryan." His mom acted like nothing had happened and waved him inside her door.

"Yeah, I took the day off. Mom, I'm sorry we haven't seen much of one another lately."

"It's all right. I had food prepared like I always do but I know you are busy and of course I understand. I threw it out each day, knowing you guys hate leftovers. Everyone eats so differently that I would have had too many dishes to fill and my refrigerator isn't that big."

Ryan was confused. "We never once said that we didn't eat left-overs. You just never have any. We have them downstairs all the time. You could have sent stuff down also. And I thought you were telling me the past two weeks that you were too busy for us and not to come up here."

Maria looked horribly shocked and sat down with a melodramatic flop. "Ryan, that's a terrible thing to say. I would do anything for you, you know that. I would never make things up and I would never say no to you."

"Wow, Mom, I'm so sorry." Ryan cringed when he heard her high-toned voice. She used it on him and his father many times when they did something out of the ordinary. Still, he felt terrible for upsetting her like this.

"I mean Clara could've told me she was making supper those days. Do you know how much food I wasted while waiting? I could've done other things, you know. I tried calling both of you, but enough about me."

Ryan was speechless. "When did you call us?"

Maria swung around to start the dishes and wouldn't look at Ryan.

"Mom, when did you call us?" She still didn't answer. "Mom!"

"Ryan, I'm too hurt and too..." Maria burst into tears.

Ryan sat there feeling small and broken. He knew for sure it was him who had been the one trying to connect with her over the last couple of weeks. Why would she lie like that?

John was sitting there watching the whole conversation and suddenly spoke up, "Look at those clouds. I heard there are thunderstorms coming in from the west. Did you know that those ones can bring ice storms?"

Ryan stayed quiet.

Maria turned around with her chin up as if she were a royal queen conveying her final decision on important matters. "I'll make something nice tonight. Your favourite of course, lasagna, and for the others, they're so fussy, I'll think of something."

Ryan gulped and realized his throat was tight and dry. His back muscles were sore and burning. He spoke before he could even think. "Mom, there's a reason why Clara and I have needed a bit more alone time."

His mother turned away and started folding laundry to keep busy. "Of course. Just bring your laundry up or I can come down, and I'll clean the house for you. It hasn't been touched I'm sure from the last time I was there. You guys are so busy I know that. Let me do it and that way you can go out and have fun."

Ryan felt choked. "Mom, it's not about being busy."

Maria pushed him slightly aside as she whizzed past him to gather the teacups off the table to wash. She always did things in a rush, Ryan realized. Maybe to look busy or maybe to stay cool, he wasn't sure which.

"Ryan, I understand what it's like to be married and how busy things get. You don't have to explain yourself to me. I'll do what I can to pitch in and make sure you have more time for yourselves."

Ryan thought about Francis's homework assignment. It wasn't difficult to see the program in his mom, but it wasn't going to be as easy to stay present. He felt smart and good about himself in his last session. In the real world this wasn't the case at all. He was no more than a simple fool, sitting there helpless and with zero tools to help him fix the situation.

What was this circumstance telling him, anyway? What could he actually learn from it? It looked a bit like control and victim-hood, perhaps, though it was beginning to feel more and more like incarceration. Maria seemed to be holding all of the jail keys. He was locked in a prison of guilt and shame and couldn't get out without her permission. He was beginning to understand Francis's description of the golden cage. His mom previously made his life so easy and so good that he was trapped within it, along with everyone else. How could he have been so blind? Maybe he could just try and reason with her. Something had to give.

"Mom, the house is fine. Look I have a bit of a headache today. It's why I took the day off. We'll take care of everything on our own and I need to tell you..."

Maria cut in, "No, no, I insist. Really, it's no problem. Now you sit down and eat something, you look famished. No wonder you're sick, I can tell that you barely ate anything nutritious lately. Let me take care of you properly. With a headache like that I can tell you need more hydration. Come here, sweetheart. I'll manage everything."

Even though he could see the program, Ryan felt inclined to sit and eat and be a good boy like always. It was true, she always knew what he needed best and he did feel better after he ate. She did make him feel special. Why then did he feel reassured and taken care of, yet small and incapable all at the same time? That made no sense. He wished she would just listen; that would make a big difference. Maybe if she could just be a bit more flexible. He tried to speak again about his and Clara's problems, but before he could get the words out, she waved him off and grabbed his plate. There was no use bringing it up.

"I will clean up my kitchen and come down to clean your house spotless. It'll give poor Clara a break; she isn't used to doing so much around the house. You go now and take the day off to rest and rejuvenate." Maria proceeded to do what she did best for the rest of the day, making sure her son needed nothing.

CLARA CAME HOME from work. "Hey, so you did take the day off. Let me guess, your mom came down?"

Ryan nodded his head with a slight self-conscious, tight-lipped grin. "Tonight, she's making lasagna," he announced.

Clara responded quickly, unable to hold back the sarcasm in her voice, "And probably chicken fingers for little Ryan and hotdogs for Angie." She bobbed her hand in the air as if to say sorry. "Okay, Okay, I'm trying hard not to say too much and stir things up. I know we have more important things to deal with right now, but I wish she would just cook one meal so the kids would stop being so fussy or let me do it myself. Ryan, you know that's why little Ryan acts like he does. She gives him everything he wants and then when I try and discipline him in any way, he freaks out at me and heads upstairs to get what he wants. I can't handle this anymore." Clara took a deep breath to calm down.

Ryan tried to stay focused and not get upset. "Clara, I'm sorry. I'm kind of stuck between a rock and a hard place, here. Mom hasn't seen them so much lately. She has been really upset with us and I don't want to do that to her."

Clara whipped around, "To her? Really? Is that so! Hmm, well, Ryan, I need some air before I say something that I might or might not regret! Deal with it! I'm going out for a walk." She left the house, slamming the door behind her gracelessly.

An hour later, seeming a little calmer, Clara came back through the door without explaining herself. "The kids will be here soon. I let them go next door to play before supper."

Ryan sat up on the chair and pushed his iPad tablet aside. He had been surfing Facebook mindlessly before she came in. It was helpful in numbing himself.

"Clara, I've been seeing a kind of counsellor, as I mentioned before."

What was this, another attempt to try and change her? Clara spoke as if she had a shield up. "Yes, Ryan! Francis—you told me all about him!"

Usually, Ryan would react and get upset if ever she got like this but he handled himself well this time. "He has me doing some re-thinking about how we set up our life here. I mean living under my parents isn't working for us or the kids; I see that now. So, I under-stand you are frustrated. I would be, too. I may need your patience for a while still. We have so much to work through, so much to change. I really want us to decide together what that change will be. I know it's a lot to ask, but can we just get through tonight and take it a day at a time?"

Clara felt peace wash over her. She took off her jacket and sat down to show that she was willing to listen further.

Ryan soldiered on, trying to make things right. "I may seem a bit set aside or on the sidelines for the next while, but I need you to know that it's me getting to know myself. I can't fix myself, or our relationship, if I don't know myself yet. For now, my parents are the part of me that I know. I'm trying to figure out how to make every-one happy all at once. It may not be feasible, but I'm attempting to do the right thing for the whole. Does that make sense?"

Clara nodded her head yes, while thinking that making everyone happy is impossible and can only bring more heartache. She wanted to scream but kept her mouth zipped shut, allowing Ryan to con-tinue. She had never felt so irritated in her life.

"I can't say if I'll ever be a perfect man, but I'm certainly looking to be a man who is more presently aware. That's the project that Francis gave to me last session, to be more present and aware. I'm working on the aware part first, so I can eventually become more present in all areas of my life. So, please bear with me. Mom will cook for us tonight and maybe I can work on her a bit and try to change that to once or twice a week or something. Would that help?"

Clara nodded in agreement outwardly. Inwardly, she wanted to go upstairs and have words with her mother-in-law. Maybe even slap her.

Ryan felt torn by the commitment he had just blurted out. It wasn't what he wanted because he knew that to get to that point of change also meant he would disappoint Maria more. It was getting to be apparent that something had to change, or Clara was going to burst or leave, or worse.

Clara couldn't hold back the tears. She never thought in a million years that Ryan would ever talk this way. In the beginning, it was so helpful having his mom come to their aid. She was away from her family and it was hard with two kids, and so she loved having his mom there. But after some time, that help turned out to be like a smothering. Then she got lost in some emotional trap, mixed with guilt of not wanting his mom around and gratitude for having had so much support. It resulted in her shutting down.

She had even started drinking by herself, which wasn't Clara's character. When she realized what she had been doing, it scared her so much that she stopped drinking altogether and avoided telling Ryan about it. A jumble of emotions washed over her while seeing these changes in Ryan. This was a miracle, wasn't it? She felt jealous that he could have these great epiphanies and she was left to suffer.

Should she trust Ryan or not? In the past he had always sided with his mother. She knew that he was trying but she was afraid that if she didn't speak up, he would fall into those old patterns again. Finally, she got out of her head and spoke out loud, "I want to start by saying, thank you for wanting things to change, Ryan. I can see that you're trying, and I haven't been easy on you. Sorry I've been so silent lately. I just needed time to let it sink in. I'm stuck on the fact that you broke my trust and my heart. You did that, you chose to do that, and my feelings about it aren't going to go away. I won't be magically forgiving you and I don't know if I'll ever be all right with what you chose to do to me, to us, and to our family, but I'm still here, so..."

Taking a deep breath, she continued on. "So, I see now that I also chose to look away, to not do anything about it and to not speak up. I have so many emotions flooding through me right now. I feel as though from the very start we were never given a real chance to make our relationship work. We never really had a chance to grow as a couple since the kids were born, or even to grow as a family. I let this happen because I felt overwhelmed by it all. It was easier to let your mom help when I went back to work; it seemed to make sense. Doing it the easy way became harder and harder, though. I became trapped in the plan that made sense at the time. I couldn't backtrack and say I wasn't all right with it anymore. I didn't want to hurt anyone but all it ended up doing was to hurt everyone in our household. I see that now.

"Don't get me wrong, I'm thankful for your mother's help, but our lives have revolved around your mom all these years, and I do mean literally around her. I feel as though I've been living on lifesupport, slowly dying a little bit more every day. I can't breathe. I've tried to keep the peace for so long that I've lost my ability to bother participating in my own life and those of our kids. Your mother comes in and corrects everything I do. I can't even choose my own laundry soap or clean my house with my own hands or in my own time. When I do anything, I feel like it's never good enough for her. No matter what I do or don't do, I can never get her approval. I can't make even the smallest of decisions on my own. So, I stopped trying." Clara seemed to know that Ryan needed a pause; she lowered her head and took a few moments to think.

Ryan connected the dots internally. All this time Clara had sat in agony and in silence. Inside that golden cage. No wonder she was drinking by herself at one point. He remembered finding empty bottles in the house and saying nothing. He knew when she stopped drinking alone because the bottles stopped appearing. Even though she hadn't mentioned anything out loud yet about the drinking, he was picking up her thoughts about it. They were more connected than either realized.

Clara resumed. "I don't feel confident or competent as a wife or as a mother. I just can't reach her standard of what she wants me to be. I feel sad, depressed, and alone all the time. Other times, I feel angry and mad at you and her, but mostly with myself for not stopping it from happening over and over. I want things to change. No, I *need* things to change. I can't keep sleepwalking through my life anymore. I want to feel better about myself, to become a better version of myself. I want to be your wife and to be a mother to our kids, but there are no boundaries, privacy, or even a possibility of intimacy in this place. I deserve better, the kids deserve better, and even your parents deserve better. So, please hear me when I say that this is me saying something, wanting you to say and do something, so that we can all be happier. If you don't know what that could look like, I'm willing to help you but I won't do it for you."

That was quite the rant. Clara had so much bottled up inside that Ryan hadn't known about. He knew now that he should have known. Saving his marriage was his priority, pleasing his mother was his duty, and trying to stay sane was becoming increasingly more difficult. He couldn't change his mom overnight and shouldn't try to change anyone but himself. He didn't see how any changes could make matters better. This was never going to be a win–win situation. He had a horrible knot in his stomach, anything that he would do or say could cause him to lose one of these two women. *How can you choose between your mother and your wife? You shouldn't have to, right?*

If something good came of this, it was seeing a new Clara emerging, but his mother was refusing to budge. Ryan had to be brave and find a way to allow Clara to be herself in her own home. There was only one side to choose and that side was Clara's. How, though? The answer became clear. He was figuratively holding two pots in his hand and needed to water just one.

***

RYAN'S PHONE RANG. It was his mother telling them that everything was all set and that they could come up for dinner. Clara's prediction was correct, chicken fingers for little Ryan and hotdogs for Angela. Ryan sat through dinner from a heightened conscious level and watched the programs unravel. The kids acted like their grandmother was a waitress, demanding their orders. His father ate quietly and quickly and spent the rest of the meal teasing the kids. Maria fluttered around like a butterfly making sure everyone was happy. Nobody served themselves, as she insisted on doing everything herself. She helped magnify all the old patterns and programs for Ryan to catch. He didn't have to look far to find them. He sat in the same chair, was served his meal the same way as always.

Clara wasn't in her usual polite position. Tonight, she sat folded into herself like a shrunken child on a playground, scared to be noticed, pointed out, and made fun of by others.

Suddenly feeling brave, Ryan addressed his parents. "Mom, Dad. I appreciate everything that you do for us. I want you to know that I decided to go for counselling just recently, and it opened my eyes to the fact that I need to be more independent." He decided to correct himself. "My beautiful Clara and I need to be more independent." He looked at Clara as if to say, *I did that for us.*

Clara snapped her head around in shock, checking to see what their reactions would be.

"Of course," Maria tweeted like a sparrow on a cloudless spring morning. "I told you. I'll take care of everything. I'll be there each day to get things done and you two can be independent and do…" She paused for a moment and switched over into a more polite voice, "You can do whatever you two want to do. How can I help you?"

Ryan was beginning to show his agitation and annoyance. His mother's kindness had become too much. Words poured out before he could mould them into something kinder. "Mom, you don't need to come downstairs anymore to do our stuff. Clara wants environmentally friendly products and she told you that many times, but as always, you weren't listening to her. Enough is enough! We'll buy our own soaps and do our own laundry, do you understand?" As harsh as it spilt out, he thought he got through to her with clarity.

"How could you speak to me that way Ryan? I would do anything for you. Of course, you can buy those products. I can use whatever you want on your clothing. We'll just use the other stuff here because it just cleans better anyway. You'll see. You bring yours and the kid's clothes here and Clara can do her own stuff. I'm not hard to get along with, whatever works best."

Ryan felt he was living inside some ridiculous drama. So much so that his mother's smile was starting to remind him of Cruella de Vil in the *101 Dalmatians* cartoon movie. He shook his head and shivered at the thought. "Mom, I told you we'll do our own laundry."

Maria turned around and rushed over to cut the three types of desserts that she had prepared, catering to everyone's different likings. Ryan was fast losing respect for his mom.

John raised his eyebrows and looked at Clara encouragingly. He leaned toward her, "Sweetness wins the day," he muttered aside.

Clara smiled and tried not to laugh. Ryan smiled, too. He used to see his dad's smart remarks as goofy comments. For the first time he realized it was a direct message to Clara, to comfort her. John knew what it was like to deal with Maria, but Ryan had never put the Lego pieces together till now. His father and Clara were so much alike. Moulded from the same set. Francis was right—he was only able to handle the junior Lego set.

Ryan felt the sudden urge to retaliate against his mother. He wanted to yell at her, yet losing his cool wouldn't make things better. Instead, he decided to go with a different tactic. "Dad, I have been thinking of inviting you somewhere. Would you like to come with us to the pond? You know the one Andy and I used to swim at? I was hoping to go tomorrow, perhaps if everyone agrees. I would love to have you there, Dad. The kids would love to play with you."

His mother jumped in, "You know the flies are terrible this time of year, Ryan; they'd eat us alive, so no, no, no, not there. Why don't we go to the park on Elm Street instead?"

Ryan turned to his father again and asked more specifically. "Dad would you like to come with us tomorrow to the pond?"

His father was pleasantly surprised and accepted the invitation, even though he knew it might stir up trouble later with Maria.

"Okay, okay, I'll pack a lunch!" Maria exploded out a bit violently. "Let's leave at ten o'clock then."

Ryan spoke back with slight force, "No need for a lunch, Mom. Clara or I will handle everything. I know you hate the woods, so you can stay home if you want. You don't like the bugs, remember?" Ryan felt his face heating up.

"No, it's no problem at all." Maria threw her words back like a tennis match. "I'll bring the repellent."

"Mom!" Ryan tried not to sound annoyed, but his voice got stronger and he served the tennis ball back to her court. "You know that the kids both use natural products for mosquitos and little Ryan gets asthma from the chemical stuff. We went through this already. Please leave it alone. I asked Dad to come; you can just stay and rest at home where there are no bugs."

"All right, then. If you don't want me there, that's fine! I'll have a lunch ready when you get back. You'll be starving."

"Mom, it's not that we don't want you there. I just think this is a place for Dad."

The kids sat uncomfortably stunned, turning their heads back and forth listening and watching like spectators in the stands.

Ryan looked at Clara pleadingly as if to ask for forgiveness for what he was about to do. "Okay, we'll be ready at ten o'clock, and you are both welcome."

Maria served the ball one last time as she jumped up to clear the table. "Yes, and I'll make it easier for everyone and pack a lunch."

Ryan regretted even bringing up the conversation. He whispered to Clara as they went out the door, "I'll do better next time!"

***

ANGELA LED HER brother excitedly into the thicket of woods. The sunlight slanted down through the branches, leaving a shadow of dancing figures on everyone's faces. Angela pointed them out and noted that the outlined shapes looked like fairies jumping on everyone's cheeks. Ryan could see it clearly. It really was quite magical, he admitted, as if they were watching some old-fashioned picture show.

Ryan asked the kids to come swimming with him. Maria intervened, opposing the proposal immediately. She didn't want the kids to get dirty and wet, so she encouraged them to pick flowers instead. Again, Ryan asked the kids to get ready to swim.

Little Ryan slowly prepared to go with his father. Angela followed suit but suddenly acted panicked, now raising Maria's point of how dirty the water would be. Little Ryan got scared straight away, started crying, then struggled against his father, refusing flat out to go in the water with him. He wriggled away as if he was being held against his will and abruptly stood back with Angela, arms now folded. Ryan shook his head out of frustration. He tied a new rope to the tree, swung off of it, and jumped into the water himself, yelling out, "Screw it!"

Angela felt instantly bad for her father. Seeing him swim all by himself didn't seem right. Even though it would defy her grandmother, she finished preparing and decided to join in on the fun. In no time, she was having a great time playing and splashing about. Ryan brought her to the deeper part of the pond. He put his hands out so she could climb up and jump over his shoulder to do a shallow dive into the water. Seeing this, Little Ryan had a change of heart and wanted to join them. Maria wouldn't have it. She gave him a grimacing look and shuffled him by the wrist toward the toys she had brought; busying him back into submission.

To forget about her son's insolence, Maria turned away to occupy herself with the picnic that she had brought for everyone. She fussed with the blanket, making sure that it sat just right and placed the plastic plates from the basket in an orderly fashion. Everything was perfect.

Little Ryan played and from a distance watched his dad and Angela having fun. Though he was saddened by the feeling of being left out, he listened to his grandmother's every direction and continued to stay out of the "dirty" water, as she kept calling it.

He was now convinced something bad would happen if he went in with them.

John sat to the side, chiselling away at a branch he had just taken off a walnut tree and silently watched everything from afar. A little later, Ryan got out of the water and shuffled up to his Dad while drying himself off. "Wow, Dad! What is that for?" He wanted to show enthusiasm.

"My grandfather used to make toothbrushes for us with branches from hazelnut trees. I could only find the walnut tree here, but it works, too. I'm making some for us."

"That's pretty cool. What other skills have you been keeping secret from us?"

Maria interrupted, asking if anyone was thirsty. She had elderberry juice that she had made herself and proudly announced her accomplishment loud enough that everyone could hear.

Ryan nodded his head yes, then swiftly turned back to his father. "So, Dad, did your grandfather Edward teach you about the woods?"

"Yes," John admitted. "Granddad was a woodsman in many ways. In fact, he was pretty much able to live from the woods, which became a useful skill, especially after the war."

Ryan was stunned. "You never told me much about him, or about the war." He was hoping his dad would say more.

"Yeah, I guess he knew his mushrooms well. He was able to tell which ones were poisonous just by putting them on his tongue."

"Why did your dad never speak of Edward?"

John paused and shuffled about uncomfortably. "My grandfather never had any time for play. He only knew hard work. Dad felt alone in many ways; it was like he was orphaned. His father wasn't always present in his life, and his mother was too busy for him."

"So, what hardened your father so much? I remember him being a pretty angry guy."

John explained more. "With hard work sometimes comes hard play...and, well, alcohol was the escape. My grandfather was sober at the end of his life, but was a hard alcoholic for years. All kinds of things happened that are best forgotten. The apple doesn't fall far from the tree, though. Dad ended up living pretty much the same way, crawling inside a bottle."

No wonder John ended up with someone like Maria—someone who would take over, sweep things under the rug, and allow things to go unsaid. She was the master of covering things up. It made it easier for him to avoid dealing with the unpleasant aspects of reality and to sit in the background happily and completely unattached to the world around him. A prick of pain hit Ryan in his heart as if someone had stabbed him with a letter opener. He grabbed another towel and got Angela out of the water, first checking for leeches before drying her off.

Maria made noise beside them to distract them and threw John a look of disgust. She then turned to Ryan showing an over exaggerated sad face. She volunteered while making sure her voice echoed the misery of her story of despair, "My life was hard, Ryan. If only you knew the pain and suffering."

Was everything always going to be about her? Why couldn't she just console her husband and thank him for sharing finally, after so many years of silence? It was apparent she wanted him to feel bad for taking the attention away from "her" special outing. John fell back into silence for the rest of the outing.

Ryan gave up trying and turned his attention to Clara. She was sitting hunched over with a piece of long grass in her hand swaying it back and forth in the water. She seemed to be off in some faraway land. Angela now sat beside her, reading a book. It was quite some time before Clara noticed his gaze. She smiled and turned as if to stare at something in the distance again.

To any onlookers this family event would seem like they were the happiest family ever. In reality, no one was together, everyone sat apart, and there was no unity in what seemed to be a picture-perfect moment.

Maria took charge and called everyone over to eat. They sat in a circle no different than how they would at the dinner table. Each knew where to go based on their favourite-coloured plate. The kids enjoyed their preferred snacks, sang songs, and teased one another.

John watched Ryan with intensity, as if to be picking up on his thoughts about Maria's control. He squinted his eyes and ate his sandwich slowly. He was in no mood to tease the kids.

THEY RETURNED TO the house. "It was the perfect day," Maria kept repeating. "I would love to do it again really soon." Any other day, Ryan would have agreed, as ignorance used to be bliss, but today, from his awakened viewpoint, he felt an agonizing torment within.

Clara organized the kids to help their grandmother bring the basket back upstairs and went into her own kitchen. Ryan came up behind her at the sink as she got a glass of water from the tap. He brushed her hair back and grabbed her hips tenderly, whispering in her left ear. "I saw you, Clara, I saw it in your eyes. I don't know where you went in your mind, but I saw that you had to go there in order to deal with this mess I got you into. I'm sorry."

Clara spoke nothing and drank the water while staring out of the window over the kitchen sink.

Ryan knew he needed to say more. "How about we take advantage of Mom's eagerness to help us and plan a date for tonight? I would love to take you to another special place later tonight."

Clara laughed and turned about impishly. "I will call her and ask her myself!"

Ryan snickered slyly, asking gently, "Could you let me go up? I would really like to get one of Dad's toothbrushes. My teeth could use some cleaning."

They both lunged forward the same awkward way, almost bumping heads as they walked. Then Ryan almost stumbled and fell as he ran upstairs to ask his mom if she would babysit.

"SAM'S DINER?" CLARA giggled. "I haven't seen this place in years. We're really going here?"

Ryan opened the door to the diner, allowing Clara to go in first. He politely asked the waitress to lead him to the most romantic place in the house. The woman twinkled like a fairy godmother and led them to a booth in the corner by the window. She had a candle lit for them and placed a flower on the table. It was obvious that he had called them ahead of time to set it up. The wall had old photos of the town from the 1800s to early 1900s. This was all quaint and somehow comforting for Clara.

The waitresses were getting used to having Ryan and Andrew coming around now; "two formal gentlemen," they called them.

"Shall we have a glass of wine?" Clara wasn't really sure why she had asked that because she had no desire to drink anymore. Perhaps it was in her program to ask, she thought. She shook her head.

"I caught on to the fact that you haven't been wanting to drink at all anymore and I have decided to put alcohol aside for a while, myself, so don't worry—I'm ordering tea tonight."

Clara looked at him from the side with a suspicious glance. He was never this observant. She felt flushed and a bit nervous. *Maybe he really is changing*, she thought.

Ryan nudged forward, "What do you say? Black tea with a shot of milk to go with it? and maybe a cola, too?"

Clara laughed. "Wow! You *are* wild tonight. All right, then. I'll have the same." Both giggled and ordered hamburgers and fries. They talked for two hours straight just like they used to back when they were dating.

"I haven't had a burger since forever," Clara said.

"I know," Ryan chorused, "but somehow it feels like the best meal I've had in a very long time. I would like to take you out again sometime. Would you agree to start dating me again? Maybe to slowly get to know each other?"

"I would like that." Clara's smile was vivid.

Ryan could suddenly swear he saw an irresistible yellowish glow around his wife. Adjusting his gaze and thinking at first that his eyes were just blurry, he rubbed them. The hue then flipped between a tiger orange to a tangerine and then to a sharp scarlet red. The colours actually changed as she spoke, he realized. As he focused on her words, he lost the vision. He shook his head and blinked his eyes.

"It doesn't mean that all is forgiven. We still have much to work on, and I still hate what you did," she admitted.

Ryan knew somehow to console her. "I know and I don't blame you. It's okay."

Clara was happy. The conversation seemed to flow easier without alcohol. Him being more present and in the moment helped also.

Ryan was staring intensely again without grasping what he was seeing. She still glowed. This time he saw lime green around her. As someone walked by the table, he lost his focus.

Later when he'd tell Andrew about it, he would learn that he was indeed seeing her aura. Andy would explain that the yellow was when she was speaking commandingly or was within her power. The orange and red meant that she was feeling angry or fearful. Green was her feeling connected to her heart.

Ryan had never seen anything like it in his life. Clara was up and down with her emotions from one minute to the next so the colours around her shifted just as quickly. A yellow-lime appeared again briefly as she was feeling safer. She had something on her mind, though. Ryan shook his head to come back to attention.

"I was thinking a lot today, Ryan. I want to ask you a lot of questions. I don't know yet if I'm ready for the answers, so I admit I'm holding a lot of them back. Sometimes, I just want to kick and scream and demand all the details of what happened. I think I know why you did it, but I can't get past who you did it with."

Ryan continued listening without speaking and trying his hardest to get a glimpse of whatever it was that he was seeing glow around her.

"I think someday I want to go see that guy by myself, but I'm not ready yet."

Ryan smiled gently. "Francis would be a good choice for you. I have a feeling he'll be a little more tender with you than he has been with me."

Clara looked surprised. "Really? What has been happening there?"

"Let's just say he has been putting me in my place and not letting me off with much."

"Then I *do* have to meet this guy!" Clara laughed out loud, making the waitresses turn and look at her. She lowered her voice, "I would like to get his contact information from you when I'm ready." After her recent outbursts, Clara felt braver now to speak up whenever something was on her mind. "I don't see my family often. I don't want to involve them in our healing at this time, but I need to see them and I want to have them over to the house for a visit."

Ryan smiled and suggested while laughing, "Maybe we should buy a lawn tournament game and let our moms battle it out. What do you think?"

Clara giggled out loud too. "To be honest, I think you misunderstand my mom. She's not what you think. I was listening to your dad at the pond and I was visualizing our fathers hanging out and having a good time. I don't think your mom ever gave anyone a chance to ever get to know one another outside her cooking and then us eating it. Her having to prove constantly that she's the best mom ever seems to eat up all the attention whenever they do see one another. My dad likes to make things like John does. Maybe we can put our dads to work and ask them to set up those swings that little Ryan has been asking for."

Ryan smiled deeply and stared softly into Clara's eyes. "Beautiful and smart. Exactly why I married you."

"Don't push your luck, Ryan. You aren't out of deep water with me yet!"

Clara now had one hand on her hip. It was obvious where Angela got her powerful stance from. The tsunami wave he saw in his dream suddenly came to mind. Ryan heeded the warning and backed off quickly from trying to charm her. This was one of those appropriate times to follow her lead instead of trying to be the controller in the situation.

Chapter Eight

The Roles We Play

R YAN CHECKED HIS phone calendar to discover that he was a half
hour ahead of schedule. An extremely unpleasant pungent smell
curled his nose and stopped him in his tracks.

"What the hell is that?" Ryan blurted out while holding his hand
over his nose and coughing dramatically. He then waved his hand
back and forth vigorously to make a point.

Francis gently put his hand up to stop Ryan from talking and
pointed upwards with his index finger to gesture him to wait a moment. Francis almost looked like he was in a trance. His head hung
over an abalone seashell that was now enveloped with billowing,
swirling, grey smoke.

Ryan was almost sure that the smell was marijuana. He looked
inside the shell inquisitively to see what was smoking. "Whew!" He
thought. It was only sage.

Francis took a large feather and wiped his own eyes, ears and
mouth with it, as if to smear himself with the smoke. He continued
doing the same thing down his legs and feet. He muttered out a
prayer that Ryan had never heard before in his life.

Creator, my name is *Spirit Keeper*.

I come to you in humbleness. I use this sage as a medicine, to
smudge away anything that does not serve my spirit in a good
way. I clear my eyes of anything that I saw that did not serve
my spirit. I clear my ears of anything that I heard that did not
serve me. I clear my mouth of anything I spoke that did not
serve me or others in a good way and I clear anything I
wanted to speak and couldn't. I clear my mind and head of
any thoughts that I had about me or other people that did not
serve me or them in a good way. I clear my heart of anything
that I did not keep sacred within me. I clear my hands of anything that I did with them that did not serve me or others in
a good way. I clear my feet of anywhere that I walked that did
not serve me or that kept me from being on the right path.
May I see good today, hear good, speak good, keep sacredness in my mind and in my heart. May I do good with these
hands today and walk where it serves my spirit best. May I be

97

protected in all ways, body, mind and soul. Thank you, Creator, I have spoken. *Msit Nogama*, All My Relations.

Francis gestured Ryan over with lips puckered out slightly and nodded for him to put his arms out. Then, he took the feather and swiped it over Ryan's eyes and spoke in a language Ryan had never heard before. Then he did the same over his ears and mouth, hands, heart, and feet and turned him around clockwise to do the same for his back. He tapped Ryan's shoulder when done.

Bringing the feather back to Ryan's eyes, Francis continued, "You have been cleared from all that has not served your spirit in a good way. May you see good, hear good, speak good, keep sacredness in your mind and heart, and may you walk where it serves you best. May you do good with these hands always, brother, and serve Mother Earth in good ways."

A wave of emotion washed over Ryan and goosebumps popped up on his skin, covering his whole body. It was as if he'd heard truth spoken for the first time in his life. Tears stung his eyes as he stood there in silence. He wiped his face quickly to hide it.

Francis placed the feather and the abalone shell down on the table in front of him. He grabbed Ryan's hand and hugged him as if he'd just come back from a long journey. He then grabbed the sacred items again, arranging them inside a red box, and placed them up on the shelf above his head. He then jumped right into conversation like nothing had happened. "So, brother, how is the outside world? Still there?"

"Well, I certainly got to see more of a world within my family unit."

"A lot of programs being shared around like you'd share a picnic, eh?"

Ryan squinted his eyes apprehensively and squeezed his eyebrows together. How could he know they'd had a picnic? "Actually, yes."

"Good, good. The more you see, the less generational programs you'll pass down to the kids."

"Yes. Umm, what exactly were you doing just now? With the smoke. I never saw that before."

"That was what we would call a smudging ceremony or ritual."

"Okay, but what is it for?"

"Well, in technical terms, for centuries, Native American and Indigenous cultures have practised smudging rituals to clear away negative energy, to invite in peace and harmony for individuals or environments. You can use it to clear your own body from the negative you've absorbed from your surroundings or to cleanse a room or house and to put protection around you."

"I've never felt anything like that before."

"Yeah? And how did it make you feel?"

"I felt like something was tickling my back when you went behind me. Not from the feather but almost like the hairs on the back of my neck felt shivery and stuff. I can't explain it. I felt scared at first, but then after you were finished, I felt better. Does that make any sense?"

"It makes a lot of sense." Francis explained. "It's something you could do daily to help clear away emotions and to help with balance."

"Really? Could you give me that prayer or whatever that was you were saying at the beginning for yourself when I walked in?"

Francis couldn't help himself. He had Ryan right where he wanted him for this next joke. "God, Ryan, did you just ask me for a prayer? Hmm?"

Ryan scoffed and rolled his eyes.

"I had written the prayer down for someone just the other day and I have an extra copy right here." Francis passed Ryan the paper along with some extra smudge he had set aside.

"Thank you."

"You are welcome."

"I CAME EARLY by mistake, sorry."

"There are no coincidences, brother. This was a synchronistic event that lined up with your truest desires."

"Okay, whatever you say." Ryan felt stupid for not understanding.

Recognizing Ryan's unfamiliarity with the term, Francis explained more. "Synchronicities are coincidences that aren't coincidence. They are events that happen for a reason. How did you do with this week's homework assignment?"

"Oh, yeah. So much happened, I don't know where to start."

"Start where your spirit takes you."

"My spirit?"

"Start where your human thoughts take you."

"Well, I can see now how kids can be raised to be fussy by pleasing them all the time with their favourite foods. I also noticed that when people have no chores, they feel useless and shoved aside. I think you can guess who took over instead."

Francis nodded his head yes and gestured with his lips popped out again, thrusting them forward for Ryan to continue on.

"Viewing things from a bird's-eye view helped me to see that by allowing someone to control so much, it takes away confidence in other individuals even if it seemed to not affect me. Mom, for example, controls in a nice, polite way, but Dad and Clara were left feeling useless and set aside.

"I just realized this week that family events are about Mom. I used to think she was selfless but this time I could see selfishness in her, especially when I challenged her in small ways to give up a portion of that control. I saw a lot; I just got confused in trying to understand how someone becomes such a controller. I admit I'm not yet seeing how I control it. I do see, though, that by accepting the role I play in life, I'm also accepting those programs as a result. If I don't change, I can already see the future: I become my mom and Clara becomes my father. I mean we're already playing those roles, just on different levels."

Francis was impressed. "Wow! Who are you? Not the same man that I met not long ago. Good observations, brother."

"Trust me, I'm surprising myself, too. I got a question: Where does control come from, anyway?"

"Well, it usually starts in a very subtle way. Controlling begins with the controller's offering to help or rescue someone. It feels good to be helped at first so we give permission to be helped again. The problem starts when it feeds the helper's own ego. They do it at first to feel good about themselves, yet they say that it's for others. When they base their happiness on *having* to help, then this is when it becomes a kind of addiction. Right? The person being helped ends up upsetting the helper if suddenly they want to do things on their own or want some change."

"Yes! Oh my God, that clarifies things. It is an actual addiction, then. Mom *must* help others, or she's lost and upset, and therefore so is everyone else."

"I was right, then. She does have a good golf swing! Remember, victimhood is a harder habit to break than a drug addiction. Emotions and heroin, for example, involve the same neurological reactions to the same brain regions that are associated with addiction. This may be why people who cannot deal with emotions turn to drugs. It numbs and feeds the addiction all at once. Those addicted to victimhood need the fix called 'getting upset,' in order to feed their addiction."

"That is scary." Ryan shivered from head to toe with the mere thought.

"Addicts, in general, will do just about anything to feed that addiction: lie, cheat, hide things, name it."

"Or they have a tantrum for two weeks and blame it on their son or daughter-in-law."

"Ha! Yes, that too. A telltale sign of your past two weeks, is it?"

"Yup! And everyone stays quiet about mom's helpfulness and her victimhood."

"Yes, like with an alcoholic in a family," Francis observed.

"That is exactly it. We sometimes tip-toe around her like a person would around an alcoholic.

"Also, it hit me when I was talking to my dad that they both come from a different time period than this one—a time when people lived through much harder circumstances. I see that my mom saw her own generation and the generations before her as suffering. With the wars and stuff, that makes sense; they did suffer. So, she babied me, yet expected a lot from me as the oldest. My mom had another child that died young, before I was born. She often laments about him and says she'll never get over it. My siblings live out of town, so my kids became her focus. It's like the addiction stems from her need to ensure that we'll never suffer. She means well; I see that."

"It's a little too much saving others from suffering, though, eh, brother?"

"Yes."

"You are a bunch of postwar smothered victims."

"What?" Ryan was lost, yet his curiosity was piqued.

"She loves you so much that she's almost smothering you. This is because she's the result of a generation after the wars. It's based not only on suffering, but also on shame and pride. Everyone has their duty to ensure the next generation won't suffer like their parents did. Without a sense of duty, some are lost souls. Right?"

"Yes, and I don't even know where to begin to help her."

"I told you before, you begin by helping yourself, brother."

"Living with her and speaking about her are two different things. If I'm going to be there, I need to know how to better handle her."

"Again, help you and only you. She may or may not want help." Francis sounded stern.

"True. I find she won't hear anything I have to say anyway. If I try and talk to her, she falls into the old program of victimhood, and then so do I, like a controlled setting."

"You aren't in the war in this generation, and yet you still fight it, eh?"

"I don't know about that, but I do see the war between the women of the household. I would say that Clara is the smaller country about to be taken over."

"Yes, she's the minority, it seems."

"Okay, I get that people suffered, and maybe the control is based on the old lifestyles where people did have it harder. Life is much easier now, though."

"Yes, in this generation not many know much about what it feels like to suffer. In fact, things changed so quickly in just one generation that we confused and exchanged surviving with controlling, didn't we?"

"Wow!" Ryan sat up straight. This rang true.

"Before, we needed control to survive. Instead of healing the postwar problems, those problems turned into family smothering situations. A whole program and belief system got built around these postwar problems. Plus, no one dared make waves, out of the fear of being shot."

"Yes, and they seemed to have kids earlier back then. Babies having babies," Ryan realized.

"Yes, circumstance causes one to grow up quick. We have to remember that they were also allowed to grow up faster. Today's child has been overprotected and watered down, which could now cause opposite issues in an already hollowed-out society. Envision making all the choices for the young men and women back in the day like we do with kids today. Society would have crumbled or crashed and burned without some kind of personal independence."

"True, but still, shouldn't we protect kids a little bit, though? It is a cruel world."

"In my experience, a child taught nothing is an adult later who knows nothing and can't help himself. An overprotected child is a smothered child. A smothered child is a controlled child. A controlled child becomes a controller or even a bully. So, you figure it out, brother. The leg bone is connected to the hip bone, etcetera."

"True. I think people don't know when they're controllers, though."

"This is why we need to keep working on our consciousness and to be aware of our own ability to control."

"The more aware I become the more daunting it is."

"As you change yourself, aspects of your life will unfold and heal themselves without you trying."

"I'll keep working on me. I can see that smothering aspect within myself. By living with my parents, I get a lot of decisions made for all of us, a type of enslavement that I signed up for. What I say and do ends up being under their authority...well, under my mom's authority, really. Dad lets her run the show. She chose my career, decided that we'd live there with her, and even picked my kid's names, overpowering Clara's choices for both kids—mainly because I didn't want to upset my mother and sort of set the boundary at that time with Clara not to defy her.

"My mom loved my first girlfriend more, and Clara has suffered deeply because of my mom's disapproval of marrying her instead. I don't blame my mom. I take responsibility for it. I did succumb to her complaints about Clara in the end. I feel like an ass for saying it, but I know it's true. She poisoned me in a sense because I started believing it, so I see now where it stems from. I feel good in one sense to discover all this, and, in another sense, I can't help feeling sorry for my mom and for Clara at the same time. I'm not sure what side to be on."

Francis shook his head and raised his hand as a reassurance that everything would be all right. "The situation will remedy itself when you fix yourself, trust me."

"But if I'm living in that house, I can't see fixing myself being that easy."

"By fixing yourself, leaving that house will become easier."

"Did you just say what I think you said?" Ryan asked.

"I think I cleared your ears earlier, so you heard me very well."

"It's like you're reading my mind, I have been thinking about moving."

"Are you sure you don't mean running?"

"Yeah, maybe, but..."

"First things first. Stop using the word 'but' so much and use 'and' instead sometimes. It'll help you flip things more easily into the positive within that jumbled brain of yours. Secondly, this is what I think about your home situation, brother: In order to get yourself to move toward the kind of freedom that you seek, you first must mourn and grieve the old you as the changes happen within you."

"But I don't even know if I understand what mourning and grieving really means."

"But?"

"Sorry—'and' I think I *did* grieve. I have felt like crap more this past while than I have in my whole entire life. It's really starting to get annoying."

"Nobody ever said that growth or change was comfortable. Each time we let go of something or someone or even when we accept something new, we grieve. Think of it as letting go to make room for the new."

"I just want the new now and the old done and over with."

"You have to let the process happen. Each person we meet, each new level we reach is a 'new' us. To grab onto that newness, an old piece of ourselves then dies. Like in the autumn, we need to let the old leaves wither and die and fall away naturally. In life, we go through a winter of contemplation and before we know it, fresh green leaves pop out as a result of having let go of the old. They say that seasons are for a reason and in their own timing. It's true. If a tree processes too quickly, the result is shock and the tree dies. We are no different than nature, brother. We must allow our leaves to draw inwards so that the tree regains needed nutrients before plucking them off and causing a shock within our core."

"Here you go getting all deep on me again," Ryan complained. "I think I only take in a quarter of what you say in these sessions."

"Your spirit is listening to what your mind thinks it can't hear. You also ask deeper questions and call forward more involved teachings than you realize."

"My spirit? Okay, Kemosabe!"

"And who are you? Tonto on your horse? Lone Ranger, eh?"

"Yeah, I used to watch that show a lot as a kid. Maybe it's why I was disappointed when I saw you in normal clothes and not in traditional regalia." Ryan suddenly noticed that when Francis chuckled, his cheeks actually rounded out like a squirrel with a mouth full of nuts. "I do get what you are saying," Ryan admitted. "To work with Clara and to be fully myself, I must let go of the programs that I was given by both my parents and by society and from myself. This is a kind of letting go and a process that takes time and effort. I need to let the old nurture me by learning from it. So, I have got to take in as much as I can from the situation and make the best of it for the future. Right?"

Francis looked moved. "And you thought you weren't taking it all in. Grade 5 graduation is coming soon, I see. Furthermore, if you want to have freedom with Clara, then you first need to have freedom from those programs. Otherwise, you are headed toward a divorce, brother. Those programs come from people who don't want to try and change themselves. Don't waste your energy chasing after them on that horse of yours. Change yourself instead. Everyone came to Earth with their own karma to deal with, and each to walk their own journey. If you want to change them, then you take their karma. Good luck with that, brother! I don't advise it."

"Yeah, I have enough of my own karma. I see that now. Can karma be passed down from generation to generation, too? I don't really know much about it." Ryan looked concerned.

"Yes, it can, and it already has been passed down. For example, your relationship looks a lot like your parents', doesn't it?"

"Oh, you got me there. Yes, it does. Clara is my dad, like I already gathered from before, but I hoped it wasn't real that I'm my mom."

"But?"

"*And* I hoped it wasn't real that I'm my mom."

"Glad you stated it, not me."

"You're glad I stated what? The word 'and' or my being just like my mom?"

"Both!"

"Okay, funny guy. The kids have also inherited the karma, then. Is that what you are saying?"

"Yes, and to not pass down the programs and karma further down the line, something will need to change. You must work on yourself so that the generational patterns can break. The work you do will help heal others around you indirectly. There's a reason why I'm pointing out the 'but' in your phrases. It's not a judgment. The more we pay attention to our words, the more we become aware of what we really mean to say. You can speak how you want. Just become aware of the programs is all."

"So, like break old unneeded cycles in order to create a new life?"

"Yes, Ryan, very good. How can you show your kids a new way? Is it by living in that house? Or do you have to move and create a new life, a new world so that the kids can get out of the box? Don't answer that, just think about it. Moving is just an example of breaking that chain.

"Sometimes we can make changes alongside those people who don't want to change. Some people's programs are too deep. They may not come to the same healing that you'll come to. Do you understand?"

"Yes, but!"

Francis smirked at Ryan with a sour face.

"Just kidding!" Ryan was smiling from ear to ear.

It was wonderful that Ryan was able to take things more in stride. He was clearly ready to see outside of himself a bit more now. Now Francis could come across as less stern and serious.

FRANCIS DECIDED TO share some guidance that his former teacher once gave him. "The eagle couple doesn't raise their young to stay inside the nest forever. They feed their young until they know that they're strong enough to fly off from that nest. Then the parents fly away just far enough to try to force their young to choose to leave and find food for themselves. The parents keep themselves at a distance so that the young will be strong enough on their own in the wild to fend for themselves. The youngsters instinctively fly away from the nest alone when their wings are strong enough. The parents stay back deliberately and without intervening, keeping a watchful eye only."

"Holy, that gave me goosebumps. That sounds like Andy's father and how he raised him."

"Yes. I call those bumps 'truth-bumps.' It means you just heard something that resonated with your higher self. This is when you know that you have entered the honesty aspect of your medicine wheel. You heard truth. And you're now a young eagle ready to catch his first fish on his own. You can stay in the nest, but who will feed you when your parents die?"

Ryan turned his head to the side and lowered his eyes gently, feeling oddly humbled. "I never ever thought of things like that before."

"The elders say, 'I could fish for you. Or I could take you fishing and teach you to fish for yourself.' A community would die if only one person knew how to find the food source. Wouldn't they? If the provider died without passing down his knowledge, then all of us would die with him. It makes no sense for the survival of the whole, now does it?"

"No, it doesn't make sense to do that. That is why we have grocery stores, isn't it?" Ryan asked. "I mean, we don't know anything about finding our own food. I wouldn't have a clue how to find food without the store, and that's a scary thought. I feel like a boy, to be honest, still too young in the nest to even understand how to fly."

"Basically," teased Francis, "you're still only in Grade 5, brother, so don't worry about growing too fast. Exercise those wings and get them strong. The time to soar will soon come. Once you do fly, don't stop hunting for your own salmon, your own destiny. The catch will be worth all this change and growth someday."

Ryan smiled broadly. This guy was really starting to grow on him. He felt a love in his heart so deep that it was bottomless and expansive. In truth, Francis had become the dad that Ryan's own father didn't know how to be.

Francis continued. "New and modern grocery stores are a part of a system that has been set up to numb us into becoming a sleeping society. We follow the cart in front of us like sheep, don't we? We're all guilty of supporting that, including me. We can grow our own little gardens like I do; however, there is always going to be some need for the store. If you look around, most of the world is set up in that very same way. This dysfunction stunts our growth, and so we need to avoid falling into the entrapments of the social set-up when possible. Or at least become aware that we are inside that box and try to have a backup plan."

Ryan felt the need to be honest with his ignorance. "I have heard the word 'dysfunction' before, but could you maybe explain it to me in simple terms?"

Francis thought for a moment. "All right. We made a good comparison earlier between your mom and an alcoholic. Imagine the alcoholic is a man. Everyone loves him but he's a weak link in the family chain. Everyone else stays on high alert working to keep things together. Each person within that family unit becomes dependent on one another to ensure the unit stays stable. Each one plays a different role, yet each role has a defect or a flaw of some kind. Some of the role players take charge, some hide their heads, some cover up the alcoholic's tracks. Somehow, at the end of the day, things seem to function okay. At least on the outside everything looks fine. The team effort it takes to cover up the truth, which isn't all that fine or stable, is called *dysfunction*."

"Sounds a bit like my family for sure, but—sorry, and—if I go down the generational line, we were functionally dysfunctional and there were actual alcoholics in the family."

"Functionally dysfunctional is exactly what it is, I like that. It's functional on the outside but if you look within, it's actually very dysfunctional. Family members each play their roles because they get something out of it, maybe it even feeds an addiction. They can be dependent, independent, codependent; and some get lucky and learn to be *inter*dependent. Some part of the role they play makes them feel good for whatever reason. It becomes comforting, even if the role has its defects."

"Is interdependent still dependent?"

"Well, yes, it is. Let me explain it a different way. Have you ever seen those soulmate pictures that women love? You know, ones like dolphins swimming together?"

"I can't say I have, no." Ryan giggled shyly, feeling like a novice.

"Well, the dolphins swim together, and yet separate. It's like a dance as they swim upwards through the bubbles. It looks like a parallel line that never touches. That is interdependence. They never bump into one another and swim equally balanced in strength, poise, and grace."

"You're not getting all romantic on me, are you?" Ryan teased.

"Why? Do you need dance lessons?"

"Don't even put that in the airways! Clara will get one of her great ideas."

"Two left feet, eh?"

"Something like that. So, what you're saying is that my family has all the dysfunctions. I need to work on interdependence with

Clara. First, I need to identify all the dependencies I have because of the codependency in my family? I'm responsible for myself and the role I play."

"Yes. Great job, brother, you are getting it. Ego has us play many parts, many roles. Doesn't it? Dysfunction helps us play those roles. A fun example would be to go through old folk tales, fairy tales, and stories to see who plays what role in your family."

Ryan laughed hysterically. "That's crazy, but it would be cool to do that, actually."

"Okay, for example, if I asked you who was the big bad wolf in your family, who would you say fits that role best?"

"Well, he isn't living but that would be my grandfather. Actually, he would be the alcoholic I mentioned."

"Okay, so who is Cinderella?" Francis asked.

"I could say Clara because my mother makes her feel like she doesn't belong in the household."

"Who is your father?"

"I would say he's the father of Hansel and Gretel."

"Interesting choice. Why?"

"In some of the stories, the father isn't strong and is unavailable to his children. By not accompanying them and expecting them to be too grown up and on their own leads them to danger, and as a result they get captured and overpowered by the witch."

"I'm impressed how you thought that one out. Anyone else in the family you can identify?" Francis couldn't wait to hear more.

"Let me think. Okay, I've got it. I'd compare my sister to being Cinderella's stepsister. She's my mom's one and only. My mom sees her as perfect and a great catch for the world and too good for any ordinary man. Her feet are too big for the glass slipper. She certainly has a big head and is all about herself. She's a good duplicate of my mother, being an even bigger controller."

"Good one. How about your brother?"

"My brother, on the other hand, is one of the three little pigs. He's the non-diligent pig who wants to play and play and never builds his own house. He expects another pig to always bail him out. That person is usually my father."

"You're the one living in your mother's house, right? So, are you the diligent pig?"

"Yeah, you could say that, but in all honesty, I feel like I'm Snow White just awakening. Clara is my prince. Please tell me you don't tape these sessions!" Ryan chuckled again and covered his mouth out of raw embarrassment. "Basing my family members' characteristics on fairy tales really puts it into perspective. This has been great."

"Yes, and you did well, actually. Now, tell me, where do your kids fit in to the fairy tales?"

Ryan took a long pause to think. "Well, I see Angela strong and giving, like Robin Hood, and imaginative like the kids in Peter Pan. And little Ryan is Bambi—he is sweet and innocent and new to the world, or at least he used to be. I can see he has the least programs out of everyone, that's despite the fact that he acts so bad at times. I can also see the kids in general haven't picked up our karma yet. They have a better chance now than if they grow up with the programs, as long as we stop them from happening. Their roles are not the darker fairy tale roles. So, I am hoping little Ryan will be a knight in shining armour soon."

"Some programs are there, but not all of them, and yes, they can be changed. How about your mom? Who is she?"

"But? Did you just go on autopilot, Francis? I will have to think of some homework for you to help you reprogram!" Ryan wagged his forefinger like a disciplinarian.

"Oops, and thank you for helping me catch my old programs also, Ryan." Francis winked.

Ryan continued. "My mom, eh? Now, that's a good question. I can't fully say that she represents the wicked stepmother, but I can see her as Little Red Riding Hood, that's for sure."

"I'd like to see how you fit this one in."

"Well, Red Riding Hood brings the basket through the woods to help the grandmother and is completely unaware of her surroundings. Her grandmother gets eaten and she's so dutiful in getting things done that she doesn't even notice or recognize the fact that she's talking with a wolf. The story becomes all about her and she never seems wiser in the end. She learns nothing from the experience or at least not until things go all awry."

Francis laughed loudly. He was pleasantly surprised with Ryan's natural ability to problem solve using these creative exercises. This was an important insight.

"I love your imagination, Ryan, and your descriptions. So, with the roles that we play in the family, now you can see how the ego develops. We play a role so well that we don't want to give it up. Do we? We take comfort sometimes in these roles. Even if they don't turn out to be the perfect fairy tale character or role.

"Some roles become addictive. Some play for gain; however, ego traps us into developing programs. That's when we get possessive over those roles. Whoever is added into these lifestyles, like kids and wives, they end up picking roles that flatter the ego of those already in the fairy tales, don't they? Instead of just one story, many stories get mixed and intertwined in the end, and then we don't know who we are or which role we actually play. Or do we? Maybe we seek roles to play out, who knows. It's also possible that we play so many different roles within our lifespan that it's possible we may never know we're playing any at all."

"Yes, wow, that's incredible when you put it into that perspective. Now I think I need a better understanding of what the ego is."

"Oh, boy, get ready, then. It's a bigger subject than it seems, so we'll commit a whole session to that next time. I'm proud of you for your commitment and for the effort you put forward today, brother. You really know your fairy tales. You've been playing roles for a time, eh?"

Chapter Nine

UNDERSTANDING THE EGO

RYAN WALKED RIGHT over to snatch two Coke cans from the fridge and handed one to Francis. Eager to jump in where they had left off a week ago, he plopped down on his chair.

Seeing Ryan's focus, Francis decided to follow suit and leapt into his speaker's position. "Ego is a long braid to unravel. However, once you do so, it can be very helpful in all your life choices."

"Yeah, I heard people say that we need ego. Well, I mean I looked it up this week, anyway." Ryan laughed, knowing not to come across too smart with Francis. "There were a lot of different views about what ego is on the Internet. I put together the fact that all the traits of the black wolf are also types of ego traits. One theory argued that without ego, we wouldn't recognize danger. For example, if something is hot, ego gives us senses that tell us to take our hand away. It's a protection of sorts."

"That's an interesting search Uncle Google sent you on. I like that you got the point of the black wolf." Francis smiled tenderly. "Those senses that you're talking about that make you pull your hand away could be what we call instincts. Fear can be an instinct also. We have natural fears and unnatural fears. The natural fears aren't ego, though unnatural fears are ego."

"And I thought I was walking in here all smart for once." Ryan threw his hands up playfully. "What are our natural fears, then?"

"They say that fear of falling is a natural fear, as are loud noises. These are instinctual fears, and, in my opinion, we need them to survive. Other fears have been handed to us by others and then became a part of the ego. For example, if our mother fears spiders, then we might develop that same fear. We get anxious and suddenly feel lack of control, and that's when other fears creep in...those unnatural fears within the ego, I mean."

"Wow, that puts it into perspective. Is it right to say that the parts in the poster that are with the white wolf are all non-ego traits?" Ryan pointed at the poster.

"Yes. The white wolf shows the natural and positive instincts we have when we're not in danger, otherwise we're living in fight or flight mode, which is a result of letting the black wolf take over."

"Okay, so the white wolf traits help us stay positive, while the black wolf traits send us flying? I don't get it."

Francis laughed, "Fight or flight occurs when we respond to our perceived harmful events or to things that threaten our survival. Things that make our adrenaline pump. Adrenaline is in our bodies for a reason. We can use that boost of energy when needed to run when in danger. If we are constantly living in this fear state, however, we end up using up our extra adrenaline. Because our mind perceives that we are constantly in danger, our brain is on high alert and tells us to keep running. If we stay in this state of turmoil too long, our bodies can't keep up and break down. In the short term, this could be as simple as feeling weak and tired. In the long term, these small things can lead to sickness and disease. There's no set amount of time for this process, it may vary from person to person. The result is the same; deterioration is imminent."

Francis first assessed the look on Ryan's face to be sure he was following before continuing on. Ryan was wide-eyed and ready for more.

"Society is full of ego and has many unnatural fears, therefore having lots of reasons to use up adrenaline. Addictions act very much in the same way. Once we feel drained and have no natural energy within us for real upcoming dangers, we then begin to look outside ourselves to fill that void. Some may turn to alcohol, to drugs, to sex, to gambling or even to shop in order to feel better, while others take over the household. This may help them feel a temporary sense of fullness. They must continue in order to replenish the needed energy that leaks out during these energy-depleting activities. Unconsciously, they have this false sense of control that soothes their unfulfilled needs. This helps them avoid the true emptiness that they feel inside. Living in this state is draining to one's self and it drains those around them. Many can only witness from the sidelines, while feeling hopeless that their loved ones may never see the light."

Ryan had a disgusted look on his face. "Draining others sounds a bit vampire-ish to me. If that's even a word?"

"That's exactly what it is. If it gets bad enough, they call it an energy vampire, actually."

"That's just creepy."

"Yes, it is. We sometimes drain others of their life force, which we can call 'energy.' It becomes addiction when we can't let go of these unnatural fears and when we can't stop draining other people."

"Addiction feeds the ego, then?" Ryan was putting the pieces of the classic Lego together in his mind. He had graduated from the junior edition.

"Yes!"

"So, how do unnatural fears fit into all of this? Like into these addictions, for example."

"Unnatural fears appear when we create a life around us that is synthetic or unnatural."

"Okay, so a plastic world makes us live within a comfort zone. We don't want to leave our comforts. And we don't want anyone to come into our bubbles who might try to change it."

"Yes. Like a wife with a different view than your family's way of thinking, eh?"

Ryan laughed. "Good point!"

"The more plastic the world we live in, the more fears we create. This includes forcing our ways of seeing the world onto other people. Forcing anything in life creates all kinds of unnatural fears. For example, we may be helping others by doing good deeds, but we may be doing it because of expectation, with attachment to the outcome, and so on."

"So, it's like we do it with the intention of causing or luring others into living within our own comfort zones. And that's an expectation?"

"Yes!" Francis agreed enthusiastically. "By forcing someone to do things your way, it's called loving conditionally. What we've been learning these past sessions is that loving with conditions attached takes away the other's freedom, right?"

"Yeah, we have, and now I see why. Can you explain more about loving with conditions?"

"If I held it against someone, saying, 'I did this for you with love, so now why can't you do that for me?' Or if I said, 'I would love you if only you would do this or that,' then it's only conditional love."

"What do you mean? Can I have an example of that?"

"Yeah, I know a good one. If Clara wears her hair like Gloria, you would love her more and if she would do this or that you'd love her even more, and..."

"Okay, enough said! You got me there."

"And furthermore, when we get addicted to having to do something good and then we expect others to notice so that we can feel better about ourselves, that is also conditional love. Not to mention, it's feeding the ego that believes that those actions are what's needed to happen in order for everyone to be happy. If we don't do these kind acts, then we become anxious and fearful that something isn't right or not well. We end up worrying that things won't be perfect. That's what we call expectation and it's also ego. Then attachment to the outcome is a direct result from there. We set ourselves up to be disappointed or to be a victim or to expect more and more."

"That sounds like my mom...she has major anxiety if the house isn't right or if someone takes over the chores. She needs to always be busy, so it isn't just her home that she cleans, she can't handle it if she isn't cleaning my house, too. In fact, if my brother and sister weren't living so far away, she would expect to be doing *their* stuff. I just happen to be the one who ended up living there, so all the conditions are put on me."

"Yes, you're the monkey in the middle, but somehow you never seem to catch the ball. Your Higher Self knew that you were the one who was strong enough to break this chain. One day, you'll catch that ball fair and square."

"Here you go again with this 'Higher Self' nonsense."

"Your spirit, in other words."

"Okay, whatever! I just hope I catch that ball." Uncomfortable, Ryan shuffled around. He was determined to get this ego thing straight. "So, if I understand correctly, my mom had unnatural fears and now they have been passed on to me?"

"Yes."

"I can see now why my siblings moved away. I was the older one and hadn't seen the forest for the trees. My God, it's like my whole life was set up out of expectation and I couldn't see it."

"When you are brought up to be set up you wouldn't notice it, no. Most don't. Your mom was just duplicating her own program and passing it on to you like an heirloom. How could you notice your own stuff or issues? She cleans up before you get a chance to notice the mess."

"True. The week I cut my mom out from making my choices, the house got messy. We were so used to not touching things because Mom takes over."

"Yes, the house is a very good example of what I'm talking about. She even cleans up your soiled pants."

"Umm? No, I do that for myself now." Ryan grimaced and decided to divert backwards. "The messier the house got, the more I got depressed, lethargic, and filled with anxiety, yet I couldn't take care of it. I felt resentment toward both women for not coming and cleaning it up. When my mom came down and cleaned, my anxiety and fear went away. She cleaned my fear before I had a chance to take responsibility for my own mess or to even feel. None of those fears were natural fears. They were ego fears, I guess."

"Yes, she came that day in order to control you back into submission."

"Oh, my God! So, she stopped me from processing that day by taking over and controlling me, yet again." Ryan felt angry suddenly.

"Yes, she did...and in order to overpower Clara so she wouldn't get the credit for cleaning up."

"She wanted me to see Clara's inability to care for me and I totally fell into that trap and believed it."

"She got you hook, line, and sinker!"

"Okay, let me process this for a moment. She was able to master the situation of these unnatural fears of mine by making me feel guilty, which gave her the possibility of getting what she wanted. This gave her the advantage to manipulate things to have it her way. My actions were feeding her addiction to control matters and also it fed both of our egos at the same time."

"Bingo!"

"Things are smoother when I let her do it her way. She says she wants us to have more freedom and so does stuff for us, then later accuses Clara of being incapable; or redoes what we do for ourselves. It becomes all about Mom, somehow. It's Little Red Riding Hood all over again. It's an impossible situation and it makes me angry to realize it. Sorry for rambling."

"Actually, I think you are doing quite well, without even knowing it. You let go and let that autopilot do all the talking. That was great. You live so unaware that the unconscious is the one guiding you, even when it's getting you out of trouble."

"I thought autopilot was a bad thing?"

"Not always."

"IT'S ALL A matter of perspective. The key to understanding the ego or autopilot is to discern what is inside the unconscious mind. Stop letting your ego move you around like a robot. By exposing it along with the unconscious mind, like you just did, you can clear out those unnatural fears, feelings, and thoughts that aren't serving you. That anger is important—it'll guide you to smoother waters, eventually. It also helps you feel what is off balance or what isn't right within your core. You can pilot your own life on a conscious level once you bring more up to the surface. Then you can shut the autopilot off and fly your own plane.

"Soon we can leave your mother out of it and see beyond her. For now, she has proven to be quite useful. Eventually you'll be able to stop feeling angry and take more responsibility for your own actions. You were her puppet, yes, but you also liked *being* the puppet— remember that. The quicker you take responsibility for that, the quicker you can move on to new phases of the healing process."

"I trust you'll eventually get me to that point. I do see that I've been a puppet and that Mom's not actually conscious of what she's doing. She also is on a kind of autopilot; the unconscious kind. Also, I know better, but she doesn't."

"Yes, and getting angry won't help her change that, now will it?"

"No, it won't. That's why you explained that you can't change another person. If I did, I would be controlling her."

"Finally, you got it! And because you are the conscious one now, you have a deeper responsibility...remember that."

"I was afraid you would say that." Ryan cringed.

"Anger is only useful if you use it as a navigational tool to move yourself out of what feels bad, while you move toward what feels good instead. You can't do that when you involve the other person in that anger. Feeling the anger is one thing, acting on it is another. Now you need to learn to live, to be, and to choose on a conscious level. She either sees it or she doesn't. That isn't your concern. Your concern is yourself and your own personal welfare at this moment. You and I both know she can't understand now anyway. Sometimes people have to be shaken up in order to want to change. The shakeup I see coming is you preparing to move out on your own."

"Then she'll learn?"

"That is when she'll have a chance to feel and then possibly learn to use her anger as a navigational tool of her own. Again, your mom either does take the opportunity to create a shift or she doesn't. That isn't your concern. That is hers alone. So, don't try and use your new-found awareness as a weapon against her. Got it?"

"Yeah, okay, I got your point. This is probably why Andrew couldn't explain anything to me before I came to you, huh? There are too many layers in a person's life situation or within their sub-conscious to understand at 'hello.' I wasn't ready to understand it anyway, even had he tried to prepare me. I had no idea what I was walking into when I booked our first session."

"Yes, narrowing your road is a long process and a journey only you can take."

"See! There's another mystery. I don't understand what you mean by narrowing the road! Andy mentioned that also."

"In simple terms, the more you live on a conscious level, the less you'll need the outside world to keep you entertained. Further understanding will come once you find reason to narrow it."

"Can you give me an example that will help me connect on the level I am on now?"

"All those things that fit into those addictions we talked about, that feed the ego, will become less and less important to you. In today's world we have our own types of entertainment: television, cellphones, sports bars, sex. You name it. There's a specialized addiction for every individual's wants and or perceived needs."

"It seems like addictions have been around for a while, then?" Ryan asked.

"Yes, brother, they have been. In fact, if we look at it from a historical viewpoint, it gets interesting. Entertainment was originally designed for kings, queens, emperors, dictators, caesars, and people with money and too much time on their hands. Courts and gladiator arenas were formed by important leaders to keep people in their good standing. Entertainment kept everyone around them sleeping, while they were busy puppeteering in order to get the people to do their work. People did what they were told under the authority of others—living, breathing, fighting for something that would never be their own.

"Kings and their queens owned everything, including the consciousness of the people. People lived unconscious and still do. Those days have changed, however—not all kingdoms have fallen: Church for one, which was highly influenced by the caesars like Constantine the Great. I could talk about that history all day. The public-school systems around the world were built from that regime and still haven't changed a lot. It has affected us more than people even realize." Francis took a deep breath after he spoke. It was obviously a hot topic for him.

Ryan was astonished. "Wow, for not being from this part of the world, I think you know our history better than we do. Someday I'll have to ask you how you ended up in Europe anyway."

Francis raised his eyebrows slightly and rubbed his lips a moment and carried on. "Our road narrows when we stop following the outside influences and begin to look inwards, which is where our true religion lies—the religion of the soul."

"Religion of the soul?" Ryan reflected a moment repeating Francis's words as if to be memorizing them.

"We have many books to read in life, many teachers to follow, many programs to learn, many lovers to ravish, and only one heart to protect. To narrow the road in our life means to put some of those influences aside and begin to allow a smaller audience of influences to guide us. The result is focus."

Francis continued. "The consciousness begins to change as we have less that distracts us. This is the only way to quiet the ego enough to allow ourselves to live consciously and obtain that focus. Once we know the difference, the ego can't trick us anymore into falling asleep by throwing entertainment at us to keep us numb. Ego will put up a good fight, though, to get our focus. When our minds become quiet and ego is set aside, it becomes possible for higher realms to communicate with us and connect with us and to teach us from a higher perspective."

Ryan honestly had no idea what higher realms were, or what a higher perspective was. Yet, somehow, and strangely enough, it was all starting to sink in. He couldn't wait to hear more. "Okay, narrow the road so we can focus and then we can live consciously, ego free."

"Yes! And to live consciously means to start each and every day like we are a newborn baby, or like a fresh spirit coming back to Earth, each and every morning. This new soul arises from bed, innocent of anything that occurred yesterday, yet knowledgeable from the experiences of the past."

"Okay, you lost me at the waking up innocent part, Francis."

"Our spirit travels every night, brother. We go to places that teach us and offer us an opportunity to wake up and live consciously. We are innocent when we wake up in the morning. That's before the ego kicks in, which for some is inevitably about ten seconds flat in total."

"I don't know if it's the same thing or not, but the old people here say something like, 'The best pillow to sleep on is a clean conscience.' Is it something like that?"

"Yes, it is. By going to bed with a clear conscience, you have no fear of dying in the night, therefore the ego has less hold on you in the morning. If it has no hold on you, then you can wake up in a higher consciousness and stay there longer without the ego kicking in."

"I hope I go somewhere soon while I sleep in order to try making sense of my life."

"Oh, you will, don't worry!"

"With that tone of voice, I automatically worry."

Francis cocked his head back up with a forced straight face. "Imagine living a conscious life and by simple rules. Less is more. You limit yourself so that things are more simplified. With less societal influence then you can live by fewer rules. With fewer rules, fewer people can control you."

"How and where can I sign up for that society?"

"Make up steps that you do each day that will remind you to stay conscious and to keep focused. Follow those steps and you'll be able to create your own world, ego free."

"What? *Steps?* That sounds like work. No thanks, that isn't for me!"

Francis smiled, "Don't worry—it's a pattern and a world you choose for yourself."

"That sounds more appealing!" Ryan threw his teacher a smirk.

"The steps you choose yourself are designed to keep you focused. Years ago, I chose ten steps that stemmed from respect, honesty, trust, and love. I do the same routine each and every day. First, I wake up and give thanks for my life, for another day here on Mother Earth and for the chance to do it all over again. Then I give homage to the ancestors that have gone before me. Third, I send out positive prayers for women, children, and men who may need assistance on their own roads at this time. Then fourth, I give thanks to the animals, the birds, and all that Earth provides for us. I give thanks for the air I breathe, the water I drink, and so on."

"Sounds like a lot to me," Ryan interrupted. "It all seems quite random, really."

"These are only examples of my own personal steps; yours can be different. Remember? The important part is to choose steps and do them consciously. Do them from the heart or not at all. Otherwise, the ego creates steps for you. The deeper you go with each step, the closer you come to becoming one with the higher self."

"I don't know if I'm ready for that sort of thing yet."

"There's no hurry in life because the finish line is death anyway."

"Thanks for the offer of encouragement! Wow!" Ryan scoffed.

"One day, we'll make all ten steps on a fully conscious level and that might be the end. We are perfecting ourselves while on Earth, getting ready to leave it so we can go back home. Earth is just a place we borrow to come and learn from. Call it Earth School. Hopefully, we can leave it with a clean heart and clean hands. Why wait until death to be thankful? Why not aim to walk ego free while living here on Earth?"

"Good point. So, what are your next six steps? I may as well ask!"

"The fifth step is, like all steps, individual to each journey. The point is by doing the steps fully conscious and with gratitude, then our journey opens up into a vast space of awareness. In my opinion, without gratitude, that door is closed. That's why I start every day with gratitude, because I trust that I can get there. Besides, gratitude helps me to be more conscious, which is the overall goal. Being fully conscious is being fully in my spirit."

"How often will I make it to step ten? I mean on the level that you are talking about, all conscious and everything?" Ryan inquired.

"You can do them all every day at whatever level you choose. Our level of awareness gets deeper with time. It's not as easy as it looks. It would be a miracle if you make all the steps in one day fully conscious and stay alive. Especially the likes of you!" Francis chuckled teasingly.

"Yeah, yeah! Can I do it, though? That's the question," Ryan asked genuinely.

"Take your time. Remember, once you get to the end of the journey, the only place to go from there is into the spirit world. Work on being your best every day; that's how we condition our spirit body to get to the tenth step. This enables us to live on Earth as if we were an illumined spirit. We should work out that muscle each and every day, much like the mental, spiritual, physical, and emotional muscles we spoke of. It's all intertwined. It all needs exercise and a good stretch each and every day."

"What about gurus and buddhas and stuff? Did they make it to their tenth step daily?"

"Yes, they did, then they challenged themselves to go to even deeper spirit spaces. Perhaps they took those steps and then they chose to take ten more steps and so on. Imagine the conscious level in which they chose to live. Now that would be something to experience, eh? On and on, higher and higher. What a trip that would be!"

"I'm confused."

"I'm not surprised!" Francis chuckled.

"Okay, funny guy! Does everybody need to come to the ten steps? Why would we want to bother going to the tenth step, and then some, if it means an end? It's literally like dying."

"It's just a death of the old level, is all. The death of an ego. Besides, not everybody's here on Earth to become a Buddha, so stick to the first ten for now."

Ryan felt the need to urge himself on. "So, I need to let my ego die and that's step ten in a nutshell. The deeper I go into opening my consciousness, the less ego I have. Therefore, the higher levels I can go. Inside those spaces I meet my spirit."

"Yes brother, you got it. You choose the steps and you practise them until you can do them fully on a conscious level, ego-free, and therefore your spirit is free to be."

"So, it's like a juggler who has to practise one ball before adding a second."

"That is a good analogy. Keep going with that thought." Francis encouraged.

"Okay, once the juggler has mastered two balls, then he can add a third one. He can't add a fourth ball without practice. Each level of his juggling skills is a self-chosen conscious level. The ego tries to tell him he is limited to three balls only. He has to push past it and open up to the possibility that he can, then ta da! He has mastered it."

"Brilliant work, brother! Once we live on a conscious level, the ego can't come back to life or take us over into autopilot. Especially within our new-found skills and conscious levels."

"Okay, I see how the ten steps is also a part of narrowing the road now."

"Yes, it is."

"Didn't you say that Einstein said not to do things over and over again because it's insane?" Ryan teased.

"Einstein meant that when we do the wrong things that don't serve us over and over, we're insane. Follow the ego's steps and you jump right back into feeding the black wolf. Be careful!"

"How do you know they are right, though? We could choose steps based on ego."

"You know they are right because you chose them from a conscious level after you quieted the ego by having fewer distractions, right?"

"I guess." Clearly Ryan still wasn't convinced.

"Think of it this way, brother: Ego encourages you to jump steps. Your higher consciousness does not."

"So, take it slow and choose consciously and you'll know." Ryan nodded.

"Yes! A conscious mind repels the ego. If we rush the journey, we miss the small things along the way, like pebbles, wildflowers, as well as important lessons that allow us to understand life on a deeper level, the life that the Creator gave us to nourish."

"Creator? I don't believe in God, I told you."

"This world had to have been created from something, right?"

"I suppose."

"Creator is that something that created the world we stand on. Some call it by different names. For myself I call it Creator; others may call it Source, Oneness, or even God. Remember, only you alone can figure out your soul's destination. No one can or should give you their belief system. It's okay to talk about our beliefs if we are sharing without the expectation of forcing that belief onto another. That would be an expectation, otherwise, and another form of our ego. Something created us and then we were sent here to Earth so that we can learn and grow. I like to think that we came here to become our own type of Creator in the process. I say that because alongside our journey, we have free will that we can use to try and figure out our path."

"I like that!" Ryan chirped. "We're here to learn to be our own Creators and that someone or something up there who originally created us is allowing us our own experience."

"Exactly!"

"Otherwise, we'd be sent here out of our Creator's expectation, and that would be control."

"Good one, brother, now we're getting somewhere. Furthermore, there are two directions from which we can create our world. That's through an egoic or a non-egoic perspective. The egoic world creates a plastic existence and the non-egoic world creates an organic exist-ence, as we already figured out. The more we stay focused on a spirit-based lifestyle, the less the ego drives us forward and so we live therefore more organically. The ego would love for us to not believe in a creator or that we ourselves are here to create on a con-scious level. Free will is the ego's enemy. Protecting free will is the only battle there is worth fighting."

"Okay, I know now it's important to narrow the road, because if we have less going on, we have less to manage. Then we have more focus while being down here on Earth to create something valuable through our free will."

"Right...and the less we have to focus on, the more attention we can give to what we're consciously focused on, right?"

"Right."

"Humans weren't sent to Earth to be mindless drones. We came to learn to be present even with all the complications that we experi-ence while being inside a body that will eventually fail us. We came instead to become conscious and aware of what we're actually creat-ing for ourselves and for those around us. And who's to say that we aren't the person that sent us to Earth in the first place? If we can succeed while in the human form and live consciously, it makes us better spirit guides once we leave this world."

"Huh? I followed you right up until the spirit guide part."

"I'm not surprised," teased Francis.

Ryan diverted the subject. "I do see the importance of less is more. We have less to handle when other stuff pops up in life un-expectedly. And the more conscious we are, then the better condition we leave the world in when we die."

"Yes, you hit it on the nail, and, as an example, what about when that sudden storm comes?"

Ryan got scared. "Huh? Is it going to be stormy today?"

"No, no. What I mean is, what if a storm falls on us in life? Snow can fall hard and heavy sometimes. We know that all too well back in Canada. Having a wider road means more work to keep it cleared.

Don't you think? Or say a farmer has a field. The larger the area, the more weeds to pull. We have a better opportunity of growth without waste if we use only what we can maintain. It becomes easier to manage. So yes, less is more in some cases."

"The bigger the kingdoms, the more servants to serve, though."

"If that was coming from the historical white man's mouth that would make total sense, wouldn't it? Keep the slaves in their places, right?"

"I didn't mean it that way."

"And yet you stated it, nonetheless. Ego put you right into the wrong type of autopilot, eh?"

"I guess even with this new way of thinking, the program is still in me."

"You think?" Francis raised his eyebrows and rubbed his lips to make his point.

"It's frustrating to see how easily I fall into autopilot," Ryan admitted.

"Yes, and the ego finds you very valuable, or it wouldn't want to keep you locked in that autopilot mode. It'll fight a war to get you back as its ally. Never forget that. The fewer distractions you have in life, the better the chance you have to walk consciously and in full control of your own life. The more distractions you have in life, the easier it is for the ego to hold you hostage."

"Okay, let me turn this around a bit. Even though I don't believe in kingdoms, I was raised in one. If my mom is the queen and everyone else has been her puppets and jesters, then I'm the prince she has been moulding to succeed her as king one day. And I can see that I fell into one of those old traps in this conversation."

"Now that you see the truth, I want you to go out, look around from the perspective of the wider road and see how it feels now that you have changed your perceptions a bit."

"How do I do that?" Ryan asked.

"Don't try to do anything, just absorb and take it all in. See where it takes you. Look around on a conscious level. See what used to surround you and take up your focus."

"What do I look for?"

"Try and see who is sleepwalking through life and why? How is society set up to make people stay asleep?"

"Sleeping?"

"Have you been listening at all? Yes, the things that make people go into autopilot, and those things that they don't realize are keeping them stuck inside their ego."

"Okay, I can do that."

"Now get out of here," Francis taunted.

"Okay, see you next week. Actually, hold on. Can I ask you one thing before we go?"

"Go for it."

"If we're learning to narrow the road, why is it that you introduce so much in one session? I mean somehow I know I'm getting it, but it doesn't fit with your teachings on narrowing the path if we're going so broad all the time."

"Good observation, brother. If I'm honest, your spirit is the one guiding these sessions, not mine. I alluded to that earlier, if you remember."

"That makes no sense at all and it still doesn't answer anything about narrowing the road."

"You know all this stuff already, Ryan. I'm just here to help you remember what you already know and have forgotten. Our sessions are just a refresher course of what you have already learned lifetimes ago—before your ego took you hostage, that is. We are just unravelling a rope with many knots. Your higher self has been leading me and telling me what to say from the get-go."

Ryan rolled his eyes. "Okay, whatever...and the road?"

"The more concepts I throw at you at once, your ego learns to shut his mouth?"

"Okay, that decodes the mystery a bit. My ego may have been leading the first session, if I recall."

"You think?"

"Why or how would that happen?" Ryan asked.

"The ego can't control you if you are aware. Trust me: In that first session you were anything but aware."

"Okay, I can see that is somewhat true," Ryan laughed.

"As you do your homework assignment, you'll get a good idea of what I'm talking about. Everything we talked about since the beginning fits into one narrow spiritual road. Oh, and one last thing, brother."

"Yes, what is it, Francis?"

"Do yourself a favour and don't let the ego take you hostage for too long this week, because trust me, now that you have become aware, it'll try hard to get you back on its side. It'll make you feel as uncomfortable as it can so that you'll think the conscious level is not worth it. Allow the discomfort and let it pass."

"Whew, okay, I'll try my best."

Ryan left with a strange feeling in the pit of his stomach. The outside world seemed lonely, empty, and lifeless. He wished he could spend more time with Francis, like a child wanting extra time with his teacher. It felt safer now than the other life he had to go back to, the one that mommy and daddy had so carefully set up for him. Juggling another ball was not going to be easy to master. A part of him was about to die in order to merge with the next level, and he knew it.

Chapter Ten

———

Down the Rabbit Hole

IT WAS AN agonizing night as Ryan thrashed around and tried to sleep. He woke up every hour, checking the clock, and becoming increasingly irritable and exhausted at each interval. Dreams crept in like a deep, humid fog that hangs over a congested city, each vision a piece of strand that intertwined and connected to the next. He walked through them as a bystander only, an omniscient figure; almost like a personal guide watching over the other characters in the dreams, yet limited and unable to stop upcoming events...all seeing and aware, yet without knowing how.

Thomas, Ryan's grandfather, was older and dressed in old-fashioned clothing. A blacksmith, he had spent his adult life making horseshoes for a king. Thomas looked as if he had been beaten down and defeated, sweat dripping from his brow and maintaining a stern look on his face. He wiped his forehead with his filthy sleeve.

Thomas had once been young and fearless, romance pouring from his loins. He lost his zest for life long before this scenario on some dreadfully harrowing night. Loving above his status brought him great agony. The love of his life resided in the castle. From noble birth, her beauty and sweetness were unparalleled. She begged to be able to marry for love. Still her family forced her into an arranged marriage, securing the families' wealth. The union would guarantee good standing for her sisters to marry noblemen. She would never be the same, her hopes ripped away forever.

Heart-wrenching shrieks could be heard from a distance far and wide, as she was snatched from her lover. He begged mercilessly, chasing after the carriage like a madman. Echoes ricocheted off the buildings, carrying her screams, as she rode off into the distance, vanishing from his grasp; she disappeared forever. He slumped to the ground, unable to fight the expanding darkness that rolled in with the fog, poisoning and taking over his soul.

There was no choice but to let her go. He settled eventually and tentatively with a townswoman whom he could never love. She paid for his loss. He treated her treacherously, constantly cheating on her and beating her physically into submission. His children grew up knowing nothing of his past or why he was such a gloomy, wretched soul. He taught them to stay quiet in public, honour the king, and keep their heads down. The oldest son followed his father's every footstep, becoming a blacksmith, and treating women as servants and prostitutes. In turn, he raised his own children the same way, forcing them to keep their heads down and to make no waves; fulfilling no dreams.

Ryan woke up with heavy and erratic breathing. He realized the son in the dream was his own father, John. Drenched in sweat, his heart was now palpitating intensely. *Only a dream*, he thought sluggishly and reached out to touch Clara's cheek.

RYAN SPIRALLED DOWNWARDS deeper into yet another dream, beginning with Thomas's birth. Soon afterwards, Edward, his father, was captured by soldiers at the age of nineteen and forced to serve in an army. It was gruelling and entailed hard labour. He was there for one year when the First World War ended in 1918. Upon returning home, Edward did what he could to avoid the community. He had settled into a simple life, all the while remaining silent about what happened while he was away and about the friends he lost along the way.

When the Second World War came around, he was again taken away by soldiers, though this time as a captive to a concentration camp near Weimer, Germany. He was harboured there with many other prisoners, mainly Jews, Poles, and Slavs, for the duration of the war. He was among other prisoners working as forced labor in a local weaponry factory.

Ryan looked on helplessly in the dream as he witnessed many outstanding events during Edward's time in Buchenwald. Ryan could see the details clearly and would later gather further information upon waking, showing that the details in the dream were accurate. Buchenwald indeed offered insufficient food, poor conditions, and deliberate executions that caused more than 50,000 deaths just in that camp alone. Over 280,000 people passed through this camp and the other units associated with it, until it was finally liberated by the US army in 1945.

If it hadn't been for his talents and skills, Edward would be among the dead. A jack-of-all-trades, he had an innate ability to fix things. He used his skills in exchange for a little bit of food or clothing, which he shared with other prisoners. When the soldiers discovered his blacksmith skills, they used him to make much-needed items toward the war effort, such as machinery parts, as well as to make and fix horseshoes for the few cavalry troops that remained.

When the Second World War ended, Edward was given inside information by one of the guards with which he had formed a friendship bond. He was told not to get on the trains bound for his own country. Without being told why, he took this information as a serious warning, immediately telling others to come with him and walk home by his side. Some of them followed his lead, and others took their chances on the trains, too weary or weak to walk. He used his woodsman skills to forage for food and led the small mob home.

The released captives returned home in numbers eager to get on with their lives. Arriving by train, many of them were now about to face further torture. They were either mocked, feared, or treated as traitors in their own villages. Fears of treachery turned neighbour against neighbour. Egos had flared, as the people became more and more anxious, scared, and suspicious. The captives, having been released from one hell, came home to be tortured or even murdered by their own townsfolk.

Ryan struggled to wake up. He took a deep breath, while trying to sit up. He was suddenly knocked back down by some unknown force, as if it were imperative to finish the dream and even redo some sections for any details that were missed the first round. As he lay in bed struggling, feeling stuck in his body, and unable to move, scenes spun him round and round like a top.

Edward and the others had their own stories to tell. Some hid in the woods, some behind sheds, and others faking terrible stomach cramps to avoid being herded onto the train. Edward himself hid inside the stench of the latrines for a long period of time until it was safe to come out. Then, one by one, he gathered his friends and led them home.

The month-long trek was worth its agonies, as Edward's sources were correct. By the time they did get back, the other townspeople had calmed down and now felt guilty for murdering the victims. They now knew more about the concentration camps and understood their grave mistakes. They no longer saw the former captives as traitors or spies, but the damage had already been done.

A darkness had rolled in like a great storm cloud and a great evil had taken over the town. There was no turning back the clock and no undoing what had been done. Many post-concentration camp survivors died with their secrets of war unspoken, their memories swallowed and covered forever by the dirt on their graves. For others, home was meant to be their safe place. However, that's where many echoes of overlooked horrors remain. These stories are unnoted and forever untold. No one took responsibility for those atrocities and no one ever will.

No one was arrested for their actions in Edward's small town. Everyone knew who had done the killings, but said nothing. Shame bubbled and festered within the community, like an unattended wound, yet life went on. What was out of sight was out of mind; a history better forgotten and unmarked.

People kept their noses to the grindstone and taught their children to do the same. Emotions were a complete waste of time. Physical durability and endurance were what mattered most. Only the strong survived. Yet, internal wounds oozed like an emotional pus, leaking out slowly, then festering and gradually spewing out onto the mindset of the next generation.

Thomas was the oldest and was still living at home when Edward returned, having taken on the role of caretaker in his absence. He stayed and worked alongside Edward and learned his skills. Many of those virtuosities later became unneeded, now being phased out by machinery that would inevitably replace manual labour. Thomas decided to build his own farm, as it was the only skill that seemed to be lasting. He worked hard for the rest of his life. His only play was foraging in the woods, a skill also passed down by his father.

Edward asked his wife only once what had gone on in his absence. Helen responded unexpectedly. With trepidation she dropped to the floor and, tears flooding down her face, she begged desperately for her husband's forgiveness.

Thomas upheld his mother's honour and said nothing of the events that occurred when the soldiers had invaded her home three times. He used alcohol to drown out the abyss he felt inside his heart, eventually succumbing to the bitterness and anger he harboured without ever understanding why. Memories haunted him. By the time John was born, Thomas was a shut-down man. He ruled his household with an iron fist.

John's mother, Julia, served her husband until the day she died. She was known for her humbleness, and for never complaining about anything. She adored John and treated him fairly. John took on a lot of his mother's good traits.

Julia's parents had gone through similar circumstances in the war. She did what she could to ensure her kids would never suffer like the generations before them had. She saved the children from her husband's angry outbursts by sweeping things under the rug and hiding their imperfections to make things easier.

***

RYAN SNAPPED AWAKE and went out of the room dazed, confused and distraught. It took some time before he became aware that someone was there in front of him, an erect figure standing in a foggy haze. For a second he could swear it was Edward's ghost with one hand on his hip. Still half-asleep, Ryan was held in a kind of acceptance, eventually becoming more alert and curious as to whether or not he was seeing things properly.

Ryan sat down for a moment to get his bearings, then stood up again to try and follow the vapour cloud of energy that was now moving horizontally across the room. It hovered for a while as if to lure him toward it. The apparition suddenly looked to be preserved in place. Only the subtle movement of transparent hair and subtle facial features gave away the fact that it was real. It looked a bit like a poorly developed black and white photograph.

Thomas's face became clear and was all of a sudden staring back at him. Ryan snapped to attention and jolted, creating a pain in his neck from the overplayed reflex. He receded backward abruptly on high alert, fumbling and almost falling over the coffee table. After a moment of indecision, he took a half step in reverse, turning to leave the room. The window was open, and the air pressure sucked inwards creating a backdraft, which unexpectedly slammed the door shut behind him. He jumped nervously, collapsing to the floor.

Thomas drifted closer to him, while still hovering in the air and flickering in and out like an old movie projection. He made a peaceful gesture with his hands to show Ryan that he wasn't there to hurt him. He spoke gently, "For too long my suffering locked me inside this prison, and I don't want that for you, Ryan. None of us do. Let us help you." In his hands he had a key as if to offer it to Ryan.

"'None of us'? How many of them are there?" Ryan wondered out loud. The air became damp and cold. Ryan lost body heat fast. He felt utter paralysis and yet he was drawn toward the hallucination, and unable to take his eyes off of it. By the time he finally relaxed and tried to speak back, Thomas had vanished.

Ryan tried to stand up and immediately dropped back down to the floor, falling into the fetal position. He covered his ears to block out the shrilling ringing that sounded like the blow that comes from a train whistle. He shook uncontrollably and pressed the side of his head as hard as he could. He rocked back and forth for the better part of an hour.

Regaining control of his muscles again, Ryan slowly got up off the floor. He made himself a coffee and tried hard not to think. The sun would be up soon. He decided to go back and lie beside Clara to get warm. Could those dreams have been links to his actual family history? Unable to shake it off, he rolled into himself tightly, curling inward and hugging his knees.

***

LAST NIGHT'S POLTERGEIST, or spook show, made Ryan want to know the truth. He banged on his father's door as soon as he heard movement upstairs. John confirmed that in this life, Edward had indeed been in the Buchenwald concentration camp, and was captured for different reasons in both wars. He had survived a close brush with death many times. He was born in 1876 and had died in 1960.

Why was he never told about any of this before? And what about Maria? Her family had their own secrets and skeletons in the cupboard, surely. Ryan was okay with not knowing his mother's family story for now. He knew enough to realize that they were all indeed postwar victims. Their actions and reactions to the world were the result of war and now they were all trapped inside a state of victimhood, hidden under a blanket of guilt and shame. It was time to expose old wounds and let the air at them.

"My kids will know the family history. I'll make sure of it. If I have to expose myself and tell all someday, I will. That I promise," he said aloud to himself.

Once having unearthed these echoes in time, his grandfather's habit of drinking and yelling was fast becoming a softer cluster of recollections. It made Ryan ask questions. "Would things have changed had my grandfather known I soiled myself? Would he have been softened by seeing that I was so deathly afraid of him? Did he ever do the same thing after experiencing the horrors he saw in the world? When soldiers invaded their home? And oh my God, that was my grandfather's voice I heard that time when I was being growled at for siding with my mother over Clara!" His hair suddenly stood on end.

IT WAS TIME to get out of the house for a drive. Nothing looked the same. Colours seemed more vivid, and Ryan's thoughts whirled everywhere. At one point he almost drove into another car, swerving quickly back to his own side of the road. To be on the safe side, he took it slower and moved to a wider highway with less traffic.

Rambling thoughts took him over. How the average person adds more debt to their life by needing more and more...the ego constantly needing to be fed new things, only satisfied for brief periods of time and then starving for something new to satisfy the craving.

Ryan snapped into another thought. "Every day, I drive to work, spending endless and useless time catching up on sports on the radio, reading magazines, and watching television. All this so I can know what to talk about when I meet up with friends for beer." Sports was a life study, and something he kept up just to feel normal. He wasted so much time and money on things that a person can't take with them when they die. He was watching others succeed and not putting time and effort into the team at home.

Endless billboards with half-dressed women on them caught his eye. Commercials for underwear and bathing suits used to feel normal to him. Today it felt different, unbalanced and almost like some dirty type of seduction. The hair, the outfits the way the women were portrayed on the billboards was about being perfect and beautiful. "Gloria! Oh my God yes. She was modelling what society was expecting from her and that is why I liked her so much. That was what my mind saw as the norm. Clara didn't fit into that box." Ryan had spoken aloud, turning his head to the passenger seat next to him as if someone were there beside him, listening.

Gloria had been a match to what Ryan was focused on in the past. His energy had always turned to her in conversation, even in formal settings; legs facing her, and connecting to her energy instead of Clara's. Clara often sat contrary to him, arms folded, protecting her energy inside a tightly nestled cocoon. Ryan used to view this as an uncooperative and non-social slap to his face. Clara was a stronger woman than he had perceived: real, organic, and unswayed by the pressures of the societal norm. Yet she had to put up with him. Why? "I was overpowering her and trying to force her to be something ornate and extravagant."

The invisible passenger next to him said nothing.

What would happen to Angela? She was untouched by the world's programs, yet exposed each and every day to these billboards on her way to school. He had made comments in front of her so many times. "Wow, look at the beauty on that sign. I wouldn't mind meeting her once. She can sell me soap any day!" He felt ashamed of himself for being so disrespectful to his own daughter, and for probably making her feel less-than. "What was I thinking? I mean, this stuff is touched up by digital technology and telling my little girl that's how she has to look, or else. How will her man treat her some day?" Ryan gulped, now shuddering with the mere thought of some boy or man putting his grubby hands all over her. "Will she be in competition with another woman someday? Women like Gloria?"

Ryan's mind spit out like a sizzling firecracker. "Damn, what'll happen to little Ryan? Is he going to end up like me? Preferring plastic women and choosing a synthetic world? I remember when we only had beepers, let alone cellphones. Technology will only get faster, better, more improved, unimaginable. Will he be caught up in all of that?"

Ryan slowed down, pulling to the side of the road, and opened the door hastily, while the car was still moving. He threw up all over his pants and inside the car. He grabbed tissues from the glove compartment to clean himself off. "Disgusting!" he yelled out, hearing his echo go out to the woods and boomerang back toward him.

A rabbit stirred and suddenly sprinted across the road, making Ryan spring back momentarily. He remembered the discussion he'd had with Francis about animal symbolism. "A hopper meant taking great leaps forward, didn't it? And it was white. There has to be some kind of significance to that, right?"

He remembered Andrew's words in their first conversation, "Awareness starts to change you..." Andrew was going to be the only one to believe or understand this radical change.

Ryan got back in the car and headed for home. He was now curious as to how many of the road signs would have images of men on them. There were some, but mostly of men dressed up in either a suit and tie or portrayed as adventurers, businessmen, or doctors. It was obvious that men were seen as doers, fixers, protectors, or leaders in the world. On the whole, all respectful roles. Ryan was actually flabbergasted by this. "I seriously have zero recollection whatsoever of ever spotting any of these signs before!"

Was he that mindless or was there some sort of subliminal fallacy set up in advertising to cause this to happen? Surely his subconscious had to have been absorbing it in one way or another. "Is society sleeping that much? Are we setting women up to be less than men? Are women victimizing themselves without knowing it? There should be a cumulative effort to alter ads and signs, shouldn't there be?"

It was obvious why the road signs showed off women's bodies more than men's. "Men like it and they support that 'need.' It's like, as a whole, society supports prostitution as some kind of backdrop or even background music, and we don't even realize it. Of course, there's a difference between the signs and prostitution, but the roots themselves are somehow connected, which causes the imbalance. It gives men the right to disrespect women. And men take no offence because the billboards aren't full of half-naked men. If they did, they'd put a stop to it."

Ryan continued thinking out loud. "We switched our thinking a bit, but the disrespect women have endured in the past is still there today—just portrayed in a different way. Women weren't always allowed to work; and yet prostitution seemed to be the only job they could get because it was considered a need. Women were barred in the past from being doctors, but they could sell their body. That is the root of the imbalance and maybe why women in need today sometimes have to turn to prostitution for money. Instead of taking care of them, men take advantage of their vulnerability. I did that. I took advantage of women."

Ryan looked at the passenger seat as if to see if his imaginary audience was still present.

A warmth of shame washed over his face. It was true; he had put Gloria in a position of joining him in a game of lies and double-dealing. They were living a life of duplicity together for a while, yet apart. He played two roles, one being Jekyll and other, Hyde. He was nice to her during sex but purposefully passed her off as some whore immediately afterwards. He got so upset when she would call between booty calls.

Instead of coming clean back then and making things right by ending the affair, he chose instead to just shrug her off because she was caught up in emotion. Underneath it all, he had been redirecting the blame and transferring the guilt onto her. One day he would have to talk to Francis and ask how to deal with that aspect of it all. She deserved his apology at least. And what kind of friend was he to poor Tom? He couldn't even go there.

"I was such an ass," he admitted.

No wonder women acted like they did with him and his buddies competing for women's attention. Now, it felt like a type of cheating. Every man he knew was from the same bubble. It was a shared addiction within a collective consciousness. He thought he was doing it to stop himself from cheating; now he saw that it was actually just leading him to it by feeding the addictive fix. Cheating was just the result of the addictive behaviours performed prior to it.

"No wonder the subconscious self takes over. The conscious self is too busy with work, life, billboards, flirting, and cellphones." Ryan envisioned the world numbed into a comfortable place of non-interaction with the inner world. "The road is way too wide." He muttered. "Too damned wide!"

Suddenly gagging violently, Ryan pulled over to the side of the road again and drove into a quiet area. This time he stopped in time, able to swing the door open and throw himself out of the car to avoid spewing on himself a second time. Lack of sleep had taken its toll. He felt lost, weak, tired, and utterly helpless. His ears were ringing again, and his skin was burning up. Was he feeling anger, resentment, or sadness? It was hard to say. A stress headache was coming on for sure. Hands now clenched tight on the steering wheel, his heart raced and everything started swirling. It took a while to calm his erratic breathing. He wished he could just die.

How could life ever be the same? Nothing looked, felt, or tasted normal anymore. There was no turning back, especially now that Clara knew. Awareness changed everything.

That voice came again. "Call Andrew now!" Before even realizing it, Ryan picked up the phone and was dialing the number.

"HOW ARE THINGS, Rye?"

Ryan answered back with a hoarse, thin voice, "I don't have words, Andy. I think sometimes that this awakening is opening a kind of craziness in me. I'm talking to the passenger seat while I drive, for God's sake! I have anxieties running wild, and my thoughts are on overload."

Andrew laughed and assured Ryan that everything was perfectly normal. The pillars of his world had also come crashing down when he met Francis, he explained. He also learned the importance of re-building in such a way that they could never be knocked down again.

Andrew was good at drawing him away from the panic, and diverting by asking questions. He helped pull out everything from the last talk with Francis down to the dreams and everything in between. Ryan was relieved to share his experience.

They laughed about Francis's jokes and his straightforward manner. "He never called me the monkey in the middle," Andrew laughed. "He saved that one just for you. I think Francis has a way of seeing each person as special. No two snowflakes are the same. You're doing great, Rye. After I met up with you that day in the store parking lot, I knew somehow that I could share my journey with you. I had dreamt of you just before we saw each other."

"Really, what was the dream about, Andy?"

"It was a bit strange. I dreamt that you and Clara were on some sand beach and you turned to her and asked if she trusted you."

Ryan stopped him in his tracks. "Okay, you're freaking me out."

"Why? What did I say?"

Ryan retracted, realizing he sounded a bit commanding. "Never mind—keep going." He wanted to see first what Andy had to say before jumping to conclusions.

"Then you ran like hell up into a building. It might seem strange to you, but I was standing at the top of the building already. I was now staring at you while Clara hung over the wall watching people wash away in this horrible tsunami."

Ryan laughed out loud. "I'm actually happy you kept that to yourself until now." He then explained the series of dreams and how they intertwined so mysteriously.

Andrew laughed, "I think only Francis could be the one to share all this with us. Anyone else would put us in the crazy house, I'm sure."

Ryan agreed and paused a moment, taking it all in.

Andrew continued, "Sometimes I wondered if he was a counsellor or a magician. He seemed to pull rabbits out of a hat from thin air.

It took some time for me to realize that he had helpers. Like people from above that know more than him even; spirits, or ancestors, or something. He was always just relaying the message. I later put it together that my guides were working with his guides and telling him stuff about me. Now it's a relief to know they're watching over me and to know I'm loved."

Ryan was baffled. Was it possible that Francis talked to spirits? Was he even comfortable going back now, knowing that?

Andrew assured him that as he adjusted to this new reality, it would all become clearer. He also encouraged him to call if he needed him at any time. Day or night. "Really, man, next time don't go through it alone. I'm there for you."

Chapter Eleven

FREEDOM

RYAN GOT UP at the crack of dawn. He took his coffee out on the patio to watch the sunrise. The first burst of light popped up over the horizon. Pale shades of purple, orange, and pink painted the skyline, changing as if a paintbrush were being swept over a fresh canvas, the painter changing the image with each new stroke. He had never watched the sun come up before. He used to make fun of people who described its ascent or descent, thinking they were melodramatic and overly romantic. Today he understood the hype. It was actually quite spectacular and dramatic. Colour tones changed within seconds, sometimes even between blinks of the eyes. It had its own "alga rhythms," functioning in its own timing, shifting with its own mind.

Shuffling around clockwise to see if any neighbours were watching, Ryan mumbled softly, "Thanks for this new day. Thank you to Mother Earth, to my ancestors, and to my mother for bringing me into this world." He ended it awkwardly with an "Amen" and drew in a long nervous breath. "Oh, and thanks for Clara. I'm even thankful for the craziness that I've been going through. Thanks for the session I have with Francis today. Okay, that was enough experimenting for today. I'm signing off. Love, Ryan."

***

"HELLO, BROTHER. I brought you a gift." Ryan hugged his teacher and passed him a box of Cokes.

"Oh, wow, my Cola fridge was getting low. I'll put this in there right now in case anybody needs a little 'fizzing up' later today. Thank you. Do you want one?"

"You're welcome, and not now, thank you. Been fizzed up enough lately."

"How were things with you this week?" Francis asked, now curious.

"Things have been very interesting, to say the least. Lots to think about."

"Excellent. You allowed yourself to go onto the wide-open road, then?"

"Yes, a bit too wide and I can see now that I need more focus."

"Good."

Ryan felt courageous suddenly and asked, "Can we do that smudge thing we did that day with the sage and feathers. I like how I felt after."

"Sure thing." Francis got out the abalone shell and sage from its box, lit it up and called Ryan over. He fanned him down with the feather and smoke, while repeating the prayer they did the first day. Then he handed the items over to Ryan and gestured for him to do the same for him.

"Are you sure?"

"Yes, please."

Ryan was nervous he would catch something on fire but proceeded to wave the feather around and saying the prayer the best he could from memory.

"Feeling better?"

"Yes, thank you."

Francis waited to allow Ryan to talk first.

"This week I had dreams, visitations, or whatever you want to call it."

"Yes, I was waiting for that."

"So you know, then. I mean you know him? My Grandfather Thomas?"

"Now I know who he is, yes."

"I saw things about him and my great-grandfather in my dreams, from this life, and past lives. They seemed to mirror one another."

"Yes, different lives are cycles that seem to come again. We are in different bodies each time, though. We play roles that seem to echo past problems, past entrapments, in order to release built-up karma we accumulated with one another."

"How do we become free of karma?"

"We need to work on ourselves on a conscious level to get there."

"I thought a lot about everything you shared in the last sessions. It's sinking in slowly. I've also been thinking about Clara and how she gives me a freedom that I honestly don't deserve."

"Yes, it's called 'freedom from' and 'freedom to.'"

"She wants to be free of me?"

"She wants to have freedom from the fear she has of wondering what you're up to when you're not home, brother. She also wants freedom to choose for herself. She allows you to have freedom from her. This freedom allows you to do what you need to do, while she's also doing what she needs to do at the same time."

"That sounds like a lot."

"It's simple."

"Easy for you to say."

"You always see things better when you view things from the perspective of being on the outside looking in. Try it out again for this subject. Step out of the circle."

"Okay, so you mean that freedom from controlling someone else allows them freedom to do what they need to do, which in turn allows them time to grow?"

"That works! Grade 6 is already under your belt, I see. It looks like you've been doing some extra homework."

"I haven't been given a choice. It just keeps coming like a fast train."

"You did ask for the fastest route through the situation, remember?"

"I did, yes! The dreams helped me get a better understanding of how the family fell into roles."

"Good. Now put it into perspective. Tell me how your family dealt with freedom and what you need to do about it."

"Well, because Mom and Dad were unconscious, they couldn't allow a freedom to others. They didn't have it to give."

"Good, keep going," Francis said encouragingly.

"I need to create my own freedom from the sleeping spell that the family has been under for generations. I need to live my life without any expectations of them changing unless they want to. I need a better reason to want to move out than anger."

"Meaning and purpose getting deeper each day, eh?"

"Yes, it is. I have a sense of relief when I think about having freedom from having to change others. Also, knowing Clara isn't trying to change me gives me hope. Maybe she and I can one day be like those two dolphins swimming side by side. What did you call it, interdependence?"

"Yes, I did. Good memory. Now who's the one getting all romantic?"

Ryan chuckled, "I want my kids to have freedom from the 'sleeping pill existence.' That's a new phrase I made up."

"Good one."

"Thank you. I can see how my actions caused our family to stay caged. I'll affect the kids if I don't make changes. As I looked around the world and saw the billboards, television, and how people acted in society, I realized I used to look outside of myself for a type of re-assurance. I used the outside world as a surrogate."

"Surrogate, eh? Interesting way of putting it, brother. Give me an example."

"Well, sex. So, the Gloria situation essentially was a surrogate."

"That is a great example. You used sex with her to replace love. Brilliant!" Francis praised.

"Yes, and furthermore, flirting with women was one of my biggest discoveries. The more women noticed me, the better I felt about myself, my body, my existence. I never thought about how Clara would feel when I did those things in the past. I had the wrong intention."

"Yes, at home we create a certain energy and it builds up when we nurture it. By going out and spreading that energy, the woman at home gets robbed of her energy, doesn't she? It can happen both ways, but the one at home gets drained and is weakened. Then they too need to replace what they're lacking. Some drink, some look for a replacement in other things."

"Yes, and that is what happened to Clara. My actions weakened her, causing her to have less confidence, and she needed alcohol for a while to cope."

"Yes, and Gloria got more and more confident, right? What do they call it, great hair days?"

Ryan laughed. "Yes, giving attention to other women gave away the energy that Clara and I built up."

"And, therefore causing further emptiness at home, eh?"

"Yes. What was I thinking?"

"Well, you weren't seeing the whole picture, were you? If you had, you would've seen how the spouse at home was being syphoned off of."

"Oh my God, another vampire situation."

"Good thing I ate garlic today. You would get me next. Holy!"

Ryan smiled and continued, "I had practised cheating so many times in my head that when I finally went through with the real act, it didn't even jar me. It left me feeling empty and unsatisfied and needing more. Orgasms became a mindless and automatic physical response. I felt some guilt. It was more of an annoyance to tell the truth, like a fly I wanted to just slap off my arm. My guilt was more about betraying my friendship with Tom."

"This is important stuff, Ryan. It takes some people years before they come to understand themselves the way you just did."

"The funny part is that before I met you, I rarely even spoke. I said that before but I mean it."

"I heard that Einstein didn't speak full sentences for the first five years of his life. He was considered a fat baby with an enlarged, angular head and everyone expected him to be slow and treated him as such. When he was asked why he hadn't spoken much, he replied that he had no reason to speak until that moment. He broke all kinds of limiting perceptions in his lifetime, as well as concepts of space, time, light, mass, and energy."

"I'm no Einstein, for sure," Ryan admitted.

"No, however, you are a man who now has a reason to speak. That reason is important enough to prompt you to take an honest inventory of your life and to create a situation much more worth sourcing out your energy now. Right?"

"Yes, and now with Clara, I see things differently. We haven't been intimate yet and I don't want to push her until she's ready for that. I can't describe it, but I suddenly feel so much respect. I see now how special she truly is. Thankfully things have changed in me. Now I look at her and see fullness and beauty. When I look into her eyes and see her smile, it takes my breath away to see her happiness, to see her inner light shining, and I feel so humbled."

"Yes, brother, looks like you finally figured out something called 'making love'! It isn't the act of it, it's what you feel—right?"

"Oh, my God, that's what it is, yes: making love. I couldn't go back to having sex if someone paid me to. Clara is too pure in my eyes now for anything but making love; and when or if we do get physical again, I want to be there fully with her and only when she is ready."

"Good. Now, how does freedom fit within that for you with this new-found perspective?"

"Well, I'm free from the past and more real in my thoughts, if that's what you mean."

"Good—keep going."

"I'm free from the thoughts of porn-type scenes that used to be in my head when I was around Clara. I'm not proud of it, but both kids were created with those scenes inside my head to get off. I see Angela and she speaks so wisely. She's so pure, and yet I gave sperm in that way to help create her. How could that be good for her?"

"It isn't."

"Can that be cleared?" Ryan asked, feeling disgusted with himself.

"Yes, and you just cleared it partly through your honesty. You're changing the intention. Send the rest of that energy up with your gratitude for her life the next time you watch the sun rise."

"How did you know that I watched the sun rise today?"

"I didn't, but now I do."

"You are a mysterious man, Francis."

"Thank you."

"I'll get up again tomorrow and send up that old energy I once smeared onto both kids and ask for only innocence to walk with them. I feel like I'm starting to sound like you. Oh, my God!"

"You're starting to sound more like *you*. You've gotten to know yourself. Congratulations! And God, too, I see. You mention him more and more."

Ryan laughed, "Well it's a 'me' that I never knew was even possible before."

"Welcome home, brother."

"LOOKING BACK, FRANCIS, this has been a pretty intense time. I wonder if I should take it slower."

"That's up to you. You wouldn't be here in the now if you weren't ready to take the steps that you have. Normally, by walking slowly we create a more thorough healing. However, the Creator knew a mental mind like yours would have put us on pause. It would have forced us to do what we did just within months, over a period of ten years instead."

"Why would my mind get in the way?"

"The mental mind is too rational. It's heavy when it's unleashed. It would be impossible then to balance the four quadrants. Your mental mind fights a good battle."

"Wow, I think I needed to hear it that way."

"If you live by the medicine wheel concept that we talked about, you'll never lose balance again. Not within your mental, physical, emotional, or your spiritual."

"I got it and I remember also respect, honesty, trust, and love go along with those."

"Yes, you have an excellent memory, brother. A photographic one, I would bet." Francis lowered his eyes and waited for Ryan to process. "First time I saw you speechless, Ryan."

"It's just no one ever made me feel so smart before or listened to what I had to say."

"Yes, and so now it feels rational to be listened to, I bet. In the past, you never had to process anything—it was processed for you because others assumed you couldn't or wouldn't. Maybe that's what Einstein went through, eh? Your physical body grew but the emotional self is still incubating. That's why when you finally opened up to the teachings, they came to you so quickly. The less ready you were, the faster it all had to come so you could catch up those parts of yourself that were left behind. The rational mind held the rest of you hostage, along with the ego. When you finally had freedom from that rational mind, those teachings ran like a wild horse to you, didn't they?"

"Wow, yes, they most certainly did. But why?"

"They knew they may have had only a short window of time and opportunity before your ego would come roaring in to take over again."

"That seems right."

"You have more on your mind, don't you?" Francis asked.

"Yes...I have noticed changes in people around me also. Some good and some bad."

"Yeah? Like what?"

"Well, I know I have been fixated on my mom, but truthfully, she has been my whole life. My world has always revolved around her. I see now that she took control of the kids because I wasn't present in our household. Because of this, little Ryan loses his cool with Clara more and more. Clara has become increasingly uncomfortable with my mom coming down and taking control of little Ryan, even though she seems to be doing it out of kindness.

"Angela is busy with activities, so she has been saved from my mom's grasp, for now. I see our little guy becoming more and more spoiled. He's refusing to eat healthy foods and he's having tantrums. He knows that Mom will give him whatever he wants. He was sleep- ing by himself for a while but now he's insisting that Clara sleep with him again. If I scold him, he doesn't understand because my mom has made it normal for him to get his own way. If she hears him screaming, she comes down and takes over. I'm the bad guy now if I try to enforce vegetables. I want to take Mom aside to speak to her, but I don't know what to say."

"Speaking openly and honestly around your children with your mom would show your children how to problem-solve. It looks like ego is setting in for little Ryan already. It's better to let him kick and scream now rather than as a teenager, trust me. Put him in his bed and allow him to feel. If he's upset, let him know that things are going to be okay and that you love him, but that you're going back to your own beds. If he tries to get into your bed with you, gently guide him back to his room and tuck him in and say goodnight. Console him inside his own room so it becomes the comfort zone instead of your bedroom being his safe place. Don't get into big discussions, don't let him manipulate you by his words or his actions, or get into a power struggle in the middle of the night. Be kind but firm;

eventually he'll get it. Give in just once, and you'll show him that he's in control of you and then the process starts all over again. The one with the strongest will wins. Right?"

"Yes, and wow, I never thought of it that way. Maybe I let him off easily in order to save him."

"Like mother like son, eh? Now your gentle but firm consistency is the best way to remedy this situation."

"Should I say something to my mom in front of little Ryan?"

"Secrets solve nothing. They just divide people. That's how wars start, my friend. Things that go unspoken give away our power to those who should never have it."

"That's a good line. It should be a quote," Ryan suggested.

"Thank you. Furthermore, discussing problems and finding solutions in front of children can be very helpful. Be open and honest in loving ways. Remember, freedom to speak is freedom *from*. Freedom from fear, and, just as important, freedom from having children who think the world is some Disneyland theme park. You can't be Mickey Mouse forever, you know. Well, maybe Goofy!"

Ryan smiled and wrinkled his nose.

Francis continued. "Show them that you are looking for the solution, even if it doesn't come during the conversation. Eventually, you'll be able to brainstorm with them to find solutions together. It'll help them know how to discuss things with you in the future or how to handle their own children. Otherwise, they'll never be aware that there was a problem. Therefore, they never learn the meaning of problem solving. Say nothing, and they'll always see your mom as the alpha dog. She's that because she's the one always fixing the issue in front of them and you're sitting there doing nothing. They're your children to raise to become conscious adults, not hers. Be active and open, and they'll follow you instead of her."

"True—and then there is Angela, who never causes any problems. It's like night and day."

"Different child, different reactions. She's the good little girl, groomed to never leave home. Familiar?"

"That does resonate. Hopefully this kid is smarter than I was."

"Be smarter for her and don't let her fall into ego traps and programs that won't serve her."

"Angela is super aware of her surroundings. I'm not sure what program she's taking in. She seems to adapt and shapeshift easily. She knows exactly how to speak, and jumps in to fix a situation right away to create flow."

"That's the functionality of dysfunctional behaviours: playing differing roles as needed."

"Oh no! How do I help her?"

"There's no need for correction or constructive criticism with kids like Angela. The kids today come from a different mindset and have a much higher vibration. Just be a positive example. Say things like, 'Thank you for being such an honest, loving person,' instead of saying, 'Don't lie.' Or, 'Thank you for always making your bed,' even if it's not made. Children often learn by the language we use and of course the actions we take. 'Make your own bed before asking them to make theirs' type thing. Correcting today's child only takes away their self-esteem.

"Living positive and speaking positive is going to be more effective with this new generation. When we speak like this, these kids will react in a positive way and will want to naturally improve themselves. A checklist on what they did right or what they can do to reward themselves would replace a chore list as an example or a list of rules of what not to do. These kids often have incredible gifts that'll cause a type of peace on Earth. We would be wise to follow their lead."

"Each generation differs so much from the last. How is that possible? We are still being raised by the older generation, so why are these kids so different?"

"They came for different reasons. They are bringing us back to a more organic way of life. The kids of today will teach us about chakras. Are you familiar with them?"

"No, but I have a feeling I will be soon."

Francis smiled at Ryan's keenness. "In short, chakras are the energy centres in the body. The lower the chakras are, the lower the vibration."

"What is the benefit of knowing about the chakras?"

"If you have a sickness in your body, then the chakras become important because you can isolate the area that needs your attention to regain your health. Get the chakra healthy and you get that part of your body working better."

"I get more headaches than anything, and a sick stomach sometimes."

"Yes, your third eye and crown chakras were closed up when I met you. Just by narrowing your path a little bit and thinking differently now, it's loosening up the cap on your head, like a Coke bottle. Our meetings shook you up a bit and got stuff inside you all fizzed up and cleared you out a bit. Now information can flow more easily."

"What does each chakra do for us?"

"Take the bottom two chakras. These are located here at the groin and abdomen areas. They're dealing with more earthly matters like the right to be here on Earth and also with our thought patterns, surrounding home and safety, and such. Those chakras help us feel safe to create. If people aren't okay with their lives, then health problems show up in those parts of the body.

"The sacral, and better yet, the centre by your ribs, is more connected to the ancestors, like grandparents who fought wars and lived for survival. It's called the solar plexus. The grandparents we know come from a time period where people lived more from that chakra or the chakras just below, like the sacral chakra that I mentioned. They lived lives filled with power and control issues. Their kids, being our parents, were born from that power and control centre. We came as a result of that control.

"We're stronger in our desires in life and we work from a higher place than that. We work a little bit more from the heart. However, our generations were born in the heart but came to be big speakers in the world. That's why we need to free up our throat chakras and get out there in the world and speak our truth and help people."

Ryan interrupted Francis for a moment. "Does living based on certain chakras affect our ego?"

"Yes, for centuries, our ancestors stayed in a war cycle and circled around the three lower chakra issues for way too long. Egypt started out with the right intentions and eventually fell into ego. It's an example of what got us stuck. There are many societies before Egypt that fell. Maybe for the same reasons."

"When did things start changing?" Ryan asked.

"In the late '60s and into the '70s, the hippies took their place in the world, and things started changing because of their new thought patterns. They were born from the power and control centre, and yet they moved themselves from that and into the heart chakra centre through their accumulated words and behaviours. Babies like you were born into that new energy field or bubble of consciousness. Your generation came to the world to make great changes and to go up against authorities, to take on great feats and to take great journeys.

"In the '80s, people learned to speak up. Freedom of speech turned people's heads. More new thought patterns were being formed, and again great changes came into the world. Music began changing, and women started to go out into the workplace more. Within the time period of the '90s and onwards, 'seers,' knowers, and shapeshifters came into the world. Much like your little Angela, who came as a kind of scout.

"These small beings came with a struggle, though. Some felt a large gap between the generations and still do. Many children weren't as lucky as Angela. Some came quite sensitive. Some were so sensitive that instead of raising the vibrations of the Earth to help them adjust, the medical world found ways to diagnose them and put titles and labels on them.

"Now, in the 2000s, our little Ryans are being born. They have rainbow energy in them. They seem to adapt better, thanks to the generations that came before them that cleaned up the energy. They do love to be spoiled, though. Sugar replaces their need to be back in Heaven…something to become aware of and later to try and wean them off of. We do that by helping them create heaven on Earth through nurturing their passions.

"These children will be our teachers, lawyers, and doctors of the future, which Angela is also a part of. She needed to be born first to lead rainbow keepers, like our little Ryan, to their purposes. She's a strong force and will walk both worlds. The kids today will have star seed children, who will bring more peace, more knowledge, and lead us back to a more organic way of living. They'll hold this consciousness for generations to come, taking us beyond the stars."

Ryan cut in, "I could see Angela being the one to hold things together. She seems to be above the nonsense of the world. I don't exactly understand this talk about rainbow and star children."

"Yes, Angela is the teacher holding the light between the generations. As I told you before, the teacher appears when the student is ready. All you need to know is that those new generations will become softer, more gentle, and they won't support negativity, control, or wars. They'll hold peace through their example of how they live. They'll help us live and eat better."

"Okay, I get that."

Francis continued. "Angela will be one of many young women who will bring the new generations into the world; that will be from the crown chakra and above. They'll carry a bright light with them, like a lighthouse beacon for lost ships in the night, navigating us to the proper waterways of our lives…to the places our ancestors lost the maps to, many generations ago. All people, not one culture. We'll all find home. As time passes, you'll notice that people won't have to talk as much, yet they'll be open when they do talk. Again, more like Einstein."

"Do you mean we'll be able to communicate through telepathy?" Ryan asked.

"Yes. People are already using telepathy and just don't know it. We think of someone just before they call, for instance. We've picked up their thoughts. This type of thing will become natural again. Everyone did this in the original cultures. We're just going to remember how to do it again, is all. Our chakras are clearing through these new children. We'll rise again through those chakras. Now on a much higher level, all a part of something we call 'ascension.'"

Ryan piped up, "Will everybody become aware of this? Some of the people I know, I can't imagine them ever becoming aware."

"Some will become aware of it and some won't. If we don't have to fight anymore for the right to be on Earth, then peace will begin to change people's awareness. They won't have to live based on survival, and therefore there will be less reason to compete with one another.

"But those of us like you and me have no excuses, now do we? Not anymore. Yes, the rest of the world may be unaware, but we are aware now, right? Remember, the hippies changed the world by changing the conscious bubble. The new generation will affect the new energy field in their own way. Change and the world will change around you. It's called evolution. If we become the stronger species, others change to be able to keep up with us. It's nature's way."

"I like that. What other changes do you see happening? I mean, like with the Earth, there has been a lot of damage done already."

"I see Mother Earth being honoured in new ways. We'll live in harmony with her and protect her so that the new generations can be nurtured in good ways. They can and will have a healthy environment with good food, water, and air. We'll achieve this by collaborating together and making crucial changes. I see the world lowering its population by choice, eating less meat and nurturing healthy minds so individuals will take healthy actions. An example is conscious gardening and farming so that we stop taking wildlife areas. We'll only grow things where it's already cleared."

"What if we don't succeed? I mean what if humans don't wake up?"

"Then the Earth falls, wildlife diminishes, trees vanish, and then humans are next."

Ryan looked horrified, "That's a scary thought."

"It's a reality and a freedom we all have. We either save her or we don't. I hold the intention that we will heed the warnings. First, the conscious bubble needs to change. We are all creators. What we pay attention to happens."

"What about kids like little Ryan who are spoiled? What will happen to him?"

"That depends. He's a teacher who's showing you what'll happen if we don't take responsibility for our actions. So, create good around him. He isn't testing you—he's merely pointing out the divide in your relationship. An example of this is by his taking her from you to sleep with him or by getting in between the two of you at night. He's showing insecurity because it's what he sees in the two of you and making you conscious of it. He's letting his grandmother lead him during the day because, right or wrong, she has full belief in what she says and does; so he follows the strong one. It's another type of evolution. He's evolving into her teachings. Get it?"

"Clara and I need to start being stronger and know what we want so he'll follow *our* lead."

"Yes, and becoming conscious changes that bubble."

"How can we teach kids how to change the world if the school system is so limited?"

"I thought you would never ask!"

Ryan and Francis laughed simultaneously.

"I won't get into it too deeply. In short, school systems will have to change in order to facilitate the vibration of these new children. These kids cannot be coaxed into falling asleep. They won't align with the old systems or old regimes and they'll act accordingly if they're put into the old programs. Little Ryan is your example of that. He'll shine that light into the eyes of those who get in his way and act "bad" so often or seemingly follow the wrong person, that eventually you'll need to make changes. That's his way of bringing the light to the world around him."

"Go little Ryan, go! Wait a minute—that means that *I* need to change. Never mind."

Francis laughed. "New schools will be formed and eventually governments will have to align and support these schools. The movement has already begun, and when the mindsets change to this new way of thinking, then existing systems will have to change along with them. If it doesn't happen in this generation, it will in the next."

"For their sake I hope it happens soon."

"Well, I read somewhere about deer in a field, and how they work as a whole. When you have one hundred deer in a group and half of them decide to go to the watering hole, the fifty-first deer is the deciding factor. All will follow once the scales tip past the fifty-first percentile. In my opinion, we're almost there at that tipping point of the scale. The more people who awaken, the faster the scale tips."

"GETTING BACK TO the now, how have your friends been dealing with your changes, anyway?"

"Funny you asked that. The other night I decided to go out with some friends. I made a personal decision recently to not drink. I want to keep my head clear while I'm making these changes in my life. I had a hard time trying to avoid their persuasions, like I was being forced to drink. In the end, I gave in and ordered one beer to keep them from hounding and teasing me. It made me realize that we're expected to drink in our culture. What an eye opener.

"I tested my theory, and when I ordered something different other than my usual food, no one said anything. But with alcohol it was like they insisted. Talk about control! I used to be that guy, though, doing the same thing to them in the past. Now I see it was wrong."

"You really got to see first-hand how society controls us into having to do things, or we are cast out of that group of conscious-ness, eh?"

"Yeah, and we are of that consciousness unless we change it. I also noticed that every woman who walked by was giving attention to my friends, and the men were following them as they walked by. I didn't connect with that anymore. I felt distant."

"Once we make changes in our thought processes, we send out a different wave of energy. Your chakras spin at a higher vibration, now. The distance you feel with some people will get even further, I assure you. At times you may feel like it's not even worth it and you'll wish for your old life back. But even if you try and go back, you won't be able to anymore.

"In time you'll get over those feelings by connecting more with people of the same new vibration. The women in the bar matched the vibration of your friends, that's why they were aligning with them. You couldn't connect because you've shifted since you last saw them. The men had the intention to look, and the women had the intention to get them to look. It was a perfect frequency match."

"I noticed that Andy draws a lot of respect to himself now. He used to be the guy every woman fell for. He seems more settled in himself, and determined. Being around him more has helped me, though I am still a bit wobbly and nervous around women."

"Yes, it's an evolution. Life lessons will keep coming back around and hitting you from every corner until you are settled. And maybe even afterwards. Don't call any lessons to you that you've already learned, or they'll come back again even harder next time. Look for meaning and purpose only, and you'll be more able to sit back and watch others figure out their lessons."

"I like the sound of that. The day I got hit by that thunderstorm was as exciting as I would ever want it to get."

"What's your next step then in this new version of you?" asked Francis.

"I think I need to begin thinking about my future living arrange-ments, for one. In the meantime, I need to call and invite my in-laws over for a much-needed visit."

"I would like to be a fly on the wall watching that one."

Ryan hugged his teacher with a crossed heart and left the session with no response.

***

RYAN CALLED OUT for his son to come upstairs with him and kept him close. He knocked on his mother's door.

"You know you don't have to knock, Ryan. This is our house."

"Mom, just so you know, Clara's mom and dad are coming for a few days to be with us." Ryan spoke with an upbeat whistle in his voice.

Maria turned to start washing the dishes. "Where will they stay? There's no room for them. Every other time you complained that they took up too much space in your house."

Ryan laughed to himself. It was always her complaining about them coming, not him. "Well, I decided that I'll set up a tent outside for the kids and they can have a camp-out."

Little Ryan beamed with excitement and asked his grandma for a flashlight.

Ryan stopped him, "We have flashlights downstairs, Buddy, but don't worry, I'll get yours ready and check the batteries tonight." He turned his attention to his mother, "Mom, Clara and I will sleep in Angela's room. We've got a pull-out sofa in there now."

"That's ridiculous!" Maria snorted while waving him off like some fool.

"I know—and that's why we're going to do it!" Ryan shot back.

Maria couldn't hide her jealousy and whipped around to dry the dishes that she had just washed. "I'm not ready for them to come. Clara should have talked to me first. It's very selfish of her," she explained. "I wish I had more notice given to me. I guess I'll find something to make. That family eats so different. I have to think about what to make."

"Actually mom, I decided to let this visit be about Clara and her parents and not about us. I invited them myself. I'm asking that you guys come down and allow Clara to be the boss downstairs. We'll handle the food and everything. I'm letting you know that you are invited."

Maria looked heart broken and slumped into a forward position like a Labrador retriever who had just been scolded for grabbing food off the table. "Ryan, what has been going on with you? You aren't the same boy I raised. Why are you being so hard on me? What did I do wrong? I don't deserve this. You're treating me like I'm second."

"Mom, Clara is my wife. I've learned with my counsellor that I need to allow *her* to be first. I'm letting you know that things are going to be different. I married her, I love her, and I want her to be happier with her section of the house. Do you hear that, little Ryan?" Ryan looked down into little Ryan's deer eyes. He looked a bit confused but happy at the same time.

"Yes, Mommy is the woman," he spouted.

Ryan smiled down at him warmly.

"I would hardly call it *her* house, Ryan. This was my house since you were a child. She came here afterwards," Maria bickered.

Ryan lost his cool, "Mom, I think you're right, this is your house. Maybe I need to find another house to live in."

Ignoring Ryan's comment, and now grumbling, Maria stated, "I'm actually busy tomorrow anyway. I have a gathering with my friends. My good friend's son is getting married. He's a lovely boy, and so kind to his mother. She needs me, the poor dear. She says that I know a lot about these things, so I offered her my help. People often want my help. I really put a lot of work into what I'm focused on and everyone trusts me.

"When you need me, just let me know, I'm sure Clara isn't used to having a chef position, God love her. I have all the ingredients here if she forgets something. She really is such a busy woman, I understand. You know I would do anything for you guys. Her mother will probably have to take over the cooking anyway. I'll leave it with her to save Clara."

"Thanks, Mom, for understanding. I'm happy you found a purpose in your friend's son's wedding. When you come back, you're certainly welcome downstairs."

"Of course, honey. Enjoy your in-laws." Maria turned to look busy again.

Ryan left with a sense of pride. It went well even if she was hard on Clara. He expected her to act more like a victim and he was surprised to see her semi-open to some changes. She managed to not control. He began to bring little Ryan downstairs.

"Little Ryan," Maria yelled down the stairs, undermining her son's authority. "Here is the flashlight that you asked for, and there are new batteries in it, so you don't have to worry."

Ryan sucked back his enthusiasm. He almost spit out mindless words and decided instead to go a different direction. "Wait—we have your flashlight downstairs, and I have the batteries ready to put in there. Would you like to learn how to put them in?"

Little Ryan squealed out a yes and turned back down the stairs running toward the kitchen door to get his own flashlight.

Maria stood there feeling like she had just been slapped across the face.

Ryan quickly felt a beam of energy on his back and he knew that if he turned around that he wouldn't like the look on his mother's face. "Thanks anyway, Mom." He didn't bother turning around. The door closed loudly behind him.

"Freedom from and freedom to," he muttered.

Chapter Twelve

WHO ARE YOU?

CLARA AND THE kids ran to the end of the driveway excitedly.

"Nana, Pops!" Little Ryan chirped and jumped up into his Grandfather Anthony's arms.

Monica held Angela in her arms and complimented her, "How is the smartest girl I know?"

Angela gleamed. "I read that book you gave me, Nana, the one about the unicorns."

"Great! Now we can really start searching for one in nature together, huh?"

Ryan stood back. He had no idea that the unicorn book had been a gift from Monica. He welcomed his in-laws and offered to take their bags into his and Clara's room.

"Thank you, Ryan, for inviting us. This was perfect timing. We had thought about calling you and inviting you guys to our place," Monica said.

"I think the visit was long overdue, and the kids have been wanting to show off our new pool," Ryan contributed while grabbing the bags. He wanted to stay busy to hide the shame he felt.

Usually, Maria took over the show at the driveway. Her being gone made things feel different—smoother and effortless. It was nice to see Clara so relaxed and settled.

When Ryan came back, John had made his way downstairs, already making conversation with Anthony. "Clara told me that you were being put to work with the swing set."

"Yes, little Ryan already asked when I would start," Anthony laughed.

"Well, if I could be of service to you, let me know. I wouldn't mind getting my hands dirty. They seem to think around here that I don't know what I'm doing," John blurted out honestly.

Ryan cringed to think that they had acted in a way to make his dad think that about himself.

Anthony was eager to get moving. He was never one to sit around. "Yes, let's grab the tools. I think it's a two-person job, and so it's probably why they waited for me, so I could help you."

Clara looked like an eager teenager, smiling from ear to ear. Ryan wondered what life would have been like if they'd had their own house from the beginning. Yet a part of him knew that he wouldn't be the same person he was today or have the same kind of understanding.

Monica gave the kids one small gift each and watched while they opened them. They were simple, everyday things. She was always thoughtful without being extravagant or expensive. Angela got another book to add to her unicorn series and a purple bookmark. Beaming, she ran to hug her grandmother before sprinting to the sun chair to start reading it.

Little Ryan tore his bag open to find a book of mazes and labyrinths and a pen. He ran and hopped onto Monica's lap asking her to play with him. She suggested for him to use his finger to do the labyrinths so that he could play with it again, this way it could stay special longer. He took her advice and played with that book for an hour straight, imagining himself being the adventurer that found the treasure inside the maps in the book. He slayed dragons and fought robots and used his imagination wildly. He ran back and forth a few times to see the progress his grandfathers were making on his swing set. He picked up some tools and played with them for a few minutes at a time, then he would run back to his book.

Ryan had never seen his son act so happy, calm, and co-operative.

Clara shyly asked her mom to help her cook because she was scared to make a mistake. Monica jumped up immediately to be by her side. "You're an amazing cook, Clara. I think you'll do just fine. If you need help, I'm here. However, I think being the chef looks good on you."

"Thanks, Mom. I can't say I had a lot of practice. Maria usually runs the show."

Monica stopped her. "There comes a time when mothers need to step aside and let their children raise their own children, which means allowing a woman to run her own household. There's only room in a kitchen for one head chef. If you don't like cooking, that's one thing, but I know you better, Clara—I raised you. You bumped me out of my own kitchen as a kid and you had a great interest and pride in learning old family recipes. I watched you enough times to know that you're a natural."

"Why didn't you ever say anything to me, Mom?"

"It wasn't my place to influence you into being someone I thought you should be. My job was to teach you what I knew to be right and then to let you leave the nest and live your own life."

Who would have thought that Clara used to cook? She made basic meals in front of Ryan. He used to laugh and tease her in front of friends saying she was useless in the kitchen. She'd just turn away and put her hand up to him as if to say "enough."

Ryan couldn't breathe for a moment. His chest tightened and he felt squeezed. His whole body was suddenly flushed with embarrassment and shame. He had been a complete jerk!

Monica continued praising Clara, "The kids have grown. Angela is like a little woman now. I need to shake my head sometimes. You spoke the same as her, you know, much wiser than your age. You dreamt of finding unicorns and fairies. I remember that all too well."

Clara laughed feeling a bit silly. "Yeah, you know, life changed me."

Ryan stumbled over his own feet accidently. To not look like he was spying, he spoke up. "Uh, is there anything I can do for you ladies? Everyone's busy doing something but me."

Clara jumped to attention. "Umm, maybe take the husks off the corn?"

"Where is your mom today, Ryan?" Monica asked.

"She's apparently helping with some wedding. She should be back after supper."

Soon everyone gathered around to eat. Monica made sure that the kids ate the vegetables that their mother had prepared, before offering to cut the cake; she first asked Clara's permission.

***

MARIA SHOWED UP a couple of hours later. "Oh wow, look at that swing set, little Ryan. Oh, hello, everyone, nice to see you all. Hope you're enjoying yourselves. Sorry I couldn't be here to help you. I've been so very busy lately. Excuse me for a moment but I can see little Ryan needs to be babied a bit. He misses me so much if I leave for even a short time period."

Maria gave the kids the toys that she had picked up from the local store. Little Ryan threw his book of mazes to the side and shuffled through the bag of multiple fun-sized playthings and games in Maria's hand. Angela thanked her and asked that she leave her bag on the table, as she was reading her book that her other grandparents had brought.

Maria whipped her a look and frowned sideways to show her disapproval. She then stood straight as if to reset her composure, then turned around directly to go play with little Ryan. She hugged him with so much enthusiasm that it looked almost violent to Ryan.

She carried on with her over-zealous act as if to show that this is how things always play out and that this was just a normal everyday thing. The disruption in the energy was already starting.

Ryan decided to intervene. "I have to say that these two grandpas did a great job on the swing set. It was certainly a two-man job. I wasn't aware that it had a slide, too. Thank God for their expertise. It looks great, eh, Mom?"

"Oh, yes," Maria jumped in, "it's nice, Anthony," leaving out her husband. "You were working hard, I see. I was busy today myself. I had a lot of work helping prepare my friends' boy's wedding."

Monica thanked both men individually for their efforts on the playset and then marvelled in how busy Maria was and wished she could've joined them for supper. "Are you hungry?" She asked.

"I already ate, but thank you. I see you put on quite a spread of food, Monica," Maria offered her sweetest voice.

"Actually, our Clara did us the honour. I have missed her cooking. It's been a while," Monica said, smiling back sweetly.

"Really? You cook, Clara? I never saw you prepare a meal." Maria sounded sharp.

Clara looked at Ryan for help as if to be suddenly drowning in the family pool. The energetic glow she had gained earlier was now being sucked out of her.

"Well, Mom, you might have forgotten. I told you that Clara is going to be cooking our meals more often downstairs and that you and dad are welcome to join us." Ryan smiled at Clara, hoping he had saved the day.

"Oh, isn't that wonderful," Maria tweeted, smiling gently and gesturing to pick up the dishes.

"I will get them, if you don't mind," said Ryan.

Maria whipped back, "Actually, since you are okay with the dishes, Ryan, I'm going to go upstairs and lie down to nurse this awful headache. Enjoy your stay, Monica and Anthony."

Clara released her tense stance as soon as Maria made her way up the stairs. Ryan hadn't realized until then that she was clenching one fist and nervously chewing her nails on her other hand.

For the next couple of days, Maria made short, erratic appearances downstairs to drop things off for them to munch on. Her headache still lingered.

Ryan thought about the chakra teachings, the energy centres in the body, and how flow stops going to certain parts of the body. He could see now where he got his migraines from and that he was much more like his mother than he cared to admit.

John came down occasionally for visits but mostly stayed upstairs. He didn't seem as talkative or as comfortable as he had been that first day, remaining polite and congenial. Something was brewing upstairs.

Ryan went up to check on things. "Are you okay, Mom? Do you need anything?"

Maria looked away. "I just need peace. You can go down and have fun, I'll be fine."

***

AFTER HER PARENTS left, Ryan asked Clara how things went the last couple of days from her perspective. She turned around slowly and bided her time before she spoke. "I love you, Ryan," she whispered. Her gentle tone was a good sign.

Ryan spoke back tenderly, "You really are a great cook, you know. The meat was perfectly tenderized and juicy. I was particularly surprised that you knew traditional recipes. I'm sorry I made fun of you before."

"It's okay. If you really liked it, I could cook it again and maybe even more traditional foods. I don't want to step on your mom's toes, but I would love to cook for our little family."

Ryan chipped in proudly, "Well the kids ate everything up, so I know they'll be happy. And don't worry any, I have already stepped on my mother's toes enough for both of us."

"I noticed that she's been acting extra distant the last while. I wasn't sure what it was all about." Clara looked concerned.

"I've been thinking something over. I know we still need time to work on us; I also know that we can't do that living so close to my parents. I don't expect you to want to stay with me, but have you ever thought about moving?"

Clara's body jerk reaction spoke for her. She almost choked and lost her voice for a moment. "Really?" She ran to the sink to grab a glass and gulped down some water. She suddenly burst out laughing while trying to stop coughing. This was so unexpected. "You want to move for real? Why? Where? And are your parents moving with us?"

Ryan knew this was a bit much to ask of her on the spur of the moment and besides he needed to earn trust back. He took her by the hand and looked deeply into her hopeful eyes. He spoke respectfully, "No, I mean just the two of us and the kids. In all honesty, I've been slowly preparing for these changes so we can move forward. With your permission, I could do some research and go to the bank to check out our finances and what we could manage. It may not be big, but it would be our own."

Clara grabbed Ryan by his shoulders and kissed him like it was their very first kiss. It had been a long while. "Yes! I really want that, but where?" she asked.

"Anywhere—just somewhere other than here."

"I can start packing right now! Get some boxes and some packing tape! I'm going to be busy and will need to hide out for a month after you tell your mother!" Clara laughed and cried all at once. This was a huge moment. She was excited and angry at him in unison. "Why did it have to come to this point for you to finally realize what I needed? I mean, don't answer that...I am just saying..."

"Sorry, Clara. I'll work things out with my dad first, as he's more reasonable. I've learned that when I tell Mom what I plan to do, she has a special way of influencing the outcome. My parents did let us live in the house free of charge, so I won't put any monetary expectations into that conversation with Dad."

"It's like that old saying, say what you did, not what you're going to do."

Clara knew he had more expectations of her than she was able to offer, but she also knew that the only way to get past her pain was to get some help outside of herself. Maybe it was time she had counselling, too. She needed to know if this was a show Ryan was just putting on or if it was a real, viable change that he was making. "Ryan, we aren't out of the woods yet, but I feel hopeful. I have noticed a big change in you since you started going to that counsellor. I'd like to go there someday. In time."

***

RYAN SAW THE smudge and abalone shell on the office step, knowing somehow that Francis had left it at the door for him to use. He lit it up himself outside and cleared his energy before coming into the building. He shivered as he let go of the old and made room for the new.

"Well, hello, Ryan—glad to see you looking so happy. Good news?"

"Yes. It's been an amazing week. How about you?" Ryan asked.

"I've been great also. I did a fast this week and prayed for those in need of healing. It was a beautiful cleanse and a great honour to send strength to those who need it, through the prayers."

"Wow that *is* different! It sounds awesome, though. A real fast?"

"Yes, awesome is a word for it, for sure. A real fast, with no food and no water for two days. I usually do four days. This was more like a mini one to keep up with my disciplines. And you? What did you discover this week?"

"My week? Well, I killed a few flies at the family gathering, I had wondered if I got you."

"It would take a bit more than a good smack to get me down. The in-laws doing okay?"

"They're doing great. Things went better than I could've hoped for. I stood back and observed. I have to say, my mom-in-law is a lot easier going than I had painted her to be. I let my mom know that she needed to step aside, and I thought World War III was going to erupt but she managed to find ways to avoid us, so things played out differently."

"When something changes, then something changes, eh? You were the eagle looking down?"

"Yes, and I also found out that Clara loves cooking. She hid it because I used to tease her. I mean, I had to ask myself if I was that selfish or just clueless toward her?"

"Both," Francis said plainly. He locked his lips tightly together a moment, opened his eyes widely and shrugged his shoulders. "Just saying!"

Ryan giggled, "Yeah, I know. It's all right, I already know. I've begun to wonder who I really am, without beating myself up with who I was. I'm trying to figure out who I want to be instead."

"Imagine setting up a world where you're the same person wherever you go?"

"I thought I was the same person."

"Think of how you act when you're with your friends having a beer: what are your thoughts, what are the conversations that you have with them? And how do you act at the job? Are you the same guy? Acting the same way, having the same conversations with your boss that you have with your friends?"

"No, of course not. That would be a little weird!"

"Would it really?"

"I can't have a conversation with my boss about sports or women or about whatever. It wouldn't be professional."

"Why can't you be professional with your friends, then?"

"Because they'd think I was crazy or faking it. It wouldn't make sense to bring professionalism inside a friendship."

"Why wouldn't it make sense? Do you fake who you are around Clara?"

"Are we talking in the past or in the now?"

"That depends—is that Ryan in the past?"

"Yes, I can say that I'm my true self around Clara now."

"You tell Clara everything without holding anything back?"

"Well, there are some parts that I may have left out. Okay, yeah, maybe a lot." Ryan squirmed in his chair while screwing up his face purposefully and sticking out his tongue. He was caught.

Francis laughed, "When you become your true self, you can move that self into your everyday relationships and be the same person no matter where you are. Being your true self around the boss and around your friends would help you be your true self with Clara. And then you would have nothing to hide. Again, just saying!" He stuck his tongue back at Ryan.

Ryan giggled. "Okay, okay! I can almost understand being myself around my friends. I just can't see how that would make sense in the workplace."

"When we can be one person in all areas of our lives, then we live consciously. If we need to shift and change who we are, then the ego can get us. Right?"

"Yes. Okay, I see. I can still be professional at work but be centred and present."

"Simple, eh?"

"Sometimes things are so simple that I have a hard time understanding."

"Should I put you back to Grade 5?"

Ryan smiled while raising his right hand as if in school, "I think I got this one, thanks. It's all sinking in a bit more day by day."

"Great, then we'll put you in Grade 6 again."

"I'm feeling like a big boy now." Ryan paused, suddenly thinking of the kids. "But you said that kids like Angela change who they are. Isn't that going to be a problem also?"

"Wow, one subject ties into the other with you, doesn't it? Good. Well, I assume we're talking about how Angela shifts for everyone around her."

"Yes."

"Okay. Well, I would have to say that intention changes the outcome. Angela's intention is based on an instinct and hopefully it won't become a learned behaviour. She adapts to others to show them their true essence. It's a different situation altogether. She came for peace. You came to shake the peace."

"Disturbing the peace for sure," Ryan laughed.

"I believe it! You're ready to embrace who you are now, though. Once we know who we are, then we're more willing to admit our former weaknesses, and peace follows. We know what to watch for so that we don't fall into old patterns and programs. It also means that we learn the lessons of what the meaning and purpose was in order to move forward from the past."

"Yes, so that means that when I know myself, I also know my ego better."

"Yes, it does."

"And when something goes wrong, I can catch the ego before it affects me or it affects those around me. So, I won't disturb the peace so often."

"Yes, if you can. It's not so simple at first but it does come with practice. If you're yourself—I mean your true self without ego—and you disturb someone else's peace, that's their issue, not yours. Remember, you aren't here to change them, just to work on yourself."

"I know it'll take time. It's easier said than done. This week I caught myself a few times losing hold of my convictions." Ryan admitted.

"Your convictions, eh?" Francis was proud of him for opening up and not having to hide himself anymore.

"I have been looking up big words lately to try to look smarter," Ryan joked.

They both laughed.

Ryan continued, "I managed to avoid a few situations, though, just by allowing myself to be more of that 'fly on the wall.' And no one squashed me, by the way! I did find it hard when managing my mom, as her program runs deep. However, the parts of her program that had to do with myself, I did catch successfully. I was able to not add to those programs. It seemed to not suit her, but I was able to stay strong despite myself. I'm still learning how to find a way to do it so as to not always upset her each time."

"Very well done, Ryan. You may have just mastered part of Grade 7 right there. You're learning faster than you thought you could. Maybe borrowing from the dictionary, a time or two, isn't such a bad idea, eh?"

Ryan laughed. "I spoke to Clara about moving. We're going to start looking for our new home. She mentioned coming to see you someday, so I thought of couples counselling."

"It may be a good idea to do couples counselling later on, though I feel she'll need to see if I'm a good fit for her and not be one-sided before she commits to it. We'll let her call the shots."

"That's fair. I also decided to talk to my dad first in order to avoid mom's influence over me. I don't feel quite strong enough yet to stop her from taking over."

"That statement alone tells me a lot. You're ready for meaning and purpose, which we'll take up in our next session. Take a few weeks off and let it all sink in. See what unfolds."

"Yes. I think I'm ready for that next step."

"Now, for the rest of the session, let's go outside and walk without talking."

"I'm not so sure if I can do that," Ryan admitted.

"I'm not sure either, though I'm always open to miracles, brother!"

Ryan chuckled. "Okay, what do I need to do?"

"Put one foot on the ground and practise feeling the ground under your feet. Make sure that your foot fully touches the earth beneath it. One foot needs to always be touching fully before moving the other one. This is called 'conscious walking.' Also, it'll help you ground. I'll show you how and that'll be your homework for the next three weeks. When you get a chance, go outside and practise what I'm about to show you."

"Okay, sounds easy enough. Let's go."

Francis knew full well, now that Ryan had found his voice, a half hour of silence was going to be a torture in itself, and the major part of the lesson—quieting the mind.

"Yup, easy-peasy!" he said tauntingly, while opening the door and showing Ryan the way out. "After you, brother!"

Chapter Thirteen

─────────

Meaning and Purpose

"Meaning and purpose is something that we've skimmed over so far, but you seem ready to talk about it on a deeper level now."

"I haven't made much progress, if I'm honest. I just feel as though I've lost myself and my focus since the last time I saw you. I did try that conscious walking thing that you showed me. However, I think it just made things worse. I couldn't stay quiet in my mind; it was impossible. I feel stuck."

"Letting go seems to be the likely culprit...and then I would say the ego plays a part as well. That conscious walking exercise is a way to practise the art of letting go and a way to learn to be in the here and now. It'll help you focus inwards instead of getting all frustrated with the world around you. Keep practising it. One day you'll love it, trust me"

"Yeah, I admit my ego seems to keep me from getting there. Especially when it comes to my mom. I used to be blind to what she was doing. Life was a lot easier back then," Ryan admitted.

"Ignorance really is bliss, eh?"

"It sure is. Now my struggle is with my anger. I'm wanting to take out my irritation on a woman who isn't even aware of what she's doing, and that isn't right. I tried letting go of control, but I find the more time passes, I only want to get cross at her and force my new way of thinking onto her."

"Yes, and you would just cause everyone around you great pain and anguish if you went that route. Wouldn't you?" Francis clarified.

"Yes, I know, and that's exactly where I'm stuck. I feel like a devil is on my shoulder leading me into anger."

"That's a good analogy to view this situation from. We all have an angel and a devil on our shoulders, in a sense, don't we? The devil keeps us in our ego. You're a valuable ally that the ego is losing, and it isn't happy about it. It can find anything wrong with the world around it except itself."

"Exactly, and nothing has changed. I simply shifted where the judgment went—from Clara onto Mom."

164

"You haven't healed the judgment yet and that's why it shifted to another person."

"Now, how do I get that angel on the other shoulder talking?"

"Think of it like this: that angel side only sees love and light in all situations. It can find the good in anything. It's a good ally to have when you want to find meaning and purpose in hard situations, a beacon in the darkest of nights. However, that angel side becomes quiet when ego takes over.

"Like that sleeping pill you spoke of one day not too long ago, the ego knows how to drug us into submission. The Angel self, or higher consciousness, is what needs to be woken up. While it's coming around, the ego still runs the show. Sleeping pills take a while to get out of the system, after all. Once in you, you have no choice but to let the drug run its course. That ego pill knocks us down and holds our angel personality hostage until we are free of its effects. When we do wake up, we are dazed and confused. We're useless until its effect wears off."

"I love how you put stuff together. I know better now and yet the ego is having a field day causing havoc! No wonder I can't find my balance," Ryan explained.

"If we were balanced most of the time, the ego wouldn't be such an evil thing. It would just be seen as the part of us that challenges us to continue to be balanced. Working toward that balance is key, and being able to maintain balance is an invaluable skill."

"Yes, okay. The angel gives us the good and the ego gives us the flip side to things. The world isn't all good."

"Yes, and the world isn't all bad, brother. The other shoulder is our flip side, yes, and without the two sides we can't actually obtain any kind of balance. We need both the ego and the higher self to get the whole experience."

"Do we really need the ego?" Ryan asked.

"Yes and no. We must find a middle road. We do this by obtaining and maintaining balance, and that is easier achieved with a narrow road."

"Yeah, okay, I got that lesson already. The narrower the better, gotcha. What about people who are negative about everything, always expecting the worst and totally led by ego. If they're sleeping in the world, how can they function?"

"That's the autopilot that I mentioned before. Be thankful for those people. They're there as a reminder for you to seek out the positive."

"Got it. Also, can you tell me more about the higher self? I still don't know what it is."

"Our higher self is that part of us that stays connected to heaven. That self knew us before we were born. It knows where we've been in other lives and why we came to planet Earth this time around. It knows our purpose. It helps us get on track."

"Does the angel self or higher self ever fizz us up so we'll listen?" Ryan inquired.

"That isn't the question I figured you would come out with, considering you lost focus at home these past few weeks. However, the answer is yes."

"It's easy here in the office. I lose perspective when out in the real world."

"Glad to see you're honest. The sleeping pill is starting to wear off, I see."

"Hopefully it'll be totally out of my system soon, so I can get through the next maze of my life."

"Yes, and I like how you use these analogies as comparisons to your life. Let us use that maze example as we go on further."

"Sounds good. If you can break it down in simple terms, I'm all ears."

"OKAY, SO WE'RE in a maze and we have a door at the top of it, from which we will exit one day." Francis demonstrated while drawing his finger into the air as if drawing out a map.

Ryan sat up straighter, following Francis's finger with his eyes, to not miss anything.

"We have walls that we could possibly bump into along the way." Francis knocked the wall next to him to make his point. "Those walls are there to teach us and guide us. Visualize it like this: if we hit our head against those walls enough times, our noodle gets sore, right?"

Ryan added, "Yep, been there, done that until I figured out not to go in that direction anymore."

"Exactly!"

"Like the Pac-Man game, right?" Ryan asked. "Where our brains try and figure things out while we're sleeping, except now you mean that we're playing the game awake?"

"Yes, exactly. The ego is the ghost that chases Pac-man, so that he panics, thinking he'll never find a way out. The Higher Self Pac-man is you as the player watching the screen. You can see if you should turn left or right or straight, but it's not so easy at first to coordinate your hands with the screen, is it?"

"No, it's not." Ryan agreed. "So, does that mean the higher self knows the direction we're supposed to go at any given moment, but just can't control our reactions because of free will?"

"It does. The joystick needs to be connected to our consciousness in order for it to do that."

"So, we're in control of our own game and yet we continue to do things that make us hit that wall. Are we humans just clueless? Wouldn't it be better if we just let the higher self do things for us?"

"If it did, though, it would be controlling us. The higher self knows humans are smart and that if we give someone a chance, they can catch on quickly. You're a good example of that."

Ryan reached over as if to slap Francis on the arm.

Francis carried on as if nothing had happened, "And yes, if we get to the point of being consciously aware, then we can learn to step aside and let the higher self control the joystick a bit. Of course, we have to be present and aware and veto the decisions made by the higher self. After all, it is our free will and our life. This also means the end result is our responsibility."

Ryan sat listening intensely.

"We have a limited amount of time on Earth to get all of our lessons in," Francis explained. "The harder and quicker the lessons, the better, sometimes. If we are not awakened, lessons make sure that we are. We may need time to sit on that path, within the maze, and seek out healing before we can move forward. From there, we take time out to find meaning and purpose. Some may get it a lot quicker, while others may need to hit their head again. Some make no progress at all."

"Some sit in level one of the Pac-Man game longer than others?" Ryan pointed at himself while letting out a belly laugh.

"Yes, and sometimes a lot of ghosts haunt them while they're there."

"Yeah! Tell me about it. I may be stuck at level one for a while."

"And, you may have to stay there for a while longer until you have mastered that level...and that's okay. That or until you figure out that hitting your head again and again hurts!"

"The ego, then, is also conscious of what's going on? I mean can the ego know our path and act like the bad guy to help us attain that knowledge?"

"You have very good questions for someone who is seemingly living life half asleep. I think you've been more awakened than you'd have others believe!"

Ryan shrugged his shoulders.

Francis continued. "So, yes, the ego can act like a bad guy to help us gain that knowledge. The ego is much like how people view the snake. He isn't necessarily meant to be the bad guy—he just plays a role like the rest of us do. In truth he's meant to be part of the healing. Remember, the snake bites us and we use the venom to make anti-venom. Anti-venom is knowledge in a bottle. The bite happened for a higher purpose. Meaning and purpose come when we realize that without that bite, we could never save others. We can't save them from getting bitten, but we can help them, if they accept help, using the anti-venom."

Ryan commented, "So, with that logic, let me try to put things into perspective about my mom."

"You are still stuck on the mom subject? Why do you think that is?"

"Come on! I mean, this is the major influence that made me who I am today, so yes, I'm a bit stuck. I want to better understand so that I can see where *I* went wrong, not just her," Ryan explained.

Francis wasn't satisfied with that response. "You've played too many games of golf with your mother, I see! The program is too ingrained in you still. It's a tough habit to break. I told you so. Okay, tell me how you see things. Explain it to me in your own words."

"Okay, well, Mom is the snake that bit me. I extracted the venom from my body and I have the anti-venom now in a bottle. It contains the knowledge of what I need to do on my path."

"Okay, I'm following you," Francis said encouragingly.

"From the hurt and pain that I experienced I came to a point of wanting to make a household change. By having freedom from Mom's control, Clara, myself, and the kids will learn how to do things on our own. My parents will also be free from having to take care of us, too. They can be grandparents instead of being constant caregivers. It's going to be a big adjustment for all of us, worst of all for my mom because taking care of us seems to be her purpose, which makes her feel valued and loved."

"Yes. You'll have 'some' freedom from her and some parts you'll still have to work on. It'll take a lot of conviction on your part as well as perseverance, patience, and time so that your mom and the rest of your family can adjust to this new reality in their own way."

Ryan continued. "Yes, and if I turn this around, now I'm the snake about to hurt my mom. That really sucks, especially because she's not in a state of wanting help and I can't see that changing anytime soon. The rest of the family will also be hurting because she won't want this."

"I see now where this is going. Okay, yes, it does suck. It's a lesson that can't be avoided because of her free will choice to not want to change. We must always respect others' choices, even if that means allowing someone the free will choice to be upset with our choices. It may hurt you more than it does her, but it's necessary.

Her free will has set the tone of the lesson. Allow her to live out that lesson; it'll also serve as a lesson for yourself and the rest of the family."

"What if my mom doesn't want to talk to me ever again?"

"You may have to take that chance, brother."

"The old ego would've made me feel guilty. However, I know that in the long run by hurting my mom it's going to help her. That helps me feel a bit less guilty."

"If she chooses to help herself, then it'll be up to her to extract the venom and to change it into something good. With the venom in a bottle as knowledge, she can figure out the next part of her own personal journey. By helping herself, then she can truly help others. A cycle in and of itself."

"That sounds good sitting here, but you and I know that she'll always identify Clara as the snake that bit her because I'm choosing to leave." Ryan looked concerned.

"Yes, and so now use that angel self to think positive. Remember, the snake is also considered a healer. Once she identifies the real snake, being you, she can find the anti-venom. Getting the wrong snake would be a disaster. I agree, right now she sees the snake as Clara and so you need to lead her back to you. By not leaving the house in the past, you held her back from her pain lessons."

"Pain lessons? Now, that is a sobering thought. After all that, I can't help but wonder: Am I the first snake to bite her?"

"No, your mom was bitten in her childhood first."

"That's less pressure for me to live with. Wouldn't that mean, though, that she would have to heal that wound first before she could heal from me hurting her?"

"You are very perceptive, Ryan. I'm very proud of you. Yes, and you'll have to live with knowing the truth and not leading her to that answer too quickly. Can you do that?"

"That's the disaster part you meant. I can't help her. I need to let her be upset with me or Clara. If she never heals from her childhood, she may never heal my leaving her."

"So, who can you change and who are you supposed to start helping first?"

"I can only change myself and I need to start by helping my-self first."

"Right."

"My father is different. He may use his free will to choose to heal one day and he won't be as upset as Mom is going to be. Things are already feeling better between us. With my mom, I see now that

I have a role to play as the bad guy. It's just going to be a conscious role."

"You've graduated from the role of Snow White, I see. Now you are the big bad wolf. Nice one!"

Ryan smiled. "Oh, God! Yeah, I see those fairy tales are back. We should have moved out of the house before we got married. We stayed to save some money at first, and then we stayed because we had the kids and it was easier for us. Once the kids got attached to Mom, I thought they'd suffer if I took them from someone who was such a mother figure in their lives."

"Suffering is a big word in this case, isn't it?"

"I don't know, I thought that I had used the right word."

"It would have been a shift or a change for them and not a cause for suffering. We know the difference between the two now, right?"

"Yes, I think we do. Now I can see that if I stay, I'll be hurting the kids *and* her."

"Yes, and by staying, they walk her journey and take on her karma, just as you did. I don't think that you'd want that for them."

"No, I wouldn't," Ryan admitted.

"Okay, so it's up to you to take on the responsibility and set them free."

"How am I going to deal with this?"

"Is there such a thing as divorce from your mom?" Francis asked.

"That's what it's sounding like here. Ugh!"

RYAN COULDN'T HELP but think further. "It's funny that you say that about divorce because I have a friend who wants to leave his wife, but he says he wants to stay for the kids. I can see now how selfish it is to think that way. Everyone stays in limbo, and nobody can heal and grow."

"Yes, we teach kids with actions, not just with words. The more of a functional lifestyle kids see, the better, even if it means they become co-parents. In your case, you'll be lucky if Clara doesn't bail on you. Leaving your mom is going to feel a bit like a divorce, though if you stay, Clara will probably leave, so you either divorce your mom or Clara. Pick between door number one and door number two. What's it going to be?

"It'll look like a snake bite at first. Children need balance between male and female energies. If you did divorce Clara, then I would suggest a half and half situation. Alternating between living with one parent and then the other, it's the only way that the kids will get the equal balance of both the male and female energies.

Each has important lessons to offer the children. After all, they came to Earth knowing what parents they chose.

"Also, a mother can't fill her child's father's portion of their cup, nor can he fill hers for the child. Each parent has their own offerings to give to that child. Their own teachings to deliver. Each parent has a valuable lesson to teach them to set them on their journey. Neither should be denied when both parents are of sound mind, are responsible, and are willing to co-parent. In your case, the kids get too much dominating energy from an outside source and not enough male and female balance coming from you and Clara."

"Yes, it makes total sense. That's another reason why my friend won't divorce—his wife won't agree on half and half."

"I don't know the specifics about your friend, but in general, it's better to share. Not doing so would be selfish and hurtful to all. It would also take the kids off the path and create an imbalance in them. It would also affect the next generation because their kids wouldn't know how to deal with their own lives and relationships. They'd only end up with a bigger set of problems. Shared custody can teach the kids that their parents have their best interests as the driving force for their decisions. Living in balance is the best out-come. And also, they don't grow up too heavy on one side of the coin and with one point of view and know less about the other side."

"I'll let my friend know what you said. I see now that my mom creates a major imbalance because they're getting more of her and not of anyone else. My father and I have no real place, when my mom is present, and then Clara is completely cast aside. The kids are being brought up by one individual really, because my mom is the dominant figure. I used to think that it was Clara who was setting up outings constantly. I see now it was her tagging along with my mother's choices, or her making plans to get away from Mom's influence."

"Yes, and if you stay in that house what would happen?"

"It would be my own selfishness that would be their mirror in the future. Staying home, all this time, was easiest on me."

"Yes, and?"

"Having my mom take over kept me from being active in my own life. Non-participation allowed me to sleep in and miss out and to allow the ego to run the show. This set both Clara and me aside. Mom was feeding my ego side and encouraging me to sleep through my life."

"It gave you an excuse not to take any responsibility. If some-thing got screwed up nobody could blame you, right?"

"Wow, yes, you're right. My mom has always claimed that she did everything for me because she loved me. Now I see she was just smothering me and doing things so she could feel good about herself."

"Right, and it wasn't setting anyone up for success except her, now, was it?"

"No, it wasn't. I have been living in a golden cage, served and adored, but never free. I can see how my children and Clara are living in their own cages as well. We are separate and shut off from one another; we'll continue to be like this if I don't do something about it. The only solution I see is to move."

"By living with your mom, would you say that it put you under an illusion of freedom?"

Could it be true? Was he living his whole life within the illusion that he was free to be? When, in fact, he was trapped and blinded from the truth and stopped from living his own life? Ryan had realized this before; however, at this moment he could see an even deeper truth. "Yes, it did."

Francis decided to throw in a question to make Ryan think further, "Do you think that by her words and actions, your mom wants things to stay as is? For all of you to stay and learn to sing inside those cages? What do you think about that?"

Ryan got emotional. "I think that's the key to it right there. Now that I know better, I couldn't sing even if you paid me to. I know that I need to go—we all do. If I don't, I'll fall back into a program of some sort, make more mistakes and excuses. I'd shut off again in order to deal."

"Who's the one aware now in this situation? Who is responsible now?" asked Francis.

"I'm the one who's aware—that's why I need to be the responsible one."

"Knowing what you know now, how do you think you'll treat your mom if you stay?"

"I'd be full of bitterness. It would be better to move out, to save my relationship with her. I see myself losing patience fast. I would rather be happy to visit and share about my life, without having to share the day-to-day details. It would feel more natural and have less room for resentment...at least not any *new* resentment on top of the old, which I'm beginning to heal."

"So now it really is time to divorce your mom, eh?" Francis chuckled.

"Yes, and I see now that I married Clara on paper, but my main relationship has always been with my mom. With most of the decisions I've made throughout my life, my attention and my devotion have been to her, and no one else. I never considered anyone else's needs, not even my own. She'll think that I no longer value her, as though my leaving her is a betrayal, unless or until she chooses to heal it; and I can't see that happening."

"So, mom and son divorce it is, then?"

"When I walked into this office the first time, I would never have thought in a million years that I would be joking about divorcing my mom."

"Perspective is amazing, isn't it?"

"Wow, yes!"

"Without your mom, you wouldn't be who you are. She brought you onto this Earth. You can and should be grateful for that, each and every day. She carried you and delivered you, but that birth only happened once; brother, she can't keep using that against you, that wouldn't be honouring the "gift" of life that she supposedly "gave" to you. No matter from which perspective you look at this, it would be the taking away of the gift of life. When we give someone a gift it doesn't make much sense to ask for it back, now does it?"

"No, it doesn't."

"Your mom has some hard lessons coming up in order to get that concept. Forcing you to stay by her side would be like forcing you back inside her womb, impossible to live or to grow, and a form of abuse, brother. She can't turn back time and rebirth you over and over, to be her tiny baby that depends on her for his survival. No wonder you get headaches!"

Ryan laughed but got serious fast. "Abuse? Whew! That statement hits me hard. I never saw it like that before. I've been abused?"

"I think it is time we talk about this fully."

"Good idea, because I get lost when you bring that up."

"I think it's time to take a five-minute breather. Let's go grab a Coke. Things are about to get fizzed up; I can tell. We'll talk about abuse when we resume."

Chapter Fourteen

———

A Step Further

"**O**KAY, WHAT WAS this about my mom being an abuser?" Ryan asked.

"We don't need to be physically hit or touched in order to be abused. Your mom takes over, she gets upset if things don't go her way, or she takes away your power and the control of your own life and decisions. These are the ingredients needed for the perfect example of mental and emotional abuse. Every time she puts Clara down for not doing things the right way, that's mental abuse. When you're left feeling guilty for wanting to do something on your own and your mother intervenes, that's emotional abuse. I could give you many more examples that I've heard just by listening to you in our sessions. Did you know that you've been an abuser, too?"

"Me? How?" Ryan felt extremely hurt by that statement.

"Do we have to go back to the subject of Clara's hair and her clothing?"

Anger swelled up within Ryan's core. "Yeah, but I don't do that anymore."

Francis remained calm but pushed forward knowing that by conjuring up emotion it would evoke deeper healing. It was time Ryan got past this. "By standing by and keeping the peace for the sake of your mother, Clara and the kids are subject to her control and abuse. You know better, yet you don't protect them from it. You feel guilty about the situation, yet you let your mother get away with it. By not stepping up, you're her enabler, therefore no longer a victim, rather the accomplice to her control and abuse. You're an abuser also, Ryan."

Ryan was shocked. Francis was right. Even though he hadn't been aware of it, he was the one responsible for *allowing* the control and abuse to continue to happen. He was the only one who could stop it. "You're right. I need to get out of that house!"

Francis toned down the volume of his voice and spoke very softly and comforting. "I don't want to tell you what to do. I can tell you what may happen or won't happen. You need to be the one to decide where you go from here, brother. To make decisions based out of respect, honesty, trust, and love rather than from fear."

"I'm scared. I don't want to mess it up." Ryan's breathing was suddenly erratic, his chest heaving.

Francis raised his tone and volume again to push forward. "Breathe, Ryan. Take a few deep breaths and clear your mind."

"Okay. I'll try."

"There's no rush. I'll wait for you. Breathe in deeply through your nose. Breathe out slowly through your mouth. Repeat it as needed to find your inner calm. I'm here, brother."

A few minutes passed, and all you could hear in the office was the deep breathing. "Okay. I'm feeling calmer. I was overwhelmed and felt dizzy. My heart was beating out of my chest, my whole body was trembling, and I was sweating. I really lost it there for a few minutes."

"Ryan, you had a panic attack. You were afraid and reacted to a situation that seemed out of your control. You can get that control back. Grab another drink, take your time. You know where the fridge is. We can continue when you're ready."

Tension slowly left Ryan's body as he grabbed a water bottle. His breathing came back to normal a few minutes later.

Francis talked first. "You're processing physically what your heart already knows, brother. I know that this isn't easy, and I want you to know that you've made great progress today, but I feel as though you now have something to say. Don't be afraid—I'm here to help you process. When you're ready, say out loud what's going through that head of yours."

RYAN CLEARED HIS throat and began. "I've made so many mistakes. I've been sleepwalking and living unconsciously, repeating the same patterns of behaviour, but I want to make it right."

"Okay, go on. Remember, no judgment. I'm just here as a witness."

"I feel foolish. How many grown men are afraid to leave their family home and their parents?"

Francis spoke encouragingly. "I would say that it would be more than you think. Fear can be good. It can also hold us back. Keep going, you're getting at the core."

"I've felt weak and powerless most of my life. I compensated by drinking, flirting, and bragging, and so on. It was all a distraction to keep from feeling empty and alone. I didn't take time to reflect on my life's choices. My private life was set up so that I didn't have an opinion and I didn't make waves. Ugh! I feel so guilty that I've brought Clara into this house and raised the kids there. They're getting hurt because I don't stop the abuse from happening. We all act like it's normal. When I do step up and say something now, it feels as though I take one step forward and then I fall back. Move or not, I fear the damage is already done."

Francis interrupted, "So, you've all become peacekeepers. You, Clara, and the kids have gotten better at pretending that things are okay. Your mom is the one who kicks up a fuss, just like little Ryan with his temper tantrums."

"You're *right*. My mom is the parent but acts like a spoiled child who freaks out to get what she wants. I can't change her, though. She won't stop being a bully toward Clara and she can be a bad influence with the kids. By allowing it, I'm aiding and abetting in the abuse, like you said."

"You could change your address without changing the problem. It isn't just about living in the same house, is it? It's about bound-aries and respect, or the lack thereof. You can change that by not being a bystander anymore and by standing up for what is right for you, your wife, and your children. Take the wheel as the driver of the car in your own life. Stepping up isn't about being the bad guy, it's about taking responsibility and ownership of your mistakes, making better choices and turning them into actions for the greater good of all concerned. Face things head-on. Change is inevitable. Fighting it will only make it harder on everyone."

Ryan felt better. "I need to lead the charge and be that change, but I don't want to cause waves."

Francis spoke with a firm but soft voice. "Remember, your mom doesn't have the same kind of control over your siblings because they both live away from her, otherwise she would do to their spouses what she does to yours. The pattern is too deep now and since your mom cannot give up her role of domination, then you must make a choice between two women. If you're sure that you want to move, I suggest that you rip the band aid or plaster off and do it fast. If you're not sure, then let Clara and the kids go, so that they can have a chance at a better life."

"I don't want to lose Clara, but move out now, as in immediately?"

"I'm not saying to pack up and leave today, but you do need to act today, for it to happen as soon as possible. This will show your commitment and resolve. If you don't do it fast, everyone will con-tinue to suffer."

"Is it even possible?"

"You just need to put attention on what you want and get clear on what that is. Once you do that, your angels and guides can help you. They are just waiting for you to be sure and not just talking about it."

Ryan started to feel his heart beat faster again but took a conscious breath before speaking. "I need a game plan. I need to sit with Clara and plan this move together. Then we can get the kids on board with this new chapter in our lives. I think they'll be positive and excited about it, like a new adventure. They can participate now by starting to pack now, in order to move out of the house. I need to be clear and concise that this is what I want and need, though. I need to be the one to talk to my parents and convince them that this is best for myself, Clara, and the kids in order to move forward. I need to be calm, firm, and in control of the situation without getting into a battle of the wills, because it isn't up for discussion. The details can be attended to for the logistics of the move when I'll be ready. No matter what, I need to make a choice, then stand behind it. I can't make any more excuses. Whatever happens in the future, I need to just take responsibility for my choices. Clara needs to be my partner in life, in love, and all the way."

Francis nodded his head wildly. "Wow, you are much clearer, confident, and resolute. Your whole face and your body language changed. This is big, brother. You're taking responsibility, taking steps toward better choices."

"Thanks, Francis. You've really helped me to process my thoughts and emotions by letting me talk it out without judgment. I can't see us moving out tomorrow or anything, but I can take some steps toward it immediately. The sooner we leave, the better. Though I will need a miracle worker to get me through this."

"You do have grandmothers in heaven you can call on for this situation, you know."

"Call on them? They're dead! How can I call them?"

Francis laughed at how innocent Ryan was at times. "It's called prayer, brother."

"I'm not religious, though. I told you that."

"Prayer doesn't belong to a religion. Besides, in the old English language when they said 'I pray of you,' it meant 'I ask of you.'"

"Okay, whatever. Why would my grandmothers want to help me?"

"The reason is called karma. They created their own karma in how they raised your parents. If they want to reincarnate cleared of that karma, they'll help you, trust me on that one. Call it community service for their future resume."

"I would never have thought of that. It's strange, you know—suddenly, while I'm sitting here talking to you, I feel lighter and more grateful. Does that make any sense?"

"Yes, it does, they are already working with you to move you into a place of gratitude."

"Well, I am grateful for all that has been given to me. I see the benefits in my life, based on my parents. I got to see the generational issues in my parents because I lived with them. Now I know what to watch for in my own children, what to help them with so they can be free."

"Meaning and purpose is a powerful tool."

"I have a better understanding of finding meaning and purpose now, that's for sure."

"I have seen people who went through major events in their lives, things that would put most people in an asylum. By using meaning and purpose, they turned their lives around for the better. For every bad or hard situation that happens in our lives, there is an equal amount of good and positive that comes from it. Remember that."

"I'll remember. Thank you."

"You're welcome...and like I told you before, remember that lessons will come back to you from every corner of your life and then from the lives around you. Stay aware."

"I will."

FRANCIS FIGURED HE would end the session here, thinking Ryan had taken in enough for today. He began to get up to say goodbye, but Ryan felt inspired to take things to a new level of understanding.

"Talking about lessons, can I ask about the big things people go through?"

"Like what?"

"I don't know, like someone who was raped. How can they find meaning and purpose?"

"Wow, your mind really jumps all over the place, doesn't it?"

"I don't know, it's just something that came to me. I just wondered if a person could find meaning and purpose in everything that life throws at them, even with the hard stuff."

"Rape is a very delicate subject. It's about complete control over another individual. A raped individual may have to dig deeper in order to find purpose. I remember one person who shared about being raped. The meaning that they were able to pull from it was amazing. They explained it as having had a prior feeling, call it an instinct, to not be in a certain area at a certain time, and they had dismissed that feeling. Knowing that something wasn't quite right was an instinct that was trying to protect them from harm. From then on, they chose to live at a conscious level and never ignored their instincts after that."

"That is a harsh subject, yes. Thank you—that was a very good example. It's amazing that anyone can find purpose in something like that. They must have done a lot of work on themselves to get to that point."

"Yes, they did indeed, and it was knowledge that they carried with them their whole life from then on. It takes a very enlightened and healed individual to get to that point. To see beyond the act, to get past the trauma, learn from it, and, lastly, to grow beyond it. It's the ultimate destination."

"I really like that part about growing beyond it. So, what about murder?"

"Murder is a valuable lesson. For each life that is taken, we begin to see how delicate human existence really is. One moment we could be breathing, and in the next, that breath can be taken away from us unexpectedly. Recognizing precious moments is important. Tragedies are just that, tragic, but they also have a way of bringing us into awareness. We need to live each day as though it could be our last. Getting past murder teaches us just how priceless a life is.

"What if we all took our time in life and did things more carefully and with purpose? There would be less stress in the world around us. What if we gave ourselves time to work out emotions that could otherwise turn us toward the wrong behaviours—emotions like jealousy, anger, revenge? If we lived in a world full of calm walking meditators who respected themselves and the world around them, then there would be no reason for murder or suicide or even rape."

"You have a good point. Why would someone murder, though? Is there a reason for it? I get the whole 'emotions turn into wrong behaviours' part, but there has to be more to it than that."

"Many have tried to justify their actions. Murder is simply this: it is the robbing of someone of their gift of life. It has everything to do with control. Much like rape, a murder is the result of a choice that is made by an individual. An individual is a person brought up in a society. Unfortunately, these individuals may have come from many societies that are too busy to take their time, to slow down, to walk consciously, and/or to meditate."

"What if somebody is wrongly accused of murder and convicted?" Ryan pondered.

"The judicial system is there to protect the freedoms of all individuals. There needs to be substantial evidence and a burden of proof to convict an individual. Systems are like people—they aren't perfect, and they make mistakes. There are those who knowingly put someone in jail because of prejudice or judgment. Those people are no better than the actual murderers. They're controlling another person's life, taking away their free will and their choices. It still builds the wrong kind of karma. In the end, though, I believe that the truth will always prevail, whether it be in this life or the next. Science and the discovery of DNA is helping with these matters now, in this life that we are living."

"That was profound. What about suicide? How is it a result of society?" Ryan asked.

"Suicide is a personal choice and is sometimes a result of society. Sometimes it's just about a person's mental state."

"How do you know the difference between the two?"

"In the old days, suicide may have been done out of honour, to save face for the family and/or duty for the whole. We saw this in Asian lifetimes and in war situations. In today's world we don't see that happen as much, or at least not quite in that way. Many now claim to choose to commit suicide based on themes like depression, or from seeing no other way out of life situations; and for some, it's merely curiosity to see what's on the other side. Either way, it leaves a mark on those around them."

"A mark? In what way?"

"When someone takes their own life, they sometimes leave others behind without leaving the knowledge others would need to create solutions to common problems. By committing suicide, then the person leaving this world is teaching that in order to deal with their problems they must also kill themselves. Those who lose a loved one to suicide often say that they felt left behind and that they have to do things now on their own. They feel they need to try and find answers that they may never find."

"If a friend committed suicide, how could I find meaning and purpose in it?"

"The meaning and purpose would have to come to that person themselves in the spirit world. Our job down here is to pray for them, so that they can find that meaning and purpose up there."

"Why would we have to take responsibility for their actions?" Ryan asked.

"Praying for them isn't taking their responsibility from them, it's a part of giving it back to them to finish the lesson they aban-doned. We may not agree with them for committing suicide; however, we must accept their personal choice as just that, their choice and not ours. Once on the other side, they are much more level-headed and can see things from a different perspective. With hindsight, most regret the act."

"Why pray for them if we don't even understand why they made that choice?"

"That's exactly the point, we don't always know what lies beneath the decisions that others make in general, or even how suicide became their solution and conclusion. We want them to understand why they did it."

"It would be hard for them to find meaning and purpose 'up there,' though, wouldn't it?"

"Yes, and it's a matter of them finding and reclaiming their innocence," Francis explained.

"Is that even possible?"

"It's a hard journey the post-suicide spirit will take on the other side to find their own innocence. They'll have to come to a place of self-understanding and self-forgiveness, which will follow eventually. They need all the prayers and support that they can get, brother. Had they asked for help from others while living, then others would have known how to pray for them, or to even help them. Once they have taken their own life, the stakes change. There's no going back, and no way to return back to Earth, to try and fix what was left behind. There's no reversing what has already been done."

"That means that we shouldn't judge them, then, right?" Ryan asked.

"Right. Judgment heals nothing; it only creates more pain. Perhaps it's *our* lesson from their choice. They need our compassion even though we may not understand fully yet. However, if we can try to understand why people do what they do, then a kind of forgiveness can occur naturally within us, and in time."

"This may sound silly, but I have to ask: Why *do* people do what they do?"

"Every act is different. In the case of suicide, they do what they do based on what emotion they choose to feed. Perhaps even which wolf they chose to strengthen, up until the point of their decision to kill themselves. What wolf would they feed to get to that point?"

"The black one. Which is no different than me. I fed the black wolf and made mistakes based on that decision. So, suicidal people making the choice to go through with it and actually killing themselves is no different than me thinking about cheating and then acting on that thought."

"Yes, it's all about respecting life, isn't it? Everyone came to Earth to exercise their right to make free will choices. Some of those choices cause good in other's lives, and other choices create scenarios for others to have to try and forgive."

"Speaking of forgiveness, I have a few questions about that..."

"I was waiting for you to broach that subject. I knew we weren't just talking about the guilty deeds of others!" Francis let out a huge laugh. "What is it that you really wanted to know?"

"I've been thinking about Clara's reaction to this whole thing, and that it doesn't seem normal. Don't get me wrong, she was angry and hurt, but she kind of forgave me rather quickly. She's been trying to understand how it happened, and claims that she'd had this feeling deep inside that things weren't right. Instead of saying something, she chose to shut down from life. She seems to be sharing the responsibility of my choices. At first it was a relief to know she blamed herself, too, but the deeper we go with healing my own inner stuff, the more I see how strange it is that she would forgive so easily, or act so civilized about it."

"I can guarantee that she hasn't forgiven you yet, Ryan, and she has probably already made that clear, so don't mix forgiveness up with understanding. Clara understands you and that's partly why she'd see herself as having made mistakes, too. To forgive someone we'd need to see a change in them. That change needs to come with a consistency and a constancy. Clara will likely wait until she feels safe with you again before she'll offer any type of real forgiveness. She's still wary. Trust is something you'll have to earn from her, brother. Until then, it would just be empty words and empty promises from both of you."

"What do I do in the meantime, then?" Ryan hoped for a quick miracle.

"Your job is to focus on understanding, trusting, and forgiving yourself. That's why Clara's reaction is haunting you. You haven't had enough time to prove anything to yourself, much less to Clara. If you were to be put in a situation of temptation right now, I doubt you'd pass the test. So, don't kid yourself into feeling that you're healed anytime soon.

"Look at the conversation that we just had a few moments ago and analyze your mental state for a moment. You feel undeserving of Clara's compassion, even comparing yourself to a murderer or a rapist. That shows me that you aren't even close to understanding why you did what you did with Gloria. That's because you see the potential of cheating on Clara still within you. Think about that. It's a knowing you have inside you that popped up to the surface as we spoke through those topics. Do you understand?"

"Wow. Yes, I do. I guess I was sort of comparing myself to them."

Francis continued, "You said once that Clara mentioned feeling something in her body the moment you cheated. Even though her mind hadn't known, her body had. This is a kind of knowing. Her mistake was in not trusting that feeling. When you finally confessed, she was able to see that she should have trusted her instincts from the beginning, and now she knows that she can trust herself. Not you—she trusts herself only. From now on, those instincts will be on high alert, because she knows that she can trust them. You won't be getting off with anything anymore. The consequence may be that she may never truly trust again, and I can't blame her."

"Me neither," Ryan admitted.

"If Clara had faced you at the time of the cheating episode, you would have caused great damage to her by denying it. She would have stopped believing in her own intuition and she also would have stopped trusting herself fully because of your lie. This mistrust would have a lasting effect.

"The biggest gift that you can offer her now would be to learn to trust yourself again. Don't ask for her forgiveness or expect her to trust you. You'll need to live with the consequences of your choices. You might gain her understanding and trust by your actions some-day, and still there are no guarantees. Expecting forgiveness would be setting both of you up for another disappointment, wouldn't you think?"

"Wow, you just slapped me in the face right there, Francis!"

"Good! So, what now? What's your next move?"

"I think I need to forgive myself first."

"Can you?"

"Yes, but I need to prove to myself that I can be trusted first."

"If you don't, then guilt will haunt you at every corner and temp-tation will find you."

"You can say that again."

"If you don't, then guilt will haunt you at every corner and temp-tation will find you," Francis repeated purposefully.

"Okay, funny guy. Mean what I say, right?" Ryan laughed like a child catching on to jokes for the first time. "How do I begin the pro-cess of forgiving myself?"

"Find meaning and purpose in what you did."

"Now?"

"Sure. Go for it."

"Okay, so because I made mistakes, it caused a chain reaction of events: first trying to change her and then discovering that I'm the actual problem and that I also hold the solutions."

"Halleluiah!"

Ryan laughed again. "The life I chose was keeping me in a state of non-awareness. The more I choose to learn about myself, the more I wake up into a higher awareness. Had I made no mistakes I wouldn't be here today. Gloria was a catalyst for change. Without her I would never have seen my former issues or have found solutions to problems. Because I did seek out solutions, I can now help myself and work on helping others."

"I think you just got promoted to Grade 8 right there. How does your guilt feel when you look at it based on meaning and purpose?"

"It feels like a circle that has been completed. There have been a lot of 'aha!' moments. I feel lighter and clearer now. Is guilt supposed to feel good?"

"Do we have to find meaning and purpose for feeling good now, brother?"

"No, I think I'll be all right. The point is, I don't need to make another unforgivable mistake in order to get it. I also see that Andy saved my ass from a much harder journey."

"Yes, and that's meaning and purpose again right there."

"Would you say that the ego has served me in a good way?" Ryan felt happy to be asking questions from this level.

"Yes, it has."

"Should I talk to Clara about this again?"

"That's up to you, though it's best to let a sleeping dog lie and rest undisturbed. She knows the truth. When—or if—she's ready, she'll come to you. I think that Clara has a lot on her mind right now. I would suggest that you talk about your own journey and what you have come to understand within yourself. Remember, she's the one who must decide when she's ready to walk the path of her own healing journey, and you haven't finished yours yet."

"What if she brings it up?"

"Keep your finger pointed on yourself, and only on you. Listen to her when she's ready. I have a feeling that Clara is staying quiet for a reason and that she's naturally awakened. This would explain a lot about her words and behaviours in this whole situation. She is unconsciously giving you space to address the core issues that had nothing to do with or about her, in order for the conscious her to see if she still wants to be around the person you are becoming. That's a smart move right there. She must like what she sees, or she wouldn't be giving you the time of day. You're a very lucky man; don't ever take her for granted. You're about to enter a new level, but remember this: She's years ahead of you and just wounded right now."

"Her mom mentioned how in tune she was in her younger years."

"Once we're awakened, we never really shut off. Our senses may go dormant like a tree does in winter. You're becoming the spring in her life to force her out of hibernation. You're also the reason for her dormancy in the first place. I bet that was a long, hard winter for her."

"I'm her spring? That sounds like a whole lot of pressure!"

"You better get moving, then," Francis warned.

"Have I not been moving fast enough? Oh, my God. I kind of feel like a bear that has lived its whole life in a cave. I don't know what's beyond that cave or how to handle freedom."

"A bear's instinct gets activated the moment it steps out of that cave. Bears learn a lot from the mother bear. You should take your mother's lead and start using the tools she gave you."

"Tools? Like how to smother people? God, I'm doomed!"

"That's ego talking. Flip to the higher self. What does that angel on your shoulder have to say?"

"You got me there," Ryan said, feeling lost.

"You know how much you healed based on how much meaning and purpose you can get out of any given situation. Just take it a step further now."

"Okay, so you mean for me to find my mom's good traits, right?"

"That's up to you. The question was, what did she teach you?"

"Well, if we're talking bears and caves, she certainly taught me survival depends on tight family units."

"That's a good start. Keep going."

"What she taught me was all the stuff of what not to do."

"Perfect. Now continue," Francis pushed.

"She showed me the importance of the next generation...how to make the kids feel safe and independent so that they can follow their own instincts into the future and fulfill their own destinies. She brought me indirectly toward my helping my own kids. She taught me that baby bears need to someday leave the mother bear, and be out there in the world on their own. First, they must be given the skills to survive, even though it would be easier if they stayed as long as they wanted to. Without her teachings, they wouldn't know when it would be time to leave, they wouldn't know if they were even ready for that change. Especially if she kept taking care of them and didn't give them a nudge to leave."

Francis was impressed. "A brilliant analogy once again, brother. Now we're getting somewhere. Your mom's actions did have a much higher purpose than you thought before, didn't they?"

"Yes, wow, and now that I see Mom from that perspective, I also have a better understanding of her as a person, in general, as well as my dad."

"With this understanding comes a type of forgiveness," Francis added.

"Yes, and my folks come from the survival period. It's not that I need to forgive them, they didn't do things to me consciously, so they don't need my forgiveness. It's more about understanding that my parents' suffering was real to them, and they were just trying to survive. Although they didn't continue to suffer, self-inflicted pain kept them from mending, which made them see themselves as suffering. Did all of that just come together in my head?"

"Miracles do happen!"

"Thanks, funny guy. Seriously, I get it now. Suffering is what we go through during an actual crisis. Self-inflicted pain is after there is no crisis and no war, and yet we keep living as if there's a conflict happening and call it suffering."

"That's a good quote right there, brother."

"Thanks! I needed to process that by getting my anger and frustrations out, so that I could see above it without the emotions clouding everything."

"Anger is a type of anti-venom, then, isn't it?" Francis hinted.

Ryan sat stunned. "Wow, yes. My mom came into my life as a form of my ego to make me hit my head against walls in order to learn. Maybe her higher self knew about the plan from the beginning. This allowed her to work from the ego to help me evolve. It happened so that I could get that anti-venom in a bottle, in case I had other bites from others in my life in the future."

"Now that is a thought. Good analyzing. What else?"

"I've been gaining experience and knowledge by taking time to heal and develop so that I could move forward in the maze. Like you said before, when we go too quickly, we go straight for our death. The ghost catches Pac-Man if the game player doesn't think before he makes the right move—then it's lights out!"

"And that would suck, wouldn't it?" Francis said with a smirk.

"It sure would. Oh, man, I want to learn and grow and take my time. I'm starting to enjoy my time here on Earth. I'd like to stick around for a while without ghosts chasing me, or, worse yet, catching me."

"How wide is your road now, brother?"

"I think my road just narrowed as we sat here today."

"Good. It'll become even more narrow in time. You'll slow yourself down very soon. You can expect less to be happening once you get over the next hurdle. It's a big one."

"I know that I'm still a work in progress, but I do have a sense of pride in getting this far."

"Don't get too proud yet. Breaking your mother's heart seems like an easy thing while we sit here chatting. Allowing for her to hurt without interfering or fixing things is going to be the hardest part of your journey yet. It's a hurdle you must jump over. We identified the programs, but none are changed yet."

"So, watch my program of wanting to please Mom, right?"

"Yes, and let her feel without fixing her. The art of non-interference is the biggest and hardest journey any human can ever undertake. Remember, you can only intervene in your own life. Helping others who aren't ready to help themselves is taking on their karma and their pain. Your mom will be acting out even though her higher self knows that it's in everyone's best interest for change to happen. You must take a step back and get outside the circle, especially since you have chosen to move. Don't get involved in another cycle of karmic ties—the second time around it'll be a lot harder."

"What do I need to look for to not get caught up in another karmic cycle?"

"Be aware of your own control issues. Wanting to fix someone or save them from their personal experiences keeps them from achieving personal growth. That's major control. Tread carefully."

"Thanks for the heads-up."

"You're welcome. Many blessings on the next part of the journey."

"Thanks. I think I'll need all the luck I can get."

"Luck is by chance. Blessings come from the Creator."

"You and that Creator again," Ryan laughed. Though he would never admit it, he was beginning to find strength within himself as he drew energy from that source called the Creator.

"See you in a couple weeks, brother. Don't rush things on this end. Put your time and effort into making that change happen in your life before you come back. I'll be here when you're ready. Let it sink in. I'm looking forward to hearing about the next part of life's expedition."

Chapter Fifteen

Fresh New Beginnings

"How ARE THINGS, Ryan? I've noticed a change in you lately. I get a feeling that asking me here to Sam's Diner has something to do with that," John said bluntly.

"Well, actually a lot has changed and I thought I'd talk to you about it," Ryan explained. He cleared his throat and continued, "Look, I'll be honest, here, Dad. I'm ready to make a big move in my life and the changes coming will affect you and Mom."

John sat up straight. "You're moving out?"

Ryan near fell off his chair from shock. At that moment, the waitress came to the table to take their order, unknowingly interrupting their conversation. They scanned the menu, trying to keep a normal face for her sake, and placed their lunch order. Ryan waited politely for her to leave before getting back into the conversation.

"You are perceptive," Ryan complimented his father.

John jumped in, "I've seen this coming for a while now. I'm not stupid and certainly not senile yet," he scoffed. "I told Maria that if she kept smothering you guys it would come to this, but no, no, no, she just had to do things her way! It's always her way!"

Ryan almost smirked. "Why haven't you ever mentioned anything to me before?"

"Would you have listened?" John asked.

"Actually no, probably not," Ryan admitted. "The old me was too wrapped up in myself to notice anyone else. That's one of the reasons why I've decided that it's time to get our own place. I've been changing, Dad. When we had Clara's parents over recently, it showed me a lot about the kids' and Clara's needs. I can see how Clara hasn't been able to be the mother in our home and that she needs space to grow. We all need that space, actually."

John looked intense. "Yes, I saw that myself...your mother takes over, even though she says that it's to be helpful. But I get the feeling that there's more to this story. I'm scared to know, but you may as well spit it out."

Ryan gulped. "Yeah, there's more. I'm not really sure where to start."

"Start with the truth," John blurted out. The diners next to them stirred and turned their heads for a moment to see what the commotion was all about.

"Dad, I've made a big mistake. An unforgivable one."

"God! No, Ryan, no!" John begged for it not to be true.

"I wasn't faithful to Clara and we're having some problems now because of it. Needless to say, we need space to deal with it and to try to figure things out."

John turned away trying not to attract attention. Speaking in a stressed but hushed tone, he said, "Damn, Ryan! I knew it! You have an amazing woman. What the hell were you thinking?"

Ryan sat ashamed and stammering, "Dad, it... it wasn't planned, okay? I totally screwed up and I feel so ashamed! I told Clara the truth, so I'm not hiding anything from her or anything. I'm taking time to understand how it came to that, to figure out the reasons why I did it."

"To figure out the reasons why you did it? Well, you better hurry the hell up, kid! That's all just a cop-out in my book. If we weren't in this restaurant, this would be a screaming match to get you to understand reason, boy! It would be time to man up, because you'd have one bloody nose! Do you hear me?" John swore under his breath, shaking his head from side to side, causing another stir in the restaurant. It wasn't hard to see that something was wrong.

"Dad, let me explain. I'm taking full responsibility for it—I am. This was my doing."

"You better damn well take responsibility," John insisted. His hands were trembling, and tears welled up in his eyes. He loved Clara like his own daughter. This was a double betrayal.

Ryan took the cue. "A counsellor is helping me understand where it all might be coming from. It's my mess and I'm going to clean it up and save my marriage. I can't see my being able to do that while living in the same house as Mom. You can hate me, but you couldn't hate me more than I've hated myself. I don't want to screw it up any more than I already have and end up losing her for good. Please don't judge me right now, I know that I deserve your anger, but I need your help to make this change. Please, Dad!"

John took a few breaths to try and cool down. "Okay. First of all, let me be clear. You aren't off any hook with me, not yet and not for a while. Got that?"

"Yeah, I got it."

"And secondly, for Clara's sake and for the kids', I will agree to help you, but only because of them. Do you hear me?"

"Yes, I understand."

"What do you need from me?" John asked reluctantly, still shaking his head, repulsed.

Ryan explained about wanting to get a loan, and that he didn't have any equity to secure one at a reasonable interest rate.

"What did Clara say about moving?"

"She does want to move, but we haven't gone too far into the details. I wanted to talk with you first so as not to feed her any empty promises that I can't fulfill."

"At least you thought of saving her the anguish in some way," John threw his words out sarcastically while still holding back his true anger.

"I need your support right now, Dad, not your jabs in my side."

"Okay, I'll stop. Go on."

"It's okay, I don't blame you. I just want to move forward. I'm not expecting you to bail me out and give me money. I just need you to support me for once."

"Of course, I'll be supportive, Ryan. I'm sorry! I'm just upset. No, I take that back. I'm not sorry at all. Have I ever done anything to you to make you believe that I wouldn't support you? Tell me, have I?" John's eyes were gleaming.

Ryan felt ashamed and could clearly see his father's disdain and pure heartache. "That was a judgment on my part. I apologize. Maybe I was just scared. I don't think that you and I have ever spoken this much before, so maybe I didn't know you well enough to know how you would react or what you would say."

John smiled with obvious stress showing on his face. "I speak when I'm spoken to."

Ryan laughed awkwardly. "You make a good point there. I should have spoken sooner. I know that you told me the house would be mine when you and Mom pass away. I don't want to put you out any. If you want to cut me out of your will, I'll understand. I'll check with the bank this week to see exactly what kind of loan we can get and do it on my own."

John sat silent for a few minutes. He realized he should back off a bit and try to deal with this situation with a bit more reason. "You put money into your apartment, so I don't want to take anything from you, either. I think we can work a way around this so that the bank sees the house as an asset. We could even put the apartment up for rent to help pay for your mortgage loan. The house is already paid off, so I don't need that money. Besides, it's been getting harder for us to go up and down those stairs. I wanted to switch apartments, but frankly, I never thought you would be so open-minded. Maybe you are!" John laughed.

"It looks like we both judged the situation." Ryan gave off a beaming aura of relief. The ice was finally broken. "What if we worked it out that you got your wish and created the right space for you downstairs, Dad? Would you want to rent the top half out to somebody for real?"

John was now able to set his quarrel aside enough to think and look at the opportunity he was being handed. "I think if we redid the yard and spaced it out and put another driveway in, it would work out perfectly. We have the right plan, just not the right woman living upstairs to agree to it. Maria is going to be livid. She'll seriously lose her mind."

With tears filling both of their eyes, they laughed together un-controllably like two school friends in the corner. Fear and anger became an anti-venom to allow love to shine through.

"I was thinking about looking at houses near Green River Valley. Clara and I like that area a lot," Ryan explained. "I'd like to go see a few houses with Clara. I just needed to have an idea of what price range I could afford. I do know now, thanks to you. I might also need someone to watch the kids while we're out, without having to an-swer any questions that may come up about why we're moving. It's too fresh for Clara to have to deal with that."

John agreed that it would be a good idea to keep the kids out of it for now and that he'd be happy to spend time with his grandkids. They could do something fun together outside, maybe go to a park or back to that pond, he thought. "That valley is closer to Clara's par-ents and it would be good to be halfway so that both sets of grandparents could get to know the kids."

"It was exactly what I was thinking." Ryan couldn't stop smiling.

"Let me handle your mother. She can be more reasonable than she looks, though she may not take it so well in the beginning. We can expect her to breathe fire for a while. She'll adjust once she fig-ures out the benefit of the change. She'll act one of two ways, threatened or sweet as pie. If she acts sweet, then you'll know that you'll certainly have to deal with her longer. Those claws of hers will be out in secret. If she gets angry right away, we can deal with it sooner.

"Maria isn't fond of changing something that is working, so prove yourself. She'll take comfort in knowing she did a good job raising you. She may even chalk it up to it being her idea all along. At least that's what she'll tell the neighbours," he laughed. "In her eyes, you'll be making a big mistake. Find your house first; be sure everything is set before we stir up the dragon."

Ryan smiled. "You're a totally different character than Mom is. How did you manage all these years to hide this part of yourself from me? I feel like I just met you." Ryan was afraid that he might have gone too far and overstepped, especially after today's events. He decided to allow his words to settle without fixing anything.

"I accepted her for who she is, and I stayed quiet to be there for you guys. Look I won't tell Maria about the cheating. That's for you and Clara to figure out, and it's none of our business. Some experiences are meant to remain your own."

Ryan was grateful his dad volunteered. "So now, I'm leaving for my kids' sake," he declared.

"By leaving, you're showing me how much bigger of a man you are than I am." John lowered his eyes in shame for having admitted that out loud. His jaw was now quivering, "I'll hold off on telling Maria about the move for as long as I can. It's not always easy to reckon with her when she's determined to get an answer to something—and she'll be asking."

Both nodded their heads in an unspoken understanding and began eating.

JOHN HATED LYING and was now in an awkward situation. There was no demilitarized zone in sight in which to seek refuge in this provoked war zone.

Maria was suspicious and hounded him mercilessly to find out why they had gone out for lunch without her. This never happened, not ever, so she knew something was up. John maintained his self-confidence, explaining nothing. All the while, she worked on him endlessly like a dog gnawing on a bone, intending to eventually wear him down.

After a couple of days, John had had enough of her relentlessness. Taking the bull by the horns, he had to make a barefaced move, and quick. In order to uphold his promise to Ryan and keep things undisclosed about the cheating, he chose to tell her about the upcoming move instead. It was the obvious lesser of the two evils. Redirecting her anger and scalding comments toward him would help to bide time. This gave Ryan a couple more days to get things done away from her piercing eyes. John knew that when she was angry, she went quiet. He welcomed the silent relief.

WHEN JOHN EXPLAINED to Ryan that things had gotten heated, and that he'd had to settle things his own way, things took a bit of a tumble.

Ryan snapped and accused his father outwardly, "You are nothing more than a dirty traitor!"

John was shocked and furious. "Traitor? Look in the mirror, buddy! And on top of that, you try being the one to deal with that kind of Chinese torture and not give in! Get the hell out of my face!"

Ryan stormed away.

After an hour of calming down, Ryan decided it was best to hold back his contempt. This situation was new to both of them, and he was putting a heavy expectation on his father, after all.

"I'm sorry!" he said, feeling ashamed. "I'm just nervous. You did much better than I would've done under that kind of pressure."

"Let's hope that it'll help smooth things over in the long run," John replied.

THOUGH THINGS SEEMED perfect on the outside, an invisible and uneasy stalemate remained in the household. Everyone walked on eggshells. Over the course of the following three weeks, Maria stayed quiet and remained upstairs, only inviting the kids to come see her. This arrangement was helpful in a way, as it gave Ryan and Clara the space and time that they needed to get things done. They weren't trying to punish her. They just needed the break.

Ryan knew though that the talons would have to come out eventually. He wished she had gotten her anger out and over with. The wait was a bigger punishment than he could handle. He couldn't sit any longer. He decided to go about his plans.

John came around finally and went with Ryan to the bank. The institution offered them a great percentage rate, based on using John's house as collateral. Things seemed to roll smoothly, rapidly and effortlessly. There was no limit to their happiness. Clara heard the news and started packing, taking her time to downsize as she went along.

The couple took the opportunity to spend time viewing houses for sale, imagining making a fresh start and getting to know the valley. They took in all the views as they drove along while imagining living there.

Clara asked if they could stop and walk along the shoreline of the river. She took in several deep breaths of the fresh air that Mother Nature so gracefully offered to her. The valley was lined with trees in autumn foliage, which made the river look like a golden-lined road. A riot of colour erupted in the autumn forest, with evergreens accenting the orange and yellow backdrop. The days were getting shorter, and the temperatures were gradually decreasing. A flock of migrating swallows flew overhead toward Africa to escape the falling temperatures. This was the life that she had always dreamed of. Living close to nature and having lots of space to spread her own wings. She called on her guardians from above to help her wish become a reality. "I want the perfect house to show itself to us in the next three days or something better and a sign so clear that I can't deny it's the right place."

A few days later, she got the sign she needed. The perfect house that ticked off all her boxes became available. The real estate agent said that the owner wanted a simple transition, and figured they'd be the perfect match for the conditions being offered. The owners had partially moved out and were eager to get into their new place; consequently, they offered a deal, lowering the price on the condition of a quick signing. Ryan jumped at the opportunity, with Clara's approval.

The house was small, cozy, airy, and bright, with a large yard for the kids to run and play in. It even had a tree swing, which was Angela's only request. Two huge eagles circled around the house continually during the viewing.

After having lived in fear for so long, how could it be this easy? Everything had come together almost instantly. Ryan just had to decide to put that fear aside, act, and then voilà, the right house appeared.

Clara suggested they take their time—to paint first and allow the kids to transition first before moving them to a new school. To their surprise, both kids wanted to jump right into their new life and had no issues with any and all changes. Clara took their lead and went ahead and got the kids registered in the new school. Many of the new neighbour's kids were in their classes and so everything fell into place beautifully. The only thing to do now was to make their house a home.

After a couple more weeks, the painting was done. They were all ready to move in on the weekend.

THE FIRST FEW times Ryan went up to speak to her, Maria acted like she was fine and that she was happy for everyone. She kept up a fake smile. The weekend was fast approaching. He and his dad would start to move things over to the new house on Saturday. He needed to try and seek out her approval if he could.

Ryan asked his mother over and over to come see the house. She made several excuses, including headaches and events outside the house that were keeping her busy. He had had enough of her shrug-offs and finally snapped, "Mom! Mom, please look at me! I know you're upset, and I need you to face it. Mom?"

Maria stood up abruptly trying to get around Ryan's arm. It was getting harder to be patient with her and he couldn't stand her disregard any longer. He held his arm firmly against the wall wittingly to block her from going down the hall.

Maria couldn't withhold her anger, stomping her foot and blurting with a roar, "Why are you doing this to me, Ryan? What did I do to deserve this? I did everything for you. Everything! Now, you blame me for bad things. You say I held you back from your happiness?"

"Mom, I never ever claimed that you were holding me back. We haven't even talked, so where did you get that from? What I came to say is that Clara never had a chance to have a life with me because you were always there for us. In many ways, you did too much for us."

Maria busted out and started screaming. The shriek made Ryan cringe and cover his ears. "Clara should be ashamed! She turned you against me!"

Ryan swung his arms forward. "Mom, listen to me."

Maria pushed her son backwards. "No, Ryan, you listen to me! Those poor kids, how could you do such a thing? They're my whole life. I would lay my life down for them. Who will take care of little Ryan now? He's too little to go to somebody else now."

Remembering how Francis altered his tones when helping him through rough emotional waters, he decided to change the pitch of his voice. "Mom, I appreciate you. I'm grateful for the teachings you've given me. Because of you I'm strong now. I know more about the world because of you. If it wasn't for you and Dad, I wouldn't be the person that I am today. I love you for who you are. I wouldn't change you if I could."

Ryan knew that last sentence was a bit of a white lie. He lost focus. "I'm an adult and it's high time for me to live my own life and on my own terms! I chose to move out; Clara isn't the one who asked for this. I'm looking forward to inviting you into our home and taking care of you when you do come over, so that you can feel like our guest, not our servant. Little Ryan will miss you for sure. We all will, but sometimes, it's better to be missed and loved, than to be too close and taken for granted, which is what we did to you."

Maria tumbled down into the chair in silence. She was absolutely stunned and speechless.

Ryan sat down also, feeling a bit wobbly in the knees. He had spoken the words so fast, and so from the heart, that he couldn't even believe what had just sputtered out. It was like a water pipe had just burst and splattered all over the place.

Maria faked the best smile that she could, "Ryan, I'm happy for you to feel strong and to want to do this on your own." She stopped there and held in her bitterness.

Ryan secretly hoped she'd apologize but knew better than to ask for it. He decided instead to grab and hug her. "Mom, you are the first woman I loved. I'll love you forever. You're the inspiration of all the things I do in this life. I'm so happy to have a woman like Clara in my life, also. She's strong like you. It's just time for her to see that strength in herself. I honoured you for many years, and now I need to honour her. I'm ready to be a man, a husband, and a father now. I need to play those roles now, too. I'm not just your son."

Maria was still overcome by emotion, "I don't know if I could ever forgive you, Ryan. I never brought you up to act like this. I'm an old woman and you are causing a major shock in my life that I don't deserve. My heart is beating so fast. I think my health is failing because of all this stress. Clara will someday be sorry for talking you into this. She'll never be able to take care of those children the way that I do, never!"

Ryan lost his patience and got a bit cocky. "*I* did this. *I* decided to move. Get that in your head. I asked Clara to move out with me. Can you just accept that? I'm not asking you for any kind of permission, none at all. I would only hope that someday you'll understand me. I'll pray for you in the meantime to find meaning and purpose in your own life without trying to control mine."

Maria spun around as if to be handling a whip ready to crack it. "What did you just say? You'll pray for me? Since when did you start believing in some kind of God? What kind of brainwashing have you been under? And did you say that I'm controlling your life? No, no, no, Ryan! I won't accept this nonsense. How could you ever speak to me that way? You are the one controlling *me*, here. I have worked day and night for your family and I haven't stopped for a minute. I have slaved and worked and did everything for you! This is the thanks I get?"

"Look, I just want to live my own life. And besides, we're only going to be twenty-five minutes away, for God's sake!"

Maria suddenly laughed out loud unexpectedly, like a jackal about to pounce on a kill. "It's very far, Ryan! Very far indeed! You are my baby, and I've never lived without you by my side for all these years. Who will I be now?"

Ryan tried to hug her again, but she pushed him away. He hit the wall beside him with a thud.

"Mom, I'm your oldest and I'm a man now, not a baby. Did you hear me? I am a man! It's time to accept that. I want freedom. I'm taking it and moving out with it."

Maria turned away in disgust.

"Besides, you'll now have more time with Dad to do things that you never had time to do before."

Maria snapped, "Time with that grumpy old man?" She stood up to turn her back away from him. He was now being officially shunned.

Ryan couldn't help but laugh. He wiped the smirk off his face and tenderly turned her around again to face him. "Yes, I think Dad will have his second wind, and you can be like teenagers again. I know a good little diner that you can go to for a date. I'll even pay for it if I have to."

Maria was in no mood for his jokes and nearly fell over again from exhaustion. She grabbed her head going back down into a seated position so she wouldn't faint. She put her palm toward him as if to say stop, and then pointed at her door for him to get out.

"Come on, Mom. Try to understand, please!"

"Get out!" Maria demanded.

Ryan left, hastily stomping down the stairs. He brooded while pacing back and forth for an hour. He decided he couldn't leave things there and went back up again to talk. He knocked on the door rapidly. The door creaked open and he nearly fell inside. Maria was still sitting where he left her. "Do you still hate me?" he asked.

Maria laughed through her angry tears, her makeup now smudged down her cheeks, and all over her face. Ryan thought for a moment that she looked like she had a raccoon mask on.

"I think we're too old for dates, Ryan, so I don't agree that your dad and I will enjoy our time alone," Maria barked.

"Mom, you are never too old to nurture one another and to get to know one another again. I think with a beautiful woman like you, he'll appreciate having more time alone to woo you."

"Oh, Ryan!" Maria smirked shyly.

Ryan jerked to attention. Where did this sudden switchover come from? Her emotions and reactions were whipping back and forth flippantly, like a pinball machine. He wasn't sure what character was about to come out of her next, the cuddly masked raccoon again or a pouncing black panther.

"You became such a good man, Ryan." That tone of voice was a good sign that she was calmer.

"Yes, and all because of you, Mom. Hug?"

Maria slumped down, shrunken and shrivelled like an overcooked shrimp. Ryan wasn't sure why so many situations reminded him of animals, but he could swear that this was what he saw at that moment. He shook his head to get his senses back.

Maria now wailed out, crying like a woman seeing her man go off to war. She was cut deep, but Ryan trusted his decision, and that made a difference for her. She wouldn't stop him from moving. However, he wasn't going to get off easy.

***

MARIA WOKE UP early and knocked on Ryan's door. "Well, if we're moving out, then we'd better go see that house and make sure there's a big enough kitchen for me."

"Yes, actually we've been getting the house ready, so it's a great time to have you over for a visit."

Maria whipped a look at him when he called her a visitor.

"I'll make sure that you have a special seat in the dining room, don't worry."

Maria wiped tears from her eyes. She had cried straight through the night and continued all that morning. She was utterly exhausted. She still couldn't understand why they'd do something so terrible to her. All the same, curiosity urged her on to see their new place.

John came down and saw them hugging. He winked and gave Ryan a thumbs-up, turning away quickly before Maria circled around to catch him in the act.

Ryan made the big mistake of thinking the dragon was subdued. Instead of bringing his mother to the new house immediately, he and John hung out a few minutes checking around both apartments, figuring out what needed to be done in order to prepare for those new upcoming changes. Maria took it the wrong way and, instead of waiting patiently, she lost it again, yelling at both men, accusing them of not loving her.

She started up the stairs lamenting, "They hurt me! They hurt me!"

Ryan went to her immediately, trying to cool her down. He grabbed the keys, ready to jump in and start the car straightaway. "Mom, I was taking you. I just needed a few minutes first to finalize the plans with Dad so that when I went to the other house, I would know what to look for or what to bring or what to leave here...okay?"

Maria refused outright to listen. "You ignored me on purpose."

"No, I didn't."

Maria was unable to keep her emotions in check and became hysterical, her anger now shifting toward John for forcing her to move to the downstairs apartment. She wasn't going to be ignored anymore. No one would keep things from her or do things behind her back without being sorry. She was now breathing fire! They would be sorry for crossing her. "I am in no mood to see the house today!" The upstairs door slammed shut.

Chapter Sixteen

The Inner Child

"GOOD AFTERNOON, FRANCIS."

"Hello, Ryan. How goes the battle? Fight any dragons this past while?"

"Yeah, I sure did. My whole life turned on its head. We did find a house, though, and believe it or not the papers have gone through, and we're already setting up."

"You do move fast! That's a world record, I think. How did that happen?"

"I don't know. I asked for change and a train came tearing through my life. I think the train is called Francis."

"I can see that. The Great Train of the North!"

Ryan laughed.

"How long ago now did you start this transition again?" Francis asked.

"Well, I met up with Andrew and heard about you sometime back in January."

"Really? Wow—so around nine months now...long enough to incubate a child." Francis laughed. "It took you some time to decide to take the plunge, then?"

"Yeah, back then I preferred needless suffering." Ryan laughed.

"I see that, and look at you now! Wow, you worked hard and in a short time period, too. And now a new house? It must be exciting for everyone."

"Exciting for sure. My mom was the hardest one to convince. She still isn't on board and I don't think she will be for a while but I'm letting her process without my big paws interfering. I couldn't have done it without you."

"You did it all by yourself, brother. I'm just that fly on the wall."

"Yes, or maybe the caboose on the train. My dad surprised me with unexpected support. I told him about the cheating. He was of course pretty upset. However, we did talk it through, and he told me how to handle my mom. He got her focused on being angry with him instead, in order to free me from having to deal with her. I owe him one. I'm happy with the location of the new house and we're pretty well settled in, now."

"What area did you locate to?"

"The house is just outside Green River Valley."

"You found a place right on the river?"

"Yes, I did. How did you know? Oh, never mind, I think the answer might scare me."

"Well, the name of the area kind of gave it away," Francis teased. "And let's just say I had a hunch."

"More like a dream is what I'm imagining."

"You got to love those ancestors for showing us stuff in our dreamtime state. I love the yellow siding. How did it go talking it out with your mom? Did you at least check your ego?"

"Yes, the house *is* yellow! You are freaky sometimes, Francis."

Francis threw him a playful look.

"As for my mom, I said nothing to her about the cheating, but I did face her about the move. She was a bit of a volcano that wanted to erupt but she held back for the sake of peace. I used the gratitude approach as best I could, but my ego took over a few times, which undid any headway I gained with her. She's been silent since."

"There's a lot bubbling inside of her. Let's cross our fingers that true peace will come. The gratitude approach is a beautiful way of honouring someone, and usually leaves no room for arguments. It's a way of speaking the truth without hurting someone. Just be wary. I detect something is up her sleeve. Silence gives someone too much time to think and boil over."

"Thanks for the heads-up, and yes, I can see how gratitude turned things around until I screwed up. I couldn't speak to her as direct as I would like to have. It wasn't my finest day but it felt good to speak from a place of truth even if I was a bit rough around the edges."

"Maybe gentle consistency is what to work on next, eh?"

"Yeah, I lost that consistency when I blocked her in the hallway to force her to talk to me."

"Well, then! At least you recognize it. Now you can find meaning and purpose quickly from the event and you can turn that into beautiful ways to approach her in the future. Right? I don't know anyone who ever gets tired of hearing words of appreciation and honour. But I know lots of people who close off the moment you attack their bad traits."

"I can see that in myself. I'm exactly like that. I lose focus with people like that. When my boss talks to me, for example, he starts off negative, and I just shut down. When his right-hand man comes around, he focuses on the positive first and I feel happier, more creative, and inspired."

"Remember that next time you approach your mom. Also, a person may spend a better part of their life in the workplace, and so bosses could learn a lot from your words right there, Ryan."

"Yeah, I would love to take some of your teachings into businesses and help employers see it from that perspective. That would be cool."

"You may be getting a new calling yet, brother. That's all plausible."

"That would be great, helping people like that."

Francis smiled mysteriously, "Yes, there's nothing better than helping others."

"You mentioned before about schools changing in the future. I've been thinking about the kids and what type of businesses will be out there in the future. If these new kids do vibrate at a higher level, then they will also need a shift in workplace culture, right?"

"Yes, they will. It's exactly what you could be putting time into; researching for that coming new calling, brother."

"Yes, maybe I should."

FRANCIS SWITCHED GEARS back to the now. Ryan was jumping into the future before finalizing things in the present. "Speaking of the new generation, are the kids handling the move okay?"

"They jumped in feet first and acted as though it was a normal, everyday thing. For me, it's like moving overseas, but we're only twenty-five minutes away from our old place. Maybe it's the way I was brought up, seeing anything outside my comfort zone as being far, far away."

"Like a fairy tale, eh?"

"Yes, very much so," Ryan chuckled.

"Where I grew up, I walked an hour or more just for a can of Cola. A twenty-five-minute drive is just a walk in the park. I do see, though, that in your world, this is a big accomplishment."

"Yes, I have made a lot of progress in a short time period for sure."

"I told you that if you followed my lead, I would help you get lost," Francis reminded him.

"I see what you meant by that now."

"You stepped outside of yourself and something happened."

"Yes, and like you said, if something happens then something will happen, right?"

"Indeed, it will, and it did. Now that something is happening, more can happen. Right?"

Both men laughed hysterically.

Ryan spoke up enthusiastically, "I'm excited to see where life goes from here. I'll probably look back on this moment later in life and think that it was all quite a bit easier than I first expected it to be, even though it's a lot to handle all at once."

"Oh, those expectations are killers, aren't they?" Francis chuckled.

"Yes, they are! I hope one day I can look forward in my life and have no expectations."

"Yes, and no attachment to the outcome."

"And I can take it all on unconditionally."

"I think you are onto something there!" Francis raised his eyebrows.

They laughed again. This moment seemed like a dream to Ryan. He felt so free.

"Someone wise once told me I was perceptive."

"A smartass for sure!"

"You do make me laugh. I think these sessions have taught me who I am. I've lightened up a bit."

"Not so numbed by the hum of society's mechanisms, eh?"

"Yes, for sure. I was so wrapped up in my own tunnel vision of how life needed to be, that I couldn't see outside society's perspective. There was no other version of life given to me than the one limited version I had chosen to accept. I hadn't travelled outside that perspective."

"Oh, the places you'll go..."

"As in Dr. Seuss? What's next? You'll be offering me green eggs and ham?" Ryan asked.

"If you want some. Dr. Seuss is a wise man, he is. His books take you outside the box."

"You just gave me an idea for a gift for little Ryan. I think that he would enjoy those books."

"Or maybe they're for you. They could be a self-study-program."

"Yes, and then I can bring them into workplaces to help companies re-evaluate."

Both men laughed. Yet Ryan felt like there was some strange truth to that statement. He knew Francis's tones well enough by now to know when to pay attention, which was pretty much all the time. There was always something subliminal behind his words. He took a mental note and decided to try and sound smart. "Maybe that is yet another key. We are all children, underneath the hard shell of life. We all need to hear it like a child would see it."

"Yes, that's called 'inner child work,'" Francis explained.

"Inner what?"

"Inner child work," Francis repeated.

"Is that the same as that angel self you went on about one day?"

"It's different—but it's certainly connected. The angel self is your subconscious self. The inner child is the childlike aspect of your subpersonality that's aware. Everything we learned as children or before puberty is stored within that mind fragment. We stuff it down so much that we forget sometimes to let it come out to play."

"Wow—so how do you invite it out to play?" asked Ryan reluctantly. He had no idea if this was a subject for him or not.

"There are many ways to do it," Francis explained. "Inner child work is a technique used to get in touch with the true essence of the self. When we connect with the inner child, we learn much more about our true needs. I like to call it innocence. Children are free to speak their minds, to be more honest, and they don't hide what's inside. It's usually later in life that society affects their habits. Inner child work is a way of letting that child aspect of ourselves have a chance to learn to speak freely again.

"Once affected by society, that child hides inside where it knows it'll be safe and not be forced to change for the world. Going inward and tapping into the inner child is communicating with who we were before those outside influences came about. It also touches the inner parts that were a part of us before habits were formed or became in-grained deeply inside of us."

"I have no idea how to work with my inner child or what the hell you're talking about yet, but it does sound interesting all the same," Ryan laughed.

"Your head is still stuck in your 'but,' I see. Give yourself time, brother"

"Yes, *sir!*" Ryan gave him a military salute.

"See, your inner child just spoke right there. When you're free-flowing and unafraid to blurt things out, your inner child comes out. If it feels safe enough, a few more times, here and there, it may decide to come out more. We can tap into it right now if you want."

"Tap into what?"

"Into your innocence. If you're ready?"

"I'm never ready when it comes to the likes of you, Francis. I'm here, though, so why not. I'm open to try something new today."

"Okay, then. Come over here to the table; we're going to do a bit of painting." Francis grabbed the children's acrylic paint bottles from the shelf and placed a variety of colours in front of Ryan, along with a sheet of paper.

"So, what do I do now?" Ryan asked.

"Take any bottle and drop only eleven blobs of paint on the paper."

Ryan tentatively grabbed the yellow bottle first and let four drops fall on the plain sheet of paper. He thought for a moment and then chose the red bottle next, letting out two more drips. He then proceeded to the blue and green bottles and finished it off for a total of eleven globules as instructed.

"Now fold the paper gently in whatever direction that you wish in order to create a symmetrical painting."

Ryan made the silliest face he could come up with. The adult in him then proceeded to fold the paper on a slant. He pressed down lightly, smoothing it out again and again, while checking to ensure that he had a perfectly symmetrical set of creases.

"Now open it," Francis instructed, now folding his arms and rubbing his mouth with his forefinger.

Ryan opened the paper carefully and placed it in front of him. Looking at the painting inquisitively, he suddenly jumped back in disbelief. Shaking his head, he barked, "No!" He was utterly flabber-gasted. Whipping his head toward Francis, and now thinking it was some kind of magic trick, he pushed the paper away. Francis had to have had some kind of secret influence over the outcome of his painting. "How did you do that?"

"*You* did that."

"No, I didn't. You did that, Francis."

"I didn't touch a single drop of that paint. So, how could I?"

Ryan's hair stood on end. He couldn't believe what he was seeing. A dragonfly stared back at him. It was a mix of the yellow, red, blue and green that he had dropped on the paper. The head and body were yellow with swirls of green and the wings were blue and green with a spot of red on each tip.

"Looks like a dragonfly to me," Francis commented nonchalantly.

"You knew it would make that kind of image!"

"I'm telling you, I had zero influence over it. If you don't believe me, make another one."

Ryan wasted no time. He grabbed a new piece of paper, executing the same eleven-drop scheme as he had during his first creation. He used more strategy this time, making sure to employ more paint colours. Then he folded and carefully opened the paper.

His jaw dropped. He now had a perfect multi-coloured cat head staring back at him! "Well, that isn't the same!" Ryan yelled out excitedly. Like a child with earphones over his ears, he didn't realize how loud he was being.

"No, it isn't the same. It never is," Francis explained.

"How can that be possible? Two different things altogether, yet both from the animal kingdom? Why?"

"Only the child in you knows why, brother."

"You spoke before about the dragonfly meaning wisdom. What would the cat mean?"

"Confidence."

"So, am I confident or am I wise?"

"You are neither and both. If you raise a child in the right environment, he'll find his purpose quicker. You were brought up to be unwise and without confidence. You're learning now to become wise and have confidence. That's why the cat came. To give you the confidence you lacked before. The inner child delivered it to you."

Ryan scratched his head. "Wait a minute. Is this what my destiny is? I mean, was I destined to learn and grow, so that I could obtain wisdom and become confident enough to do something?"

"Good job for figuring that one out. So, the answer is yes, and if you do something, something will happen."

"Can I do a third painting?"

"Sure. Go for it."

Ryan jumped in excitedly and plopped two colours onto the paper. This time he used only black and white. The image came out as a perfect insect.

"Looks like a beetle, but I would say it's more like a fly on the wall," Francis teased.

Ryan reached over without thinking and punched Francis successfully and squarely on the shoulder. He snapped into attention for a moment, thinking he hurt him.

Francis put on a show of acting injured and then looked at Ryan with a fatherly charm. He stood with a grace and poise that Ryan had never seen before in anyone. Francis almost looked ghostly for a moment and was sitting straight up with his head forward, as if to be posing for a photo.

For a moment Ryan saw a white glow around Francis and what looked like a huge chief's feathered headdress sitting on top of his head. An eagle bone necklace hung around his chest. He was old, wrinkled, and weathered, and holding a wooden staff with a large feather tied onto the top of it.

Ryan shook his head and readjusted his eyes. Francis cleared his throat. The vision was suddenly gone. Ryan squirmed and changed position in the chair trying to find some kind of composure.

"Are you okay, Ryan? You look like you just saw a ghost."

"Umm, I could have sworn that for a minute I saw you as some old native chief. It was like being in the presence of some great wise man or something."

Francis leaned forward and spoke tenderly. "If you see wisdom in me, then you have earned it. It was a mirror of your own wisdom, brother."

"No, I mean that I witnessed it in you. I have been inspired by integrity." That felt like such a weird thing to hear himself say. He decided to leave it at that.

Francis stared at the floor humbly and cleared his throat. "Any questions on the inner child?"

"Wow, that was intense. I think I'm okay for now."

The room fell silent.

"Can I ask you just one question before I go?"

"Ask away."

"Did we know each other in other lives?"

Francis looked in the corner of the room, as if to be listening to someone who was answering the question for them. He turned his focus back to Ryan. "Yes, we did, brother."

"Do you know who we were in those lives?"

Francis paused another moment, momentarily staring off into the same corner. "Yes, I do brother."

"Did I know that chief in the other life?"

Francis answered in an almost hypnotic state. "Yes, you did, brother."

Ryan wanted so much to ask who he was in that life but left it at that. The room remained quiet for some time before Ryan gestured to leave. He put his hand out and hugged Francis with a pure heart, thanking him for today's session.

It was apparent that the dragonfly painting today meant that there was a definite force behind the events that had been conspiring. There were too many coincidences happening for it not to be real. No one set that painting up but Ryan himself. There was no magic happening in that room constructed to convince him. He knew he had, in a sense, just come full circle.

Perhaps Andrew knew about this past life also. Ryan was now more aware of the depth of their connection. They needed to talk.

***

ANDREW ANSWERED THE phone on the first ring. "I was just thinking about you."

"I know. I've had you on my mind a lot lately, too. I can see this is the kind of telepathy that Francis talks about, huh?"

"Yes, it is, Rye."

"Can we meet up in person? I really need to talk to you."

"Yes of course. Let's head down to the park beside the diner. We can walk while we talk." Andrew knew that Francis had encouraged him to practise the art of conscious walking. He himself had gotten to be quite an expert at it, his movements now graceful, smooth, and not jerky or agitated like they used to be. He wanted to help Ryan master it, too. "Then we can grab something at the diner after. What do you think?"

"Okay, that sounds good!"

Ryan spent the better part of an hour telling Andrew the whole story of what had conspired since he met Francis. "Some of the experiences I had were truly inconceivable! Can I call them spiritual or mystical? I don't know. I can't say they were magical because there was no wizardry or spells being performed. What I do know is this: they were unearthly moments for sure.

"From who I was at the pond incident compared to who I am now is an unbelievable shift. Life has turned me on my head and basically back on my feet again. And Francis...well, I've never before felt such a connection to anyone—or to anything, for that matter. It would take a lot now to break the otherworldly connection binding us; all of us. If that even makes any sense. What I mean is that there's nothing that anyone could say or do to me now that could ever convince me that I didn't see, feel, or hear everything that I have experienced since the moment I met up with you in the parking lot that day. Absolutely nothing! How does that song go? 'I was blind but now I see'? That is me."

Ryan shocked himself. Not just because of his words. He was unable to hold back his emotions as he concluded his rant. He couldn't believe the sound he himself was making. His whimper resounded with a type of tremble that comes from a trumpet blowing slightly out of tune. "I have to thank you, Andy, because I can look you in the eye now and honestly say that you helped save a wretch like me."

Ryan stumbled forward and gestured that he had to sit down. He plopped himself down on the nearest bench and sobbed painfully.

Andy lowered himself down on the bench beside him and allowed his friend space. He knew this was a major turning point...a climax in Ryan's life story. Andy himself felt like a character in a book having just witnessed the long-awaited and mysterious reveal of the narrative. He had listened to Ryan's story, and felt every rise and every fall, tumbling down with him at every juncture before the story even found resolution or reached its conclusion. He couldn't have been prouder than he was at this moment, and to say he was the bystander and maybe even the catalyst for this change was a complete and utter honour.

After some time, Ryan began to recover his composure.

"Wow, that must have been amazing! To hear you speak with so much conviction was incredible and inspiring. Ryan, someday you have to tell your story to the world, really. You have more of a gift of words than you even realize. It looks to me like the biggest gift that Francis gave you was to bring that voice out in you. I felt those moments when I was in Francis's presence, too, and yet I can't say that I had that kind of vision happen to me. Seeing him in that headdress and hearing him admit that you knew one another in a native lifetime...I mean wow! Seriously, that's a gift all on its own, and just for you, Rye."

Andrew then sat there stunned and humbled all at once. To have been able to listen to and witness this new variation of his friend was truly astounding. There was something special about Ryan that kept drawing him back to him over and over in life. Other friends had come and gone, but with him, it was a magnet that had never lost its force, nor would it ever weaken. It only got stronger with time.

Ryan finally spoke. He was curious now about Andrew's real story. He wanted to hear every little detail.

"Well Ryan, I had gotten to a point in my marriage that I couldn't live with myself anymore. It was like I was being forced to go back to sleep in order to live and survive.

"I avoided telling you that Jenny and I had broken up when I first called you because it wasn't time, and I knew that my connection with you wasn't about me. Had I made it about me during that conversation, you and Clara wouldn't be in the same place that you are today. My words would have influenced you too much. You and Clara were meant to stick it out and save the marriage. Jenny and I had already learned what we were supposed to from one another and we taught everything that we could teach. We walked our journey until the journey ended.

"I had several signs that came to me in the past that prompted me to leave. Do you remember that barbecue we had a few years back when I joked about burning my arm for a crazy bet? I believed so strongly that I was right, that I would put my arms in a fire to prove it if needed. And you know what happened next!"

Ryan remembered it clearly. "Yes, I do. Right after you voiced it, you ended up burning both your arms by mistake. It was eerie. I was the one who brought you to the hospital."

Andrew continued. "After that, everything I spoke out loud that summer became a reality—almost like I was causing things to happen. The world was an empty canvas and every time I opened my mouth, the words splashed out, inevitably painting my future.

"It was time to find myself. I wanted to make a change in my life, and it started by my choosing not to drink anymore. I lost a lot of friends because of that. Some saw me as becoming strange for having tea instead of an alcoholic beverage. Why this would make some of them so upset, uncomfortable, or embarrassed is beyond me. I never once asked them to drink tea, and yet I was scrutinized for a personal choice. Those who accepted me are still in my life today."

Ryan thought back to the first day they met up at the diner. "And I did the same thing to you. Sorry about that."

Andrew nodded as if to say it's okay and continued on. "I began to want to live more simply. The more uncomplicated my life was for me, the more things seemed to feel heavier for those around me, especially Jenny. She said life wasn't the same without me being me. I saw right away that I had more weeding to do in life's garden.

"One day I decided to let my main business go. I then mused to myself and later spoke out loud to a friend that I wanted to lie down and rest my body and mind for two months to see what life wanted to bring to me. Well, Life responded to my words all right, and wrote a major sports injury into my story. I was playing basketball and suddenly heard a snap. I ended up rupturing and breaking my Achilles tendon. I was down for two months or more, unable to walk, and had no choice but to lie on my back. I couldn't do sports anymore after that. Eventually I got better, but Jenny was upset. I had changed too much.

"My body was never the same after that. I was torn like a yo-yo. On one hand, I read some books that opened my mind to make life shifts for good. On the other hand, Jenny over-encouraged me to get the old me back and to forget everything that I had learned. She had no interest in this new way of thinking and put exorbitant amounts of energy into putting pressure on me. She was so distraught that I had stopped having a drink along with her, that I eventually gave up on changing myself and I fell back into the old me. I drank in order to accept and control the difficult emotional turmoil I was in. It was the only way I could see myself living a normal life again, despite the confusion that it caused.

"I was lost and I felt weak but I had no other vision to hold onto. I couldn't fall back to sleep. I was way too spiritually awakened for that, without knowing what it was. If I'd had some sort of symptoms list for ascension it would have helped. At the time there was no such thing in circulation, at least not within my awareness, anyway. I found other ways to numb myself to simply stop feeling. My father wanted me to get out in the world and be myself, but even with that freedom I was being offered, I felt trapped because I didn't know any other way to be me.

"We had our second kid. Jenny was happy, and I stayed quiet while she ran the show. I went with it and allowed it, but I was giving up on life. I went from circle to circle trying to find myself. I thought maybe I needed spiritual people in my life but everywhere I went people were empty and unhealed. They were just as programmed as I was and just playing a different role. I felt lured by women and seduced by a world that was no less of a trap or a cage than I was living in at home.

"A friend told me about this guy called Francis who had made his way across the ocean and was in our area helping people. I didn't know what I had seen at the time, but my buddy seemed different, happier. He seemed more balanced, calm, at ease; and I wanted that for me. One session with Francis and my whole life changed. That's when I started dreaming about you."

"The old me would have been majorly concerned for you and Jenny," Ryan recalled. "The new me says, congratulations, brother!"

Andrew smiled and nudged Ryan's shoulder. "I appreciate that, brother."

"Can I ask why Jenny refused to follow Francis with you? I mean, from the outside, you two always seemed so in synch."

"There were many factors," explained Andrew. "She had no interest in coming for counselling with me. She said she didn't want to change something that was still working. It *was* working, but for her, not me. She was happy at the level where she was at. Unfortunately, that stopped her from growing. I had asked her to come with me, many times, in fact. When I finally told her that I wanted to end the relationship, and to follow my own path, that's when she said that she'd go with me. She begged me to come back and claimed she would do anything to keep me.

"It was a trump card that she was handing me, really, and I could've mastered the game, taken control, and turned everything my way. As you saw for yourself, with Francis, the teachings don't allow for games or control. I knew that if she wasn't choosing to do it for herself, it wasn't the right way to do it. Without the hope or the expectation of us getting back together, she wasn't interested in that change for herself. In the end, she never went to see him on her own. It showed me that I had made the right move."

On hearing the whole story, Ryan was shocked. "How did you find meaning and purpose in all of this? What were your lessons?"

Andrew thought for a moment. "Not changing others, nor influencing them, were the biggest lessons for me; and, of course, not controlling others. I honestly think that's a common theme, based on hearing your story, mine, and that of my other friend. Maybe our generation has the same issues. I can say that each and every day of this journey has brought meaning into my awareness. Just by telling my story today showed me that by losing my relationship, I can maybe help other men."

"But don't you miss Jenny? You must still love her."

"I loved Jenny but I also loved her enough to let her go. I don't miss her, I thank her. She taught me that women have their own things to deal with in this society and men in today's age have a journey of their own. Men are trying to fit into a world to become men, and they don't fit into the same box as their fathers did. Our grandfathers before us taught us one way. Guys like you and I are here feeling emotions and dealing with sensitivities that our fathers and grandfathers never had to deal with. They still don't. Imagine our boys in the future? How sensitive will they be? We have a responsibility to figure ourselves out so we can help them so they don't end up hurting themselves like we hurt ourselves.

"Relationships are a type of system. Our connections with our spouses are no different than schools and governments, or even workplaces. Relationships are alliances that will have to change in the future or else they won't last. Just like if government systems don't change with the people, they'll eventually be changed *by* the people. In my relationship, I voted for myself."

Ryan shook his head, "Were you a fly on the wall in my sessions? We ended up discussing many of the same concepts, though you put things together in ways I hadn't yet gotten to."

Andrew laughed. "Come on, let's grab a bite to eat."

Chapter Seventeen

———

Finding Balance

A MONTH LATER AND with four more of his mentor's sessions under his belt, Ryan was feeling stronger and more confident. He wanted to show Clara the new him and worked hard on showing consistency. Francis took time regurgitating concepts that they had been learning up until this point. The review was good for Ryan, allowing him time to practise steps that he missed in the beginning, based on having viewed them from an egoic perspective. Dealing with his inner turmoil and understanding his own control issues used to irk him. Now he was partial to these subjects and looked forward to going deeper into topics without bringing his mother into it.

He was preparing himself for a much-needed talk with Gloria. Francis was edging him slowly toward the correct behaviour he would need to maintain, in order to not draw any parts of the old self back. Ryan would need to cut the cord in a concise manner, without upsetting any apple crates before meeting Gloria in person. One particular crate being Clara. He needed to prove to her first that he saw himself to be trustworthy, so as to not stir up any old resentments.

Clara was seeing a difference in Ryan and was more open to allowing him to hug her here and there without hesitation. She still urged him to let her take it slowly. They continued going on their weekly dates to the diner, in order to get to know one another in the now. Unknowingly to him, Clara had scheduled an appointment with Francis for herself. She was eager to talk with her husband one day about all of these concepts he'd been learning, as they seemed to have influenced such a prolific change in him. Seeing him act so sure of himself allowed her to relax, without wondering what he was up to. Though she didn't trust him entirely, she and the kids were safe for now.

RYAN HAD SOMETHING he wanted to say to Clara and was determined to get it right. He took a long drive to rehearse. A mouse scurried in front of the car as he approached the driveway, and he avoided hitting it. He ran into the house and grabbed her by the waist, pulling her close, and tried to hide the mischief in his eyes. "How are you, wife?"

Clara smiled. "I'm wonderful, husband."

Ryan took a moment before he spoke. He hugged her again more deeply and then rested his forehead against hers with a sigh. He took both of her hands into his and looked her in the eyes.

She smiled again, a blush now developing like a burning flame crawling up her neck. She often got flushed when given too much attention.

"Clara, I know that you had mentioned that you would be interested in meeting with Francis and I was sort of expecting you to go, but after talking with Andrew and hearing his viewpoint on it, I decided to not push you. I want you to get settled and to get to know me.

"I'm happy we made this move. I know that changing houses didn't change us as people. But because of the move, I hope to make better decisions and no mistakes. I don't blame Mom for our relationship anymore. I have an understanding now that everything happened for a reason. It led us to make decisions together—and look at us in this house now, it's wonderful! From here we can grow together as a couple and as a family.

"I want you to know that I can't promise that I'll always be perfect. I won't always be aware of everything that's happening. I may not say the right things or make the right moves. I'm learning to be a better version of myself: a person who lives authentically, a person that knows himself well in the now and also knows who he wants to be in the future. If and when I ever stray from that path or I'm not being mindful or centred, please tell me. I may not always recognize it myself."

Clara was listening intently. She shook her head yes. His words were obviously rehearsed, but they were sweet and sure, as well as reassuring.

Ryan continued, "I want to thank you for being in my life, Clara, for not giving up on me, for not trying to change me. I shifted things, but I know I'm not healed. I still have a long journey in front of me. I know that before, I wanted you to change to suit me. Now I just want you be free to be who you are. Just do it by my side, is all I ask.

"I want to marry you again, Clara. I want to have a ceremony someday, a wedding, an event where I'm present and aware. I barely recall our wedding or that time period. You married a boy. I want you to marry the man..."

Ryan was hoping Clara would jump in his arms and that it would be one of those romantic scenes from a movie where they hop into bed instantly and make mad passionate love. It didn't happen. She followed him faithfully right up until the words, "I want to marry you again."

Clara let go of his hands, stepped back, and then looked into his eyes fearfully. Her insides quaked, but she braced herself and breathed deeply to keep calm and refocus her mind. "Ryan, you're right. I do feel a lot more freedom to do what I want now. After the move I have gotten a better sense of who I am and I'm enjoying this new area. Yes, you're different now. I don't know who this man is in front of me that I just heard talking, though I think that I'd like to. It's refreshing, it really is. I'm just still a bit wary and I don't want to get hurt again. If you have truly become the person that you've been showing to me, then I wonder if I'm going to be good enough for that person now because I'm not there yet. I would love to say yes let's have that ceremony, but I have things to work out before I can get there. A lot of things.

"I want you to give me some time to learn about me. I've scheduled an appointment with Francis for next week.

"I'm very proud of your growth. However, I still need time to heal and process my own feelings, first, before I can accept seeing you in this new updated format. Right now, my own inner conflicts would take that confidence out from under you. I am quite aware of that. So, my answer is not 'no,' I am just saying, speak more like you did just before the whole 'marry me again' part. Okay?"

Ryan nodded his head in agreement. He was so much in bliss that her words didn't faze him. He had a knowing that he would have that ceremony and nothing could change that.

"I've kept it to myself until now, but I have met Francis. Just once, though!" Clara admitted.

"What?" Ryan stared at her.

Clara never let on that she had met him, nor did Francis. They were an obvious perfect mysterious match, and Ryan knew she'd soon be in good hands, but still!

"Really?"

"Yes, after you claimed that you were going to see him, I was still very suspicious of you, to be honest, and I wanted to see where you were going. I must confess that I followed you."

Clara took a breath and continued, "Sometime after that, I mustered up all my courage and drove to the building. Shaking like a leaf, I went inside, took a deep breath, and knocked on his office door. I don't know what I was expecting to happen. I just wanted—no, actually, *needed*—to meet him!

"He looked like a gentle and kind man. He greeted me with a smile and asked if I was lost. I was taken aback and told him that I didn't know yet. So, we talked for a while about this and that. I can't recall the whole conversation, something again about getting lost. I thought that odd, but gave thanks and left. I didn't tell him who I was. After leaving his office, I decided that you needed to do your own thing and I needed to do mine. I knew that if you did it on your own without me interrupting it, the changes you made would be from your heart. It would be for yourself, not me forcing you or interfering with your process in some way."

Ryan chuckled to himself. He had no inkling that Clara would ever check up on him like that. Francis was right, she didn't trust him and maybe never would. He had to learn to be all right with that. His actions were what had put her in that position in the first place.

Clara continued. "So, while you did that, I started wanting more for myself, too. I started taking walks in nature, meditating, and taking better care of myself. I made a list of things that I liked and disliked in my life. I started journaling to process my feelings, and realized that before that point I had fallen to pieces. I'd lost myself along the way, and I had no passion or drive anymore. When I looked in the mirror, I didn't like what I saw. I was a broken shell of who I once was. I was numb and hungover, a walking zombie that had puffy, dead-looking eyes with dark circles all around them. I covered myself with makeup to hide it. That person looking back at me scared me straight. I knew then and there that the kids and I deserved better than that.

"I had stopped drinking to soothe myself some time before that, and I didn't want that anymore. I needed to be stronger for myself and the kids, because I didn't know what was coming and I needed to step up. So that's when I decided that I wanted to be a better version of myself. I didn't know who that person was and, more important, who she wanted to be. By the time I found out the truth about your excursions with Gloria, I was already deep in a kind of depression.

"I've made a lot of progress on my own, but I'm not done. I have so much more to learn, to heal, and to do in order to grow. I want to find that path for myself, though I'm well aware that I'll need someone to help me through that process, which I think may be Francis. If he could turn you around, of all people, then I trust that he can help me also. I've already seen the changes between us and I'm hopeful that we can build a better tomorrow. I just need you to please honour my journey and give me time to figure things out before putting me on the altar again!"

Clara had spelled it all out, and was now feeling at peace and able to finally catch her breath. She looked up at Ryan, puzzled as to why he was laughing. Why would he act like this? She was suddenly ready to club him over the head with something, but couldn't find anything dangerous enough to satisfy the craving.

"I'm sorry for laughing, Clara. Once you've gone to Francis a few times, you'll understand why I have to chuckle over all this, so please forgive me."

Clara was still confused.

"I can see how in just one visit, my mentor downloaded the path for both of us," he explained.

Clara smiled distrustfully, still not understanding what Ryan meant. She didn't want to get into it. She was more concerned about being understood for having kept from him that she went to see Francis in the first place. "I thought you'd be angry if I told you."

"No, I'm not upset at all," Ryan consoled. "I'm actually happy you met him."

Clara continued, "Francis was an incredible man and he showed me a respect that I have never felt before in my life. Each time you came home, I saw more and more of his honorable personality traits coming out through you. Now sitting here with you, listening to you and seeing all the changes that you've made, I can say that I'm impressed. It changed us both and it's rubbing off on the kids, also. It's an example of what made me want to set up the appointment with him, actually."

Ryan was curious. "What exactly did you and Francis talk about that day? I've gotten to know him better, and I would say that he did know exactly who you were by the end of it or maybe even from the beginning. He never let on to me that you came. It seems so strange and yet so *him*. Are you sure you never told him anything?"

Clara sat back a moment to think. "Actually, I'm sure that I didn't tell him anything specific. I guess maybe I did say a few things. I seemed to just babble on about nonsense, to be honest. It was like a water pipe that had busted open, and I couldn't shut myself off from talking. It was as if he had some kind of gift or like a magic wand that was drawing it out of me. Maybe I was just too embarrassed to tell you that when I first admitted that I met him."

"Yup! Francis certainly has a gift to get people talking," Ryan admitted.

"I can't remember all that I said," she explained. "The gist of it was that I was struggling and fumbling over my words. I was nervous, yet drawn to him at the same time. I can't explain it. Somehow, I left the office feeling that some kind of huge turnaround had happened within me—and yet on the other hand I could say that nothing had happened. I'm afraid I'm going to sound crazy if I say any more."

Ryan was busting a gut laughing, as this situation was getting more and more familiar. Now he knew how Andrew felt, knowing he was sending him into the lion's den (or better yet, the wolf's den), yet saying nothing at all. It was hard to hold back, but he knew it would be worth it in the end. Clara walked in that office and marched right up to the alpha wolf, all unaware. She got to see the beast for what it really was: a gentle lamb in disguise. He himself hadn't had that luxury!

Clara was innocent, and so there was no need for the wolf in Francis to become aggressive or to show the rules of conduct in its territory. She was hiding nothing from herself, and the wolf would have smelled that off of her immediately. This only meant one thing. When Ryan went to the office that first day, the wolf didn't like what it smelled. He went in with a hidden agenda, with the wrong intention, and he wasn't being honest with himself. The wolf sensed his fear and reacted to it. This is why he didn't meet the lamb till much later.

Ryan's first encounter with Francis was the mirroring of truth that revealed all. The black wolf in Ryan came in snarling, and so Francis had no choice but to snarl back. The situation was a mirroring of Ryan himself being cast back at himself. Ryan regretted meeting Francis that first day, only because he couldn't see that what he hated most was his own reflection, his own truth; his own smell. When he saw himself, he blamed it as being the reflection of others—Clara and her parents. He was so wrapped up in himself he couldn't see the truth. Now he knew the difference. He imagined himself tilting over and smelling his armpit, "Smells good now!" He giggled to himself. He wasn't giving off the scent of fear anymore.

Clara continued on, unaware of the internal comedy act that was happening inside her husband's head. "Long story short, that's when I asked him for his card for the future. I do remember one thing he did say, that we are all seeds of the Earth and what we grow into is up to us. I had no idea what he meant at the time.

"Recently I was thinking back. I remembered you brought those plants home and one day when I was watering them, it was like everything became clear. It dawned on me that I really was one of those plants and that I was actually beginning to grow. He also mentioned something about following him. I can't remember the exact words. Before that, though, he told me in a calm and fatherly voice to reach out to him when I was ready to get lost, or something like that." Clara shook her head knowing that wasn't exactly the way he said it and wished she could remember.

"Follow my lead and I'll help you get lost?" Ryan asked.

"Yes," she almost hummed when she spoke. "That sounds like it."

Ryan chuckled. "Only Francis could put things together so magically with no magic at all. Wait until you get to know this guy better. You and I will have many conversations later to catch up on, but to explain it now would ruin all the fun. I'll say no more. Instead, I'll let you have your own experience with him. We'll talk more after you get a few sessions under your belt. I don't want to influence you in any way.

"It's okay that you don't trust me and you can check up on me anytime. I don't mind. Would you want that for yourself, though? I do need to earn your trust, even though I don't deserve it. I'll try my best, I promise that.

"I know you said not to mention a ceremony. I just want to say that if ever the day comes, I don't want it to be like our first wedding and reception. That was all about the venue, the food, the decorations, and just for the show and pictures. It looked great on the outside and all. That isn't who I am anymore. I'd go for something simple and ask Francis to officiate it. I know that isn't on your radar yet, and I'm not going to push it on you, don't worry. I just want you to know that this is what I dream of. It's my personal goal to become the right man for you so that you would want to marry me again. I want the kids to be a part of that ceremony, too. So that's my focus and my dream.

"I am learning to be true to myself, and learning to change for me and not for others. I'm learning to live with integrity and stand firm for what's right. I want to be able to be honest with myself so I can fully trust myself. I want to say with absolute assuredness that I'm a man that stands for respect, honesty, trust, and love. I'm done with the old me that was the opposite of all those things! And if someone in my old world doesn't like that new me, then I'm okay with allowing them their own space to be themselves and think what they want about me. I understand that some of those people are not truthful to themselves anyway. I was there, that was me, and that's why I understand and won't judge. But I'm okay standing alone if I have to."

"Wow, I like that, Ryan. I'm happy for you!"

"But first things first. I'll wait for you to come to me. You'll know when it's time or if it's the right thing to do. If you can't after that time period and want to divorce me instead, I want Francis to officiate that, too. You can divorce me ceremoniously and I will face any trial you need to put me through. I'll follow your lead, my lady, and you can help me get lost."

***

JOHN HAD BEEN busy prepping his own house and painted it on the inside. Reluctantly Maria agreed to moving downstairs. She allowed them to move things down slowly to allow her time to adjust and to get the house in order. She had remained relatively quiet but had a few outbursts at Clara. She refused to believe that Ryan was the one who wanted to move out.

Ryan decided he wouldn't stay quiet about it anymore and stood up to his mother. "Mom, it may be best that I start keeping my distance if you're going to treat my wife like that."

Maria didn't take the threat very well, but held her tongue reluctantly.

"I don't want it to come to this. Really. So, for the sake of our family not having to split up over this situation, could you please get it through your head that *I* wanted to move out. Do you understand what I'm saying to you? I'm the one who asked her to move, not the other way around. Really, Mom, seriously. I've had enough!"

"Yes, okay, Ryan!" Maria agreed finally. "I believe you. Now stop yelling at me."

"I'll only yell if you ever put her down again, and I mean it. Enough!"

"I said okay, Ryan!"

"Mom I love you more than you could ever imagine. I still need you, just not in the way I did before. I want to invite you over and have an official visit. Not just these flippant quick little visits you've been doing. Please let us have you over for a day and let us treat you for once. Come on. What do you say?" Ryan pleaded.

"Okay, honey, how about this Sunday. I can bring lasagna."

Ryan couldn't help but laugh. His mother could be relentless at times. "Let us take care of you for a change. Let us make you the lasagna."

"Okay I'll make everyone's favourite dessert, then." Maria laughed last.

SPENDING MORE TIME at home was helpful. Ryan managed to shift his position at work so that he could work from home a couple of days a week on a permanent basis. Overall, they were gaining a strength and momentum together as a family unit. It was nice. There were a few glitches to work out, however. Maria occupied too much of Ryan's mind still. She was hot and cold, good one week and the next she was acting out, angry and bitter. It got to be too much. Angela seemed to be having little episodes herself, where she got a bit distracted and even secretive. This was a complete puzzle to Ryan.

Thankfully, Clara was a much different woman than she had been. She was confidently in charge of the household; a bit tired, maybe, but she was shining from the inside out. She had gone to a few sessions with Francis now and seemed to be enjoying them. Ryan

was careful not to ask her too much, though internally he was itch-
ing to know everything. He enjoyed watching her beam after each
session. Things were a lot smoother between them now. The shifts
he made were well worth it.

Little Ryan was doing the best of everyone. Monica had visited a
few times, staying as neutral as possible as to not overwhelm them.
She gave them some helpful suggestions on how to handle him and
her techniques were working well. He was already sleeping in his
own bed now, was eating better, and having fewer tantrums. What
a blessing!

Chapter Eighteen

All Four Corners

"Wow, LOOK AT you. A new man in the making."

"Yes, I have changed even more so, since the last time you saw me. It's why I took a couple of months off from coming."

"Oh yeah? Let me guess. Your job this time?"

"Yes, actually, that is right; and the kids have shifted also in good ways and in bad. Angela has been going through something. I figured out this week what that something is and it scares me. I have no idea how to handle this one."

"Oh, oh!"

"Yeah! I call it a stage but I'm not sure if that's the right word for it. We'll have to talk about that in the session, if you don't mind."

"Yes, absolutely."

"Firstly, I have to tell you something. We seem to have a new little boy in the house. Little Ryan is calling himself 'Bryan' now. The 'B' stands for big. So together it creates B- Ryan. He's been asking us to call him that instead of little Ryan."

"Yeah? Good for him for breaking out of that box. The new name is actually well thought out. Next, he'll be asking you to legalize the name. Talk about evolution, eh?"

Ryan sat for a moment and thought that one out. "Actually, to have his own identity and not have to carry my karma with him is not such a bad idea."

"There you go. Check! That makes for one lesson learned and brought full circle." Francis licked his pointing finger and pretended to flip a paper chart, and then drew a large check in the air. "So, what was this about Angela and some stage she's in?"

"Um, yeah, I'm battling with a gift my mom gave to her a while ago, and that we only just found out about."

"Oh, no! And what was the gift?"

"Can you believe that she gave her a cellphone?"

Francis cupped his mouth loudly with his hand. He was astounded, "For once you shocked me. Really? No way! Your mom? For Angela?"

Ryan never heard Francis so speechless. "Yup! Mom bought it, and activated it and snuck it to her before I even knew Angela had it. When I checked into the time log, I realized she'd had it for a couple of months without our knowledge. I wasn't even able to react, Francis! I can honestly say that was the biggest shock of my life. I feel like I don't even know my own child.

"Mom told her it was 'their little secret' and that she wanted to stay in touch because she missed her so much. Mom called every day after school to find out about her day. Angela had been acting funny, it was plain to see—still, I never thought this was the reason why. She was never the kind of kid to hide something. I mean it was right under our eyes, Francis! It made me realize that anything can happen to kids if parents are not paying attention. We were so busy with the move and settling in, combined with saving our marriage, that we both lost sight of engaging with the kids. We talked about that afterwards.

"No matter how much I asked, Angela wouldn't tell me herself how long she'd had it. I wasn't a happy man, to say the least. How could my mom do that? To put Angela in that position? To put that kind of burden on her shoulders? It was like the teamwork that we finally built together had been suddenly destroyed. I lost every teaching you gave me, as I went right back to my old self and then jumped directly inside the turtle shell. I wanted to stay there, to sleep in and never wake up again."

Francis was still in disbelief. "Oh my, and you thought that by moving out you would have freedom from your mom, eh? That problems would just go away if you ran away? I don't want to say I told you so, but I did say I sensed that she had some kind of trick up her sleeve. I just couldn't put my finger on what that might be. Now we know, right?" Francis tried very hard not to laugh, though he was unsuccessful. He covered his mouth and his whole belly shook.

Ryan also laughed despite himself. It was an unbelievable situation, after all. "I know, I'm just exasperated with the whole thing. Little Ryan—I mean, Bryan—is now begging for a cellphone."

"What did you do about it?"

"I gave Bryan a flat-out no. I almost took the phone from Angela but decided to wait and think on things. I also almost went to my mother to tell her off, but Clara stopped me."

"I guess you missed one corner, eh?"

"I guess I did. Angela was the last corner I would have looked in to find a problem."

"Your mom knew that, too. I told you she has a well-played-out strategy and a good golf swing!"

"Yes, you sure did. What am I going to do?"

"It's a hard one. If you take the cellphone from Angela, you take away her freedom. If you let her keep it, you lose Angela. On top of that, *you* lose *your* freedom. By allowing her to keep it, she is bound and enslaved to her grandmother's gift because of its original intention. Now that she has it, she is likely attached to it. So, yes, what to do?"

"I was hoping you would have some insight on that situation. I'm lost."

"I see it like this: number one, your mom has just taught Angela to hide things, and to lie. This now means that Angela lost her innocence and now she also lost her trust in herself. Correspondingly, you and Clara have lost trust in her. Two, Angela was given a gift that would also enslave her to technology, and somebody has to be the adult and remedy that situation."

"Yes, she is also at my mom's every beck and call. Angela said that when she doesn't answer her call, Mom gets upset. I'm seeing myself in Angela, feeling sorry for her and not wanting to say no."

"Then say no for her."

"What if I hurt Angela?" Ryan asked.

"You surely will hurt her—I can guarantee it. She'll understand faster than she may forgive you for it, though."

"That doesn't make any sense."

"Within her core, Angela knows she doesn't need a cellphone. Deep down inside she wants you to make that choice for her even if she doesn't understand it on a conscious level. She's only a child. You need to be the adult and decide, not her. Later, if you talk it over as a family and make a decision to allow a cell, that'll be different. Letting Angela decide for herself is a cop-out. What if something negative happens to her because of that phone? Who will be to blame? Not you, right? Because you didn't decide for her. So, what, then—blame it on the kid?"

"She's already so attached to that phone, though, like you guessed," Ryan excused.

"Yes, and she got attached to it because she sees nothing wrong with it. No one told her the difference. She only feels guilt because it was a secret. It's a shiny toy that outmatches all other previous toys. And a tool to help her fall asleep like the rest of society has. Everyone is tip toeing around her now and not saying anything. Letting her keep it will for sure teach her that having it is okay. By doing that, you're also teaching her that sneaking and lying and deceiving is also okay. How could she know better if you don't make that choice for her?

"This is a hard sandwich to be between, I admit, but Angela was set up. She was framed, formatted, trapped; pick a word for it. She was tricked into becoming a liar by being coaxed into hiding it from you and Clara. Now she has no choice but to play a role. What role that will be is up to you. Either way she is stuck in the soap opera of your life now and, like it or not, she's a part of the action taking place in the series. Everyone is now just watching, wondering what will happen next...yet the episodes seem to go on and on and go nowhere.

"You're the ones who need to set her free from the guilt that she now carries of becoming a liar. Her innocence was taken by her grandmother's putting her in the position to lie. That is massive control right there, brother! You either protect her or lose her to the soap opera."

Ryan nodded his head in agreement. "I see how that control works now. If I let her keep the phone, I'm also a controller by doing nothing. I worried so much about the phone becoming a habit. She started using it and didn't want to read books like she used to."

"We have an age limit on driving for a reason, right? There is an age limit on cigarettes and alcohol. What age limits are there on cellular devices?"

"Wow, I never looked at it that way before."

"Cellphones are no less harmful and could become an addiction all the same. Not to mention other harmful effects. It creeps up like a drug, alcohol, or cigarettes. Cellphones are sometimes even more dangerous than drugs for kids that age, just for other reasons."

"Yeah, like Wi-Fi going through her body and the electromagnetics. I've been researching it."

"Good. All parents should be aware of the damage it can cause to young bodies. That's one good reason why an age limit should be put on cells. Kids have no idea how dangerous it could be to drive a car right? Yet they find it fun. Cellphones and internet access are dangerous vehicles that society uses to drive themselves to different places in life. This is a subject with many layers, and parents have an obligation to think things through before simply handing over a cellular device to a child. It's a type of neglect, otherwise, which is no different than abandonment. Both neglect and abandonment are types of abuse, don't you think?"

"Yes, they are," Ryan agreed.

"Not to mention the dangers of other outsiders suddenly having access to the child through any kind of social media or platforms that they may be on."

"This is really a hot topic for you, Francis. I feel there is more to the story."

"You're right about that, brother. I have personal experience of counselling a family after their daughter committed suicide because of her experience with such things."

"Wow, really? What happened? and how old was she?"

"She wasn't much older than our sweet Angela. Just by a couple of years, maybe."

"No way!"

"Yes, way. She was being bullied. The family initially blamed it on the intimidations. Later, as they investigated and went further through the phone logs, they also found evidence of an older man who was pursuing her. Where she felt alone among her peers, she saw herself safer with a stranger, and he knew to use that to take advantage of her. He reached out to her to soothe her through the situation. She told him things instead of going to her parents. There was one log that showed she met up with him near the school at least once. Not long afterwards, she decided to end her life...if that is what really happened. We'll never know the truth behind the situation or how her life really ended."

"How could the parents let that happen?" Ryan asked, stunned.

"I will be honest with you, brother. It was a similar situation to yours. The girl got addicted to using her parents' cellphone for games and such. Her grandmother saw her as suffering from not having her own phone, and went out and bought one as a gift. The parents allowed it, seeing nothing wrong with it, and left her be with the phone undisturbed. Two years later they lost her to this situation."

"I bet they're sorry for it now."

"Yes, they are very sorry indeed."

"Did they catch the guy?"

"The only evidence they have is someone befriending a child. He got off with a warning and is now under surveillance. Of course, he could change his name on any media platform."

"How does the family deal with that situation? It must be horrible knowing now what they didn't then. I mean, it was right there in front of them, and yet they were blind to it. How could you live with yourself afterwards?"

"They use that hindsight as a kind of meaning and purpose now by giving others foresight. The family now goes to schools and to anyone who will listen. They share their story, they spread awareness, and they save others from the same tragedies. I share their story now with you because they have asked me to use it when or if I feel someone needs to hear it."

"I'm grateful for that," Ryan announced. "I can say honestly now that I was innocent to the social media part of it and what the repercussions could have been and could still be if I don't educate myself and Angela on the matter. My mom gave it to her thinking of herself, and yet without even knowing the dangers she could have put Angela in."

"Yet another corner you missed, eh, brother?"

"Yes, and it was really the first thing I should have looked into. Social media platforms could possibly allow anyone to be in contact with Angela and I would have no clue about who, what, where, when, or how."

"Yes, you would have no idea unless you were watching her each and every time she was on it. That isn't always possible. So, what is the right thing to do in this situation?" Francis asked.

"I'm clear on one thing. I'm taking the cell from her immediately. I'll choose to be the action taker in this situation because I love her, even if others see me as the bad guy. I really don't think my mom will understand," Ryan worried.

"It's not about helping your mom understand right now, it's about protecting Angela. Attention, and detail within the situation, is what she needs from you right now. Otherwise, you are again an accomplice in a type of abuse."

"Thank you, I think I know what to do now. I'm going to put an age limit on cellular devices in my house, and my mom will have to abide by the law of Ryan!"

"Good one, I like that."

"I already know that Clara will agree with my decision. I'll limit visits with my mom if ever she goes behind my back like this in the future. No matter how small the act may be, I won't ignore it. Clara was very upset about the phone, and asked me to talk to you about it to get your perspective first before we acted."

"She's a smart one to pass it over, isn't she?" Francis bellowed out with laughter.

"She is!"

"Everything will be fine. Think of it as training for when Angela is a teenager and you have to let her go out on a date with some boy."

Ryan snapped, "Oh, no! Don't even go there, Francis!"

"It's just a matter of time, brother. The more involved you get with your kids now, the more likely they'll trust you with their personal lives in the future. Make the connection before it's too late."

"Good advice. Thanks, I will."

FRANCIS COULD SEE that Ryan needed to shift gears in the conversation. "So, you talked about other personal developments. Something about your job?"

"Yes, a lot has been shifting in that area, too."

"What's your job, anyway? And what do you do, exactly? I don't think I ever asked."

"I work as a software engineer by trade. I'm using my creativity more, which I love. I report to the right-hand man now, the one who gives a lot of positive feedback."

"So, you get to avoid the other dragon in your life now, eh?" Francis jested.

"Yes, somehow it just all worked out. I don't see the big boss very often. Which works better for both of us. Our personalities were never meant to work out of the same room. Now when I do see him, it flows better."

"Probably because you aren't stuck in each other's hair."

"You can say that again."

"Again? Are you sure?" Francis asked.

"You almost got me there again, didn't you?"

"More or less!" Francis winked teasingly. "So, what now?

"Well, I work a bit from home now. It's like having a part-time job: I'm much more focused and I end up having more time on my hands to try other things out.

"I've been thinking about that day we talked about helping companies. I've made some pamphlets, created a website, and set up general descriptions for classes or courses that would be tailored to the specific needs of companies. I've already had two businesses that have hired me to come in and talk about workplace culture. They gave me an open-ended invite and will wait until I get the curriculum finalized before I jump in full-tilt. I want to bide my time and do it right. I asked them to give me four to six months to work things out."

"Wow, to agree to wait that long, they must trust that you'll deliver. That's great. What will this curriculum entail?"

"I'll be setting up new habits that will ensure workplace success. Also, it'll help new recruits and students who will do workplace training. It'll ensure a brighter tomorrow for the generations to come. It allows the students experience and helps the companies get ahead for free. Then the students have good references to put on their resumes. It's a win-win situation. In return, the students give ideas to help companies remodel their way of doing things to fit with the new generation's way of thinking.

"I want to design it around coaching people to be positive toward one another in the workplace. I'm still working out the details to know how deeply I should go into doing this. The companies loved my enthusiasm, and both were open-minded businessmen. They claimed to have a gut feeling that I was the answer to their prayers. I was surprised to hear that from them."

"That's quite the accomplishment, brother. Congratulations! You may be able to put those Dr. Seuss books to use after all!"

"Yes, maybe so—that's not a bad idea. I was thinking to have those companies come to dinner events where I can raise money for a new youth centre. I know the person who's opening the organization, and he asked me if I could help out with it. It'll assist young people in gaining confidence in themselves before going out into the workforce; or even before getting married. It all fits into what I want to do, so he and I can work together as a unit. I'll need special guests to come and do talks. Andrew is in. Andy wants to work with men specifically and help them understand themselves in this changing world. Women will be encouraged to attend his workshops to understand and support men's emotional perspectives. What do you think? Are you up for the job? I keep seeing you there teaching people. I've already told so many people how you helped me."

"Sounds like a Divine Plan to me."

"Great. I'll let you know more about it once the plans are set. I have a feeling a lot of people will be seeking out your help to get themselves focused after those talks."

"Excellent, and remember, don't put me too high on a pedestal. It may be a far distance to fall, and I do have a natural fear of falling!" Francis winked.

"I'll follow your lead in getting them lost." Ryan winked back.

"I'm looking forward to it. Set one bird free, show him how, and he'll free all the rest, right?"

"Wow, yes—from that golden cage."

"You now see the potential that was always in you. It was just waiting to be released. Just imagine what will happen as you continue on your journey of healing."

"Yes, freedom feels pretty good," Ryan agreed.

His mind took a sudden left turn. "Okay, so now I have a question for you about animals. I have had a lot of different sightings of the late and I can't help but wonder why."

Francis laughed, "Talking about animals, you are like a shark. You turn from one direction to the next in one second flat and shock your victim. I'm usually your unwary fish. What animals have you seen, brother?"

Ryan smirked, "Okay, let me see. One day, for instance, a mouse passed in front of the car just before I reached the house. Let's start there."

"Hm? I wonder what trouble you were about to get yourself into that the mouse could sense?"

"What do you mean?"

"If you had said that it was crossing your path on a highway, then it would mean that other larger animals are going to cross up ahead. The mouse crosses first to make sure they're out of harm's way. They sense movement from the ground: vibrations beneath them that are out of synch from the usual tremors they sense. If the mouse crosses near a home, then I would take it as a warning that danger is up ahead. And knowing you, that warning had something to do with when you got home. The mouse was saying: *Slow down and proceed with caution.* I would say that you were the big animal about to cross the road, and the mouse was picking up on the vibration of your thoughts and running from you. Am I wrong?"

"I'm trying to think of what that might be. Wait—oh yeah, I put Clara in an awkward position. I kind of jumped in and said I wanted to marry her again."

"Yup, I knew it! You were the big, bulky elephant walking into the situation and knocking everything over. No wonder the mouse ran."

"Yeah, I was wanting to push forward a little too quickly, and she put me in my place pretty fast. So yup, you would have won that bet. How did you know the meaning of that mouse?"

"That was an easy one. The mouse was out of place. Usually, squirrels are our markers in residential areas to let us know to prepare to slow down. That's when you'll notice things like a child suddenly running out in front of you to chase a ball that had rolled out onto the street, or a car would suddenly stop in front of you and you'd be forced to slam down hard on your brakes. Little critters like that are great helpers if you are paying attention to their world."

"Wow, thanks for that explanation."

"You're welcome. Any other animals?"

"There are so many different ones that I see now that I never noticed before. I could go on and on. I keep seeing a hawk each time I drive to your office. One even swooped in front of the windshield on the way here today."

"The hawk was telling you that you have to shift your focus on something, which we determined was the cellphone issue. And maybe there is something still to come."

"Yes, okay, makes sense. I do seem to switch perspectives a lot after spending time with you, so the hawk fits," Ryan laughed.

"Hawk is also a great helper in getting you focused to take on new positions, which ties in nicely with that new project you are initiating. I would say new inspirations and ideas will be coming each and every day, and you are being told to take lots of notes."

"Why do so many animals come to me?"

"They're your guides. Now that you are aware of them, they will come in hoards, trust me."

"I don't know all their meanings, though."

"They'll tell you their meanings by themselves. Just watch their behaviours."

"Francis, after everything we've been through on this journey, I hope you won't mind me asking you some personal questions."

"Are you ready for the answers to those questions?"

"I think I am."

"Then ask away."

Chapter Nineteen
____

WHO AM I?

"WHAT IS YOUR story?" Ryan asked with genuine interest.

"Now that's a big can of worms to ask me to open up, isn't it? I thought maybe you wanted to know my favourite colour or something!" Francis joked.

"Maybe that, too! Somehow, I feel like I need to hear it all. Your story, I mean."

"Are you sure you have the time?"

"I don't want to pressure you, but I would be honoured if you would share it with me."

"Well, to start, my favourite colour is blue."

"Good to know. Mental note!" Ryan laughed.

"I come from a different world in North America."

"Tell me about it."

"I'm the second generation and the result of what was called 'Residential Schools.' Those schools officially closed in the late '80s, and in some cases, the early '90s. Depending on what areas they were in, some had closed earlier. Most people never heard of them. They were hidden from society in a 'right-out-there' kind of way."

"What does that mean?"

"Well, people knew the schools existed and yet they never knew what was happening inside of them. Those who did know the truth turned a blind eye. For the most part, the public was led to believe that they were helping the students to become civilized. The system never mentioned the tactics they were using to enforce that change. So, no one can blame the misinformed for not coming to the rescue of these children. Those who knew what was going on are a different story. It's up to the Creator to deal with them. There has been a lot of resolution over the matter at this point. It took a lot of time to get to this point, however. There's still a lot more to go, however."

"What kind of school was it?"

"That school system was mostly for those of Aboriginal descent, and children were brought there to be modernized, so to speak. They were taught proper manners and to speak the language of the Crown. They were given basic education in Euro-American subject matters.

This meant that they had to leave their old life behind. The children weren't allowed to have any past connection with their own language or cultural beliefs, or even, in many cases, to their families."

"Do you mean that they tried to wipe out their culture?"

"They attempted to, perhaps. Some called it assimilation, and others now term it as cultural cleansing because of other discoveries that went along with it."

"Discoveries...that sounds daunting! Like what?"

"Daunting is a good word for it. Mass burial grounds have been discovered, for one. Some of very young Native American children."

"You mean like a genocide?"

"Well, yes." Francis paused a moment and cleared his throat before continuing. "As for the schools, children were often brought there by force and rounded up by trucks without parents knowing where their kids were being taken to. Most were discovered in the schools and some disappeared without a trace, never appearing again. So yes, I would say someone tried to wipe us out. The *who* is the question that remains. There's no evidence that points to anyone's guilt. Some say they were military trucks, while others say to hush that accusation."

"I read about North American history, but I never heard about any of this before. It's all news to me."

"It's out there in the unwritten history books of people's experiences. These schools were in other countries also, including Australia and in New Zealand. In any case, my dear mother was one of these children brought to one of those schools in my country. She's my reason for bringing it up in the first place. Her story is her own and only hers to tell. What I can share is my experience alone and how I'm tied to her experience. What I mean is that I came into this world as the result of that story, because she conceived me while she was there."

"Your mom was full Native?"

"Yes."

"You don't look Native, though. Like I said in the beginning, you look white."

Ryan paused and jolted back. He suddenly realized what he might be saying and stopped. A horrible unspeakable thought came to his mind like a flash of lightning. He decided to continue asking questions even if it wasn't appropriate. It was better than letting things linger unspoken. Maybe his assumptions were wrong anyway. "So, your father?"

"I never knew him, and neither did my mother."

"That's impossible. How could she not know your father?" He gulped, knowing—yet not believing—what Francis was about to say.

"No offense intended, brother. My mother never asked her rapist his name."

"Oh my God, I'm sorry, and no offence taken. I understand now. You don't have to say any more if you don't want to."

"I'm always honoured to speak about my mother. She brought me into this world. She deserves to be remembered in all ways and especially for her innocence and purity. She was raped. She wasn't the rapist."

"Yes, for sure. She does deserve to be remembered for her purity."

"And I choose to remember her for her culture and her ways before it was wiped or brainwashed out of her."

"That's a very different way of seeing things. Thank you for opening my eyes to that lesson, Francis. How did she deal with having you after that set of circumstances?"

"She was young and had no means of her own. I was given away to the nuns for a time and then placed in with a white family that took very good care of me. I'm grateful to them for their gracious hospitality and for taking me in as their own. I still call them Mom and Dad. They have both passed away now."

"Did you see your real mom and get to know her?"

"Yes, I got to see my birth mom for the first time when she was released from the school. I was about four or five years old by then."

"Wow, so she must have been quite young when she had you?" Ryan pressed.

"Yes, she was. Still a child herself, really. I would walk an hour or more to see her, rain or shine. Back then, kids were taught to be more on their own and more independent. My adopted parents encouraged me to visit her as often as I could. I was lucky that they requested to know who my mother was before they took me into their home, so that I could know her. They were good souls, truly. Creator chose them specifically for me, I know that.

"My birth mom was a beautiful woman, very kind and very sweet. She was and still is a wise soul and she gave me lots of love when she saw me. The only thing I could give her in return was a bottle of Coke. It was all I could afford and the only tangible gift I ever gave her." Francis stopped talking a moment to clear his throat again. He looked off into the distance as if he was looking at someone standing there. He continued talking. "It was always fond memories drinking Coca-Cola while sitting by her side and chatting back and forth about this and that. She loved sitting in her rocking chair, and I sat on an old blue milk crate beside her. I still love the sound of the rocking chair today. It reminds me of her."

"Ah, that is why you love blue. So, she passed away, too?" Ryan asked.

"Yes, she did. She left us abruptly one day, and I missed her greatly. She's with me still each and every day; a wise owl watching over me."

"That's why you like drinking the cola? It's all coming together now."

"Yes, I still honour her by offering a cola when people come see me."

"That's a really nice way to keep honouring her."

"Yes, meaning and purpose are everywhere if we allow them to be, and when you look hard enough."

"I'm starting to get there slowly. How did she die?"

Francis cleared his throat once more. "Sui...suicide. She took her own life."

"Wow. I had no idea."

"Now you do."

"I'm sorry. I shouldn't have asked so many personal questions."

"Ask more—it's okay. You said you were ready to hear it, so I trust that feeling."

"Thank you for opening up to me like this. Do you have any siblings? I mean did your birth mom have more kids?"

"Yes, I had a brother."

"Had?"

"He was murdered."

Ryan knew what he meant now by opening up a can of worms. He wasn't sure what to say but knew that he needed to continue on with the conversation since he had been the one to pry it open in the first place. He decided, though, not to ask details about his brother's death. It felt like one of those stories that wasn't meant to be spoken. "That's really too bad. Again, I'm sorry."

"He lived a good life before that. We were grateful to have him while we did."

"How did you end up coming to get these teachings? You spoke of learning from someone. What brought you to gather up all this knowledge that you have today?"

"After all that happened, I became a bit of a lost soul, we'll say. I spent a better part of my adult life trying to find myself, mostly in the outside world. I drank a lot of alcohol and had my share of relationships that never seemed to last. I needed to drown out a few other unmentionable sorrows and the alcohol seemed to help with that for a while.

"I disrespected enough women and myself and lost two babies of my own to sickness. I think the Creator brought the babies into my life to try to awaken me. It did for a while. It wasn't until later in life, when I lost respect from the good people that I loved, like my adopted parents, that I came to a place of being ready to meet my teacher. My folks accepted me back into their lives once I got cleaned up, thank goodness."

"It's good that they didn't abandon you after all that. How did you meet your teacher?"

"I met a man on a bench one day. To be honest, I was so drunk the night before that I had fallen asleep on that bench. He came that morning with a Coca-Cola and offered it to me. It got my attention, mostly because of the memories with my mother. I think, somehow, she came through him to help me. Actually, no, I know she did. Something sobered me up from that talk onwards. I haven't touched alcohol since that fateful moment on that bench. It was the moment I can say that my life changed forever."

"Like when I met Andrew in the parking lot. Nothing has been the same since."

"Yes, exactly like that. In my case, I had been rough around the edges for so long that no one expected a turnaround like that in my life, to be honest. I was a hopeless case in many people's eyes, even in my own.

"The man who helped me was almost blind from cataracts and yet he could see through to my soul. He asked me to meet him again the next day. I did out of respect. I went because I was feeling sorry for him mostly, and not wanting to disappoint an old man. At first, I wasn't interested in helping myself. After a while, his way of approaching life started growing on me. He was a bit of a smartass, and that made me feel comfortable because he wasn't all formal like others tried to be with me. That kind of approach never worked for someone like me. I liked that he was raw and real.

"There was nothing formal about the pain I felt, and so, raw was exactly what I needed. He never gave up on me, coming to that bench every day with a cola for him and me, whether I showed up or not. He told me later that when I didn't show up, he would offer my portion to nature by spilling one of the cans at a tree to feed my spirit. I guess it worked. Long story short, he taught me how to reconnect with myself and showed me who I was. It was a long, hard journey. I won't lie. I was full of anger and resentment and I had a lot more guilt to carry than most men.

"That old man also was a result of the residential schools, and yet he had so much wisdom to share. He changed his own life and turned it into something meaningful. Before he died, he wanted to share what he knew with someone who would listen, someone that would carry on the teachings. I guess I was that guy.

"The man spoke of a journey I had to take, one that would make me leap over a large body of water. He said that I would help lost souls find their way home. I thought he was crazy. Some years later, I met my wife; she's from here. She was at a conference in my territory and we ended up talking about small stuff.

"One thing led to another, and we ended up talking all night. I was intrigued by her grace and honesty, and of course her beauty. She, too, had teachings from elders she had met while at certain conferences with my people. She was studying anthropology and was working for a university here in Europe at the same time. She was there doing research for her thesis. Another long story short, I fell in love. The story continued and so here I am looking at the likes of you and telling you that part of my story. Questions?"

"No questions." Ryan's emotions burst out into an ugly cry. He couldn't stop his body from shaking, tears now falling down his face and onto the floor.

FRANCIS SAT PERFECTLY still and let the clock tick above Ryan's head, completely calm and showing no emotions whatsoever.

Ryan eventually found his composure.

"When I first came here, I thought I knew everything. The more I learn, the more I realize I know nothing," Ryan said feeling royally ashamed.

"There are a lot of layers to an onion," Francis expressed with an assuring voice.

"More than I ever expected. I was the tough one that figured I already had it all together."

"Yes, and the more layers we took off, the more it hurt, eh?"

"Yes, and my eyes watered a lot, that's for sure. That damn onion!" Ryan laughed.

"I told you the tougher ones are the ones who fall the hardest."

"I remember that, yes."

"You've surprised yourself, haven't you?" Francis asked.

"Yes. Nobody would believe my story if they heard it."

"Your story is for you to believe. Just like my story is there for me to believe."

Ryan sat for a moment, staring deeply into Francis's eyes, while still wiping tears and snot onto his sleeve. After that cry there was no need to hide anything.

"Don't be too sure that others wouldn't believe. Remember, humans are smart. They just need the right challenge or challenger and they'll get back on track quickly."

"Yes, back on the path to find their purpose," Ryan recalled.

"Back on the path to find themselves."

"Just a few words, Francis, and I think I will allow Clara to begin her next session with you in peace. I know she's coming later today; she told me how she's been enjoying her time with you so much. Thank you for being there for her also. And by the way, I'll allow your story to be hers to ask about. I won't say anything about my sessions until she has moved on further in her journey with you."

"Yes, she's also coming today, you're right, and that is a good idea to allow her to have her own experience. Thank you."

"WHAT WAS IT you wanted to say, again?" Francis asked.

"First, I want to go back to the day you gave me that dragonfly necklace for her. You talked about buying that gift for someone, and that you were uncertain who it was for. For some reason I don't believe that statement. You've taught me too well not to ignore my instinct and this is one of those times I know to trust it. I think you did know who it was for. Was it for Clara? Did you know?"

"I did buy it for someone; I hadn't originally bought it for Clara, no."

"Who did you buy it for, then?" Ryan asked.

"I thought I was buying it to leave it somewhere in nature as a gift to honour my mother, to be honest."

"Why did you give it to me, then?"

"I gave it to you so you could honour my mother through Clara. If you honour one woman you honour them all, brother."

"Wow, Francis. I'm speechless and honoured. I hope your mom is okay with me doing that. Wherever she is up there."

"Oh yes, she is," Francis smiled, lowering his eyes thoughtfully.

"There's something else I need to thank you for, Francis."

"Yes?"

"Thank you for being my teacher, my friend, my guru."

"You are welcome young grasshopper!"

"Okay...maybe just one more question before I go."

"I knew this would never end!" Francis smiled tenderly at Ryan. "Yes?"

"Why did you keep your story to yourself?"

"Your sessions were about you, not me," Francis explained.

"I mean, maybe in the beginning I was disrespectful. Okay, likely very disrespectful, I admit. I probably needed to hear your story to be put in my place. I gave you zero credit when I first met you. It would've changed things for me."

"Remember, that session was about you. My story isn't finished, Ryan, so there's nothing to tell. My ten steps haven't all been taken. I'm still a young man on his journey just drinking one can of cola per day on a bench, hoping to get all the answers, and doing what he can to not slip back into his old programs. An alcoholic will always be an alcoholic. I have many things to learn before I'll be fully healed."

"What about that white wolf. I thought you were healed."

"Yes, in one respect I am. Each day has a fresh beginning, however, and I have a new choice to make each and every day. I can slide backwards at any time. So even though I'm healed, I'm wise enough to take nothing for granted. I start at zero every day of my life, assuming that I could fall backwards at any time into the ways of the black wolf. One day I'll be in the Creator's arms again, and I look forward to being greeted by my birth mother again in the spirit world. There's a lot more meaning and purpose for me to find here on Earth before that happens. I need to get to the end first to know the full story. I work on myself no matter how healed I look or feel. This way I never fall into the trap of the ego that will lead me back into becoming that black wolf again."

"I get the feeling that I know only a small portion of your past experiences, and that a lot more things happened to you along the journey than what you shared with me."

"You may be right."

"To me you look fully healed, needing no extra work at all. You seem so wise, so polished, and so clean. You know so much."

"The more I learned, the more I realized how little I knew."

"That sounds familiar."

"I learn from each person I meet. I sit with them on the bench and offer them a cola. Somehow, I end up hearing their story. From each story I learn, and I grow."

"That's deep."

"I learned from you, Ryan, from our brother Andrew, and everyone else who comes through that door. Now I'm learning from our sister Clara."

"How did you learn from us?"

"By helping others figure out their own life, I help myself the most. If you look back on our journey this past while, I taught you nothing."

"You did! You taught me a lot, Francis. Come on—you can't say that."

"We walked together as brothers, sharing. That's all that happened here, my friend."

Ryan was speechless. He lowered his eyes respectfully.

"As you walk your journey, guiding others, helping them, in your own way, you'll see yourself doing the same," Francis noted.

"I don't think I'm done with these sessions...not yet, anyhow. I'd like to continue coming for myself, and maybe come with Clara when she's ready to come as a couple. Is that okay?"

"Yes, of course it is, for as long as we are supposed to. The journey you took was the small step. Life has a lot more to bring to you. I'd be honoured to walk beside you along your journey, and maybe share one of those colas each time along the way." Francis smiled gently.

"I have more to figure out before I can help people. I need to get a focus, I think, so I don't end up screwing them up."

"One day they'll be thanking you and calling you their friend and their guru."

"Yes, and when they ask me how I got so wise, what do I say?" Ryan asked.

"Tell them you're an ex-asshole that learned from an ex-asshole."

"You can say that again..." Ryan laughed hysterically.

Francis raised his eyebrows impishly. For once Ryan got the better of him.

"OKAY, ONE MORE question!"

"Are you sure just one? I should have been charging per question. I'd be a rich man," Francis teased.

"I mean I can't help but wonder what my Native name would be if I had one. I have had lots of ideas but what name would you give me if I asked for one?"

"It would depend. Are you asking?"

"Well, yeah!"

"Hm, let me think. I got one...Man who got head out of his ass!" Francis couldn't help but poke a little fun at Ryan. It was just too perfectly set up for him to not crack a joke like that.

"Good one, but really? Come on! What's my name?"

"If you're really serious then you have to do it properly. Go to the store and get me some tobacco to honour the spirits, which I will offer to them. I'll pray in your absence and ask them what they call you. That's if they feel you are ready for it."

"Tobacco?"

"Tobacco!"

"Okay."

Ryan couldn't understand why he needed to buy tobacco. He decided not to question it and left immediately for the store. He came back to the office and offered it to Francis as requested.

***

THE NEXT MORNING, Ryan woke up with gratitude in his heart. The sun was rising, the sky was bright, and the birds were singing. A new day was greeting him, and he was seeing life with new hope. His whole existence had changed so much over the past year. What a roller-coaster ride it had been. Though he looked the same on the outside, everything felt different, more vibrant and much more alive. When he looked in the mirror to get ready for the day, his eyes were clear, his smile beaming, and his joy radiant. A lot like Andy looked that day in the parking lot.

He had once thought that he was free, but now he knew with certainty that he had only been surviving under the illusion of freedom in a golden cage. He knew now that he would never choose to be there again. He was out of the cage forever.

He thought back to his sessions with Francis, particularly the last one. With or without words, they knew something, felt something, had something that so few people in the world had. It was a great privilege to have it, to own it, to touch it, whatever it was. The connection was deep, broad, and so full. It was something almost too sacred to be uttered to anyone who had never experienced it themselves. It was something connected to the strongest of impulses, to the purest of thoughts, and perhaps to the universe itself. It was something ethereal, surreal, and yet so tangible without his ever being able to describe what it was. It was comprised of four quadrants: respect, honesty, trust, and love...and then to four more joining sections: mental, physical, spiritual, emotional. Yes, it was really something!

Ryan picked up the abalone shell and lit the sage until smoke billowed out. He got out the paper Francis gave him with the prayer on it. He humbled himself, bowed his head, and called his ancestors to his side. Thomas and Edward and the grandmothers stood beside him as he read from the page, his voice shaking.

*Creator, my name is...**Storm Keeper.***

I come to you in humbleness. I use this sage as a medicine, to smudge away anything that does not serve my spirit in a good way...

Thank you, Creator. I have spoken...
Msit Nogama, *All My Ancestors.*

Acknowledgements

A SPECIAL THANK YOU to Gorazd Rožnik, my husband, twin flame, and best friend, for all your hard work and contribution toward this book and our wonderful life.

To my parents, Marcel and Judy Doucette—my rocks, my inspiration in life.

To my friends Nancy Parker, my Soul Sister who helped breathe life into the characters, Simon and Andreja Metljak, and Brandon LeBlanc.

And to Jane Karchmar for editing.

About the Author

KIMBERLEY DOUCETTE WAS born in St. John, NB, Canada, in 1974 and grew up in Miramichi, NB. A sensitive child, she endured a lot of hardships and bullying in school. Despite her beginnings, she became known quickly for her innate ability to understand symbolism, even doing dream interpretation on the playground from the age of twelve. She went on to graduate from St. Thomas University in 1997 with a B.A., Honours, in English Literature. She lived and worked in South Korea as an English teacher for four-plus years. She visited many Buddhist temples where she learned to meditate and quiet her mind. She backpacked extensively through several Asian countries. Kim lived in a tent in Australia for a year, working at farms. She connected profoundly to the land, the ways of the Aborigines, and to the animals; and, of course, the Outback. After settling in Alberta, Canada, she travelled to Uganda, Africa, where she taught orphans to read, first raising money for a Ugandan school and supplying them with beds, mattresses, desks, benches, mosquito nets, medicines, clothing, books, a new kitchen, and part of a new schoolroom.

After a stint in Brazil, and having relocated to Moncton, NB, Kim knew that it was time to put her extensive knowledge and life experiences to work. She went to Hawaii and got her Angel Therapy Practitioner Certificate and opened up business back home as a psychic medium. She specialized in helping people understand personal growth and recognizing patterns and programs in their life, as well as grief counselling.

Upon discovering her Native lineage, Kim learned the ways of her Miqmaq ancestors; going to weekly sweats for years, doing sacred fasts, working with a Native Elder and humbling herself to all of creation. She also took time out to embark on an adventure in Peru where she worked with several shamans, learning ancient techniques that she now uses in her shamanic healings, sound healings, and mediumship readings today. Kim now resides in Europe with her Slovenian husband and two stepchildren, doing online sessions, webinars, and courses. She still enjoys travelling and won't pass up an adventure. You can find her at OpenUpWide.com and join her worldwide online community for building awareness around personal and spiritual growth; or at Kimspirational.com.

"Fear of the unknown is what keeps us from living our dream. Living our dream helps make fear unknown."